Advanced Game Programming for Intellivision

Óscar Toledo Gutiérrez

Advanced Game Programming for Intellivision

Copyright © 2020-2021 Óscar Toledo Gutiérrez

ISBN: 978-1-6780-4562-3

Official website: **http://nanochess.org/**

The author welcomes your comments, suggestions and errata reports,. Please send them to: **biyubi@gmail.com**

You can also follow him on Twitter as **@nanochess**

First published in 2021

Dedicated to my beloved wife Rosa Nely (1973-2020)

.

Contents

The Book

Chapter 3

Chapter 4

Chapter 5

Appendix F

Foreword

What a long strange trip it's been

About 40 years ago, my brother and I immersed ourselves in the first video game system we owned that *wasn't* some variant of Pong: a Mattel Intellivision. We found ourselves taunted by a shifty eyed dealer, then yelled at by a strangely growling umpire telling us *"Yerrrrr out!"*, before we hopped in our cars and raced through suburbia.

We had Intelligent Television. We had *Intellivision.*

A few short years later, we became Intellivision programmers, as we discovered the ECS and its glacially slow BASIC interpreter. ECS BASIC had one neat feature that made up for its speed: You could peek into some games and reuse some of their graphics! I already had a habit of feeding my curiosity by tearing things apart to see how they worked inside. Now I could start to take the video games apart too, at least a little.

ECS BASIC didn't let you get very far, though, and dreams of looking under the hood of the Intellivision went back on the shelf. I had my TI-99/4A to keep me busy, followed by other computers and interests.

Then, sometime in 1996, I got the itch to explore the Intellivision again. I hopped on AltaVista, Lycos, and Hot Bot, to see what I could find, and... *there wasn't much!* Finally, in 1997, I started stumbling across interesting resources. I found Frank Palazzolo's archive of data sheets. The Blue Sky Rangers had opened up a history page under the Making It website. And, before long, you could download an official pair of

Intellipacks from a nascent Intellivision Productions website. Each Intellipack came with three games, and an integrated emulator.

I downloaded the Intellipacks and immediately set about reverse engineering them. I wanted to write my *own* emulator, but I didn't have the means yet to dump a ROM image. I made a little progress, scratching at the edges by emulating the CPU.

Eventually I met William Moeller and Carl Mueller Jr. online. Carl's emulator was at the heart of those Intellipacks, and also made the *Intellivision Lives!* CD-ROM possible. Carl's reverse engineering notes lit a fire under my own Intellivision emulator, *jzIntv*.

When *Intellivision Lives!* landed in late 1998, things really got interesting. You could use Carl's emulator directly, and run whatever game image you liked. Carl had a development kit of his own that ran under MS-DOS. I started developing one of my own called SDK-1600.

Mike Hayes, who had previously run ECS BASIC programming contests, ran a programming contest in late 1999 to write a new *non*-ECS-BASIC game for the Intellivision.

The Intellivision homebrew scene was officially born[1].

jzIntv went on hiatus for a bit as other emulators—Bliss, Nostalgia, IntvWin—appeared on the scene. I focused on homebrewing instead. And homebrew, we did. SDK-1600's assembler and library of routines got stronger and more capable. Chad Schell developed and released the Intellicart, once he and I poked at the hardware to close some holes in the documentation.

I commissioned Chad to develop a "dumb cart" so we could publish our homebrews in physical carts as well. That gave us the first new cartridge releases for the Intellivision in over a decade.

The homebrew scene moved from infancy to childhood.

---

[1] Note from Michael Hayes himself: "I'm glad JZ gave me credit for getting the homebrew scene started through my old website. Maybe the fact I gave him an Intellivision-II for his ECS BASIC game in a previous contest helped. He's kept my old site hosted on part of his own site all these years".

Frank Palazzolo and I reverse engineered the Intellivoice starting from little more than an undocumented ROM dump and some tantalizing clues in the data sheets. I actually interfaced a *real* Intellivoice to jzIntv so we could see how it really worked. Within a few months, we'd worked out nearly everything.

jzIntv came back from hiatus in a big way. Our reverse engineering work enabled me to write the first true Intellivoice software emulation that didn't rely on samples recorded from a real Intellivoice. I spent months poking at other hardware oddities, with an eye toward making jzIntv the most accurate Intellivision emulator available.

And, the homebrew scene chugged along, slowly. By 2004, we had games such as *4-Tris, Stonix, Minehunter, Same Game & Robots,* all in cartridge form. In 2006, Chad released a successor to the Intellicart, the Cuttle Cart 3.

In 2007, I released the largest game ever published for the Intellivision: Space Patrol. Weighing in at 16K × 16-bit, it was just *slightly* larger than the previous title holder, World Series Major League Baseball (24K × 10-bit).

And with that, the Intellivision homebrew scene entered its awkward pre-teen years. It was still young enough to order from the kids menu, but really wanted to sit at the big kids' table. The homebrew scene was about to shift gears again.

After a short crash course from Chad, I started designing my own Intellivision hardware. Space Patrol had completely filled our 16K × 16-bit cartridge design. New games wanted to go larger, and wanted other features such as additional RAM. You could play these on an Intellicart, or a CC3, but we couldn't publish them on cartridges.

I developed my first video game cartridge board, JLP, that offered nearly 8 times the capacity, and additional features such as RAM and non-volatile storage for high scores/save games. And, of course, I taught jzIntv how to emulate it. Shortly thereafter, a couple other enterprising hardware designers also developed board designs of their own that could hold large games as well, and optionally provide additional RAM.

Over the next few years, games got a little bigger as handfuls of new titles trickled out. Publishers such as Elektronite brought out interesting new titles, but progress was slow. Previously unfinished and/or unreleased titles started to appear in cartridge form to fill the gap. Overall, it started to look like our homebrew fermentation might stall out.

Since you're reading this book now, you know the story doesn't end there. Óscar arrived on the scene with a one-two punch. First, he brought us great new games such as Princess Quest and Space Raid. And then, not long after, he brought us IntyBASIC.

IntyBASIC took Intellivision programming from the arcane domain of assembly language, and brought it back to the familiar world of BASIC. But, unlike the glacially slow ECS BASIC I started with almost 40 years ago, IntyBASIC absolutely zips along.

Just like that, the Intellivision homebrew scene lit up like a teenager with keys to the family car and a tank full of gas.

Not long after, I delivered my second hardware project: *LTO Flash!* The teenaged homebrew scene now can drive a shiny new orange hotrod.

This year brings an interesting milestone for the Intellivision. 1999 marked 21 years of Intellivision. 2020 marked 21 years of the Intellivision homebrews. As of 2021, we've been homebrewing for *over half the Intellivision's life.* Amazing, isn't it?

Back in 1997, a fresh faced 22 year old Intellivision fan started banging together some bits and pieces that would be instrumental in bringing the Intellivision homebrew scene to adulthood: jzIntv, SDK-1600, JLP, and *LTO Flash!*

That somewhat-less-fresh faced Intellivision fan is excited to see what the nearly 22 year old Intellivision homebrew scene has ahead of it as it enters adulthood.

Homebrew on!

Joe "intvnut" Zbiciak
Left Turn Only
February 7, 2021

Preface

There's always more

I was pleasantly surprised by the public's response to my previous book: **Programming Games for Intellivision**. The feedback has been great and many people have started games.

I would like to mention my travel to Barcelona, Spain in October 2018 where I meet Oscar Kenneth Albero (Kai Magazine games), and I delivered in hand a copy of the book, and he went on to develop some masterpieces like Ninja Odyssey, TNT-Cowboy, and A.F. Anthropomorphic Force, which were published by Elektronite.

New games created with IntyBASIC have appeared and are technically impressive. I would like to mention Intellivania by Skywaffle, Gooninuff by Carlos Madruga, and Mad Bomber by Chris Derrig.

Also the new entries from the IntyBASIC 2018 Contest like: Deep Zone (Artrag), Upmonsters (Atari2600land), The Crimson Tower (emerson) MazezaM (postpostdoc), Boothill (digress), Princess Lydie (mmarrero), Dwarven Mine (boardgamebrewer), A Sparrow Goes Flapping (Chris Derrig again, hey Chris!), Ouranos (Carlsson), Deadly Balls (PuzZLeR), Hunt the Wumpus (Zendocon) and mInty (decle, who is doing also an important documentation project of old Intellivision hardware).

As this book is getting ready for production, there are more new games in the IntyBASIC 2020 Contest, and the quality has increased greatly because amazing team work (in alphabetical order):

1. The Depth of Nitemare (by Chris Derrig, music by Adán Toledo)

2. Eggerland Mystery (by Carlos Madruga, music by Adán Toledo)

3. Infiltrator (by Carlos Madruga, Arturo Ragozini, Adán Toledo)

4. Mr. Turtle (by digress)

5. The Pandora Incident (by Carlos Madruga, sound effects by Arturo Ragozini, music by Adán Toledo, graphics by Justin Cheer)

6. Space Combat (by fsuinnc)

7. TV POWWW (by decle)

There were several areas not covered in my first book that I wanted to cover in this new book. Especially:

- Show examples of more polished games that made the transition to being published in cartridge form. This is because a published game should be refined by having nice graphics, reasonable music, good sound effects, and excellent gameplay! Three of the games discussed in this book have been published as Intellivision cartridges!

- Show how to create amazing graphic screens with the help of IntyColor and the proper selection of video modes.

- Discuss the design of sound effects.

- Discuss the conversion of music sheets.

- Discuss briefly some things of Intellivision hardware that were missed in the previous book (like Color-Stack mode, Colored Squares, and GROM tiles)

The following games will be discussed in this book: Oh Mummy!, Pumpkin Master, Meteor Storm, and Dungeon Warrior.

I hope you'll enjoy the ride!

Óscar Toledo G.
April 2021

Acknowledgments

For all the good people

This book was planned to appear at the end of November 2020. However, my beloved wife Rosa Nely took a turn for the worse of her lung cancer after fighting it for almost five years, and sadly she died at the start of December. She supported me through all these years, she didn't understand very well what I did with programming, but in her lovely way she was always cheering me up, and enjoyed hearing of my achievements. She gave me a beautiful daughter Myriam Sofia. May Rosa Nely rest in peace, a good soul ascended to heaven.

My deep gratitude goes to Michael Hayes for proofreading this book. I still need plenty of help although my English knowledge has improved through constant practice. Also he contributed appendix E with even more tips for using IntyBASIC in advanced ways.

Many thanks to Joe Zbiciak for writing the foreword for this book. Joe is the creator of the jzintv emulator, documentation, and programming toolset. IntyBASIC couldn't exist without it.

My wholehearted thanks to Rev (Intellivision Revolution) for providing a beautiful Intellivision II console for the cover of this book.

My good friend Chris Derrig has tested some of my games at the most unexpected times (and I've tested some of his amazing games! Special mention for his upcoming Mardi Gras game), and we have enjoyed passing running jokes. Also another good friend, Michael Lünzer, has helped me by testing with his wide collection of PAL Intellivision consoles.

Thanks to Steve Craft for supporting the IntyBASIC development with small donations (he insists in a wine vase, I prefer a good coffee!)

My previous Intellivision book also got me a lot of new friends, like Oscar G. who came with his wife from Belgium to visit me, and in a second visit brought me a pair of Intellivision items that I didn't had in my collection.

Special awesomeness kudos to the rising stars Carlos Madruga (cmadruga) and skywaffle.

Kudos to Intellivision Revolution (Rev and cmart), Collectorvision (J-F and Toby), Elektronite (Willy), BBWW games (Jay), and 2600 connection (Tim). All of them are keeping the community alive by producing new games, plus one or two developed by myself. At this moment I can remember my games The Leprechaun's Flight, Frankensteins's Monster, Unlucky Pony, Sydney Hunter and the Sacred Tribe, Aardvark, Hover Bovver, Miner 2049er, Steamroller, Fox's Trek, and Zombie Madness.

Special thanks to Al from AtariAge, and I'm really sure that I'm forgetting people. To all of you, thanks!

Chapter 1

Intellivision video tricks

The Intellivision is a game console capable of displaying 159x96 pixels on the TV screen. It can show eight movable objects on screen (known as MOB or SPRITE in the IntyBASIC jargon). It also has sixteen colors designed in the STIC (Standard Television Interface Circuit).

There are 64 definable bitmaps in GRAM memory, and there are 256 predefined bitmaps in GROM memory. We'll discuss first the fine details of the two video modes.

The first important thing is the background/foreground distinction. The background is any bit set to zero in definable bitmaps or GROM memory. And the foreground is any bit set to one in definable bitmaps or GROM memory.

This difference is important for the color selection in your game.

All the information in this chapter serves to complement my previous book.

1.1 Color Stack mode

The Color Stack mode is enabled by reading the $0021 address at the time of a video interrupt (this is already handled by IntyBASIC when you use the sentence *MODE 0*).

The Color Stack mode sets the background color as an array of 4 colors that can be chosen from the 16 available. When the display starts

1

being drawn, the color stack points to the first of the 4 colors. This pointer is advanced immediately whenever Bit 13 of the card is set to one, equivalent to mask $2000 (take note it doesn't work for Colored Squares cards).

This mode also allows to show the 64 definable bitmaps from GRAM memory. The foreground color can be any of the 16 colors.

All of the GROM predefined bitmaps can be shown (see appendix C), including lowercase letters, but the foreground color is limited to the colors 0-7.

Sprites (MOB) are able to use the GRAM defined bitmaps, but also can refer to all of the GROM predefined bitmaps.

Since bitmask $2000 advances the color stack pointer immediately, it can be used to get twice as many GROM predefined bitmaps, because you can use these in inverse video mode. For example:

```
'
' Test inverse video shapes
' by Oscar Toledo G.
' Creation date: Dec/31/2020.
'

CLS
MODE 0,0,7,0,7   ' Color Stack mode, black, white, black, white
WAIT

#backtab(24) = 96 * 8 + 7              ' White over black
#backtab(25) = 96 * 8 + 0 + $2000      ' Black over white
#backtab(26) = 96 * 8 + 7 + $2000      ' White over black
#backtab(27) = 96 * 8 + 0 + $2000      ' Black over white
#backtab(28) = $2000                   ' Return to black bkgnd.

WHILE 1: WEND
```

Refer to appendix C for the GROM shapes. In this case we used GROM card 96. Notice how *#backtab(28)* is assigned in order to prevent the remainder of the screen from being white.

The Color Stack mode is useful because it allows to have lowercase letters and all of the GROM predefined cards. You have only four background colors, but repeating those two colors allows you to switch easily between two background colors. Using the full four background colors is more useful when your screen is divided in areas, for example: a top line with blue background, a middle area with black background, and a bottom area with red background.

```
'

' Example of areas in Color Stack mode
' by Oscar Toledo G.
' Creation date: Dec/31/2020.
'


CLS
MODE 0,1,0,2,0
WAIT

' The display starts with the first background color

#backtab(20) = $2000    ' Switch to second background color

#backtab(160) = $2000   ' Switch to third background color

WHILE 1: WEND
```

The fact that you have the whole GROM accessible also helps when doing full screen graphics because the GRAM only allows to define 64 8x8 cards, and this isn't enough to cover a whole screen. You can design screens using the GROM shapes, and pass these through IntyColor. IntyColor will automatically use the GROM shapes if using the Color Stack mode, and the file *grom.bin* is available in the same directory.

Another advantage of this mode is the availability of the Colored Squares mode, allowing to use any of colors 0-6 for 4x4 pixels inside the 8x8 area, and using the color 7 as direct access to the current Color Stack.

IntyBASIC distribution includes an example of how to use the Colored Squares mode contributed by Mark Ball. It is in the folder "contrib/ColouredSquares.bas".

In order to use a card with Colored Squares mode, the card bits should be mapped like this:

bit	13	12	11	10	9	8	7	6	5	4	3	2	1	0
	p3	1	0	p3	p3	p2	p2	p2	p1	p1	p1	p0	p0	p0

Where each pixel is mapped like this into the card:

p0	p1
p2	p3

1.2 Foreground/Background mode

The Foreground/Background mode is enabled by writing any value to the address $0021 at the time of a video interrupt (this is already handled by IntyBASIC when using the sentence *MODE* 1)

This mode allows to use the colors 0-7 for the foreground color, and the colors 0-15 for the background color.

Only cards 0-63 from GROM are available (again see appendix C). This is also enforced for sprites (MOB). This means that the lowercase letters and the predefined graphic shapes aren't available, but you have access to the uppercase letters, symbols, and digits.

The color stack isn't used in this mode, and the Colored Squares mode also isn't available.

However, this mode allows to draw highly detailed graphic images that can use shadow tricks because it allows all the sixteen colors for background. I've used this method to draw more recognizable faces for the game Cinemaware's Defender of the Crown, developed for Intellivision by Arnauld Chevallier, and published by Elektronite.

More recently I did a picture of my wife Rosa Nely (RIP) for an homage of three free games published in Atariage.[2]

I'll describe the conversion process as it can be useful. It is good only for small images due to the 64 GRAM-card limitation of the Intellivision. For this I've used Windows XP SP3, and Paint.NET 3.5.11.

---

[2] https://atariage.com/forums/topic/314943-in-memory-of-rosa-nely/

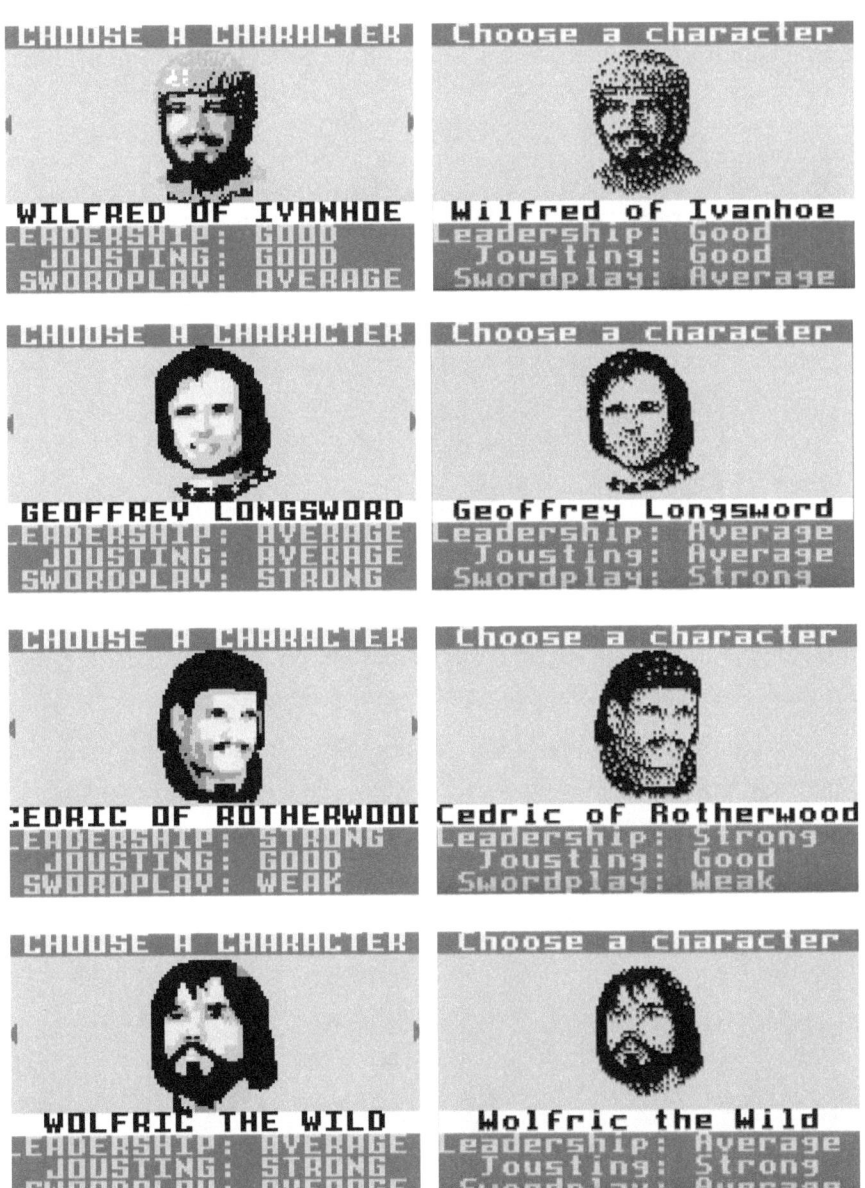

Different versions of the portraits used in the game Defender of the Crown for the Intellivision. The right-side ones were the originals from year 2012 using Color Stack mode; the left-side ones were converted by myself from original Amiga images using the same method as described below, and using Foreground/ Background mode. Notice how the lowercase letters are lost in order to have higher picture fidelity.

The first step is to have a good quality picture. It needs to have enough contrast, for example, to distinguish the background from the hair.

This picture is the best one I found for the conversion, however it is rotated in a difficult angle. I've solved it in Paint.NET by using the Layers - Rotate & Zoom option. I applied a 41 degree rotation in the Angle field.

From the rotated image I selected a 292x292 pixel square using the Rectangle Select tool (I wanted a 64x64 pixel final image), pressed Ctrl+C to copy it to the clipboard, and then selected Edit - Paste in to New Image.

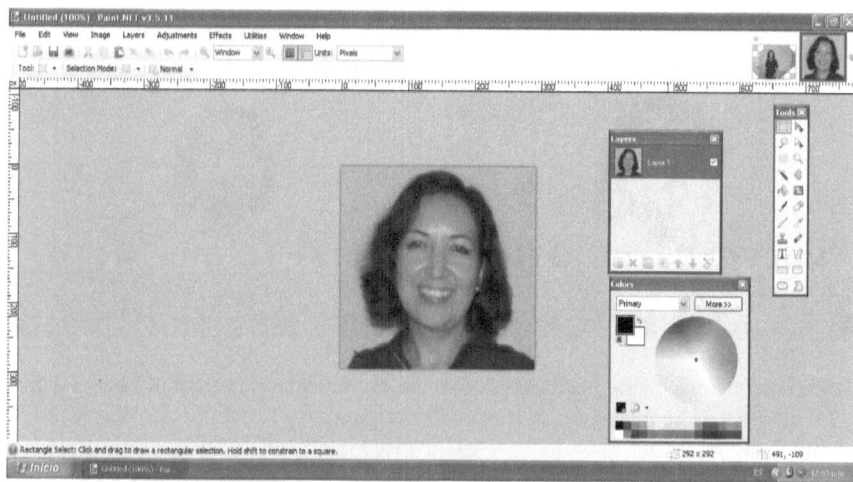

Now I do an Image - Resize... process, changing the final size to 64x64 pixels. Now comes the difficult part: getting a good contrast image in order to separate the important colors and simplify the final process.

We want a full color image, but if you want a single tone image you can proceed to do Adjustments - Black & White.

Proceed to do Adjustments - Brightness & Contrast... The values 10 for Brightness, and 47 for Contrast made the effect. I had to try several values so the following step had the desired result.

The next step is to do Adjustments - Posterize... with the value 2 in all the parameters.

From there everything is by hand. Using the Color Picker tool, right-click on one pixel from the picture to make its color the second color, and then open the Colors reference from IntyBASIC (Paint.NET allows you to have several images open at the same time), and left-click over the desired color to get the replacement color.

Then select the Recolor tool, change the Tolerance bar to zero percent, and enter 500 in the Brush Width field. Do a single click in the center of the image, and it will replace one posterized color with the selected Intellivision color.

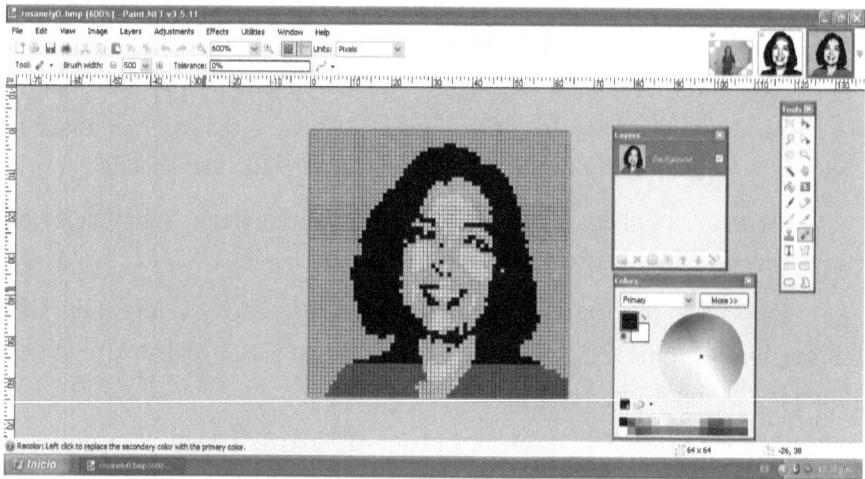

Remember the limitations of 2 colors in an 8x8 pixel cell, but we have the IntyColor advantage of having "magic" sprites, where it can use sprites to cover certain areas of the image, allowing us to have 3 or 4 colors in the same 8x8 pixel cell.

For the eyes I had to artistically add a single bright pixel for each eye, because the canvas resize lost it. This was pretty tricky because a good eye was required to make it look natural.

The final image looks pretty recognizable. This is the sprite trick sheet "rosanely0.txt" provided to IntyColor for generating the final image:

```
25,16,6,1,1,1
25,32,6,1,1,1
33,15,6,1,1,1
```

```
33,31,6,1,1,1
41,21,6,1,1,1
29,44,6,1,1,1
41,37,6,1,1,0
```

Each line describes one sprite. The first argument is the X position, the second argument is the Y position, the third argument is the color number to be used for the sprite (i.e. the color pixels that it is replacing to avoid color clash), the fourth argument is the X zoom (1 for normal, 2 for double wide), the fifth argument is the Y zoom (1 for normal, 2 for double height, or 3 for quadruple height), and finally the sixth argument indicates whether is an 8x8 sprite or an 8x16 sprite. Remember we have only 8 sprites on Intellivision, so it is a smart move to use an 8x16 sprite to cover the biggest area possible in a single sprite.

The command-line used to invoke IntyColor is this one:

```
./intycolor -b -m -g rosanely0.txt rosanely0.bmp rosanely0.bas
```

It indicates to IntyColor to activate the sprites function for more colors, and provides the trick sheet.

1.3 IntyColor utility

IntyColor is distributed together with IntyBASIC. Also it is a command-line utility like IntyBASIC. This means you need to know how to get into CMD (Windows), Terminal (Mac OS X), or the shell (Linux).

This utility takes a 24-bit BMP image file as input, and creates IntyBASIC source code able to be compiled.

Running it without arguments shows a complete list of all the options available.

Although the image width and height can be any multiple of eight pixels, typically we will use images with a width of 160 pixels, and a height of 96 pixels. This corresponds to the size of the Intellivision screen in pixels.

Before you can start designing graphics, you must have a reference palette of the sixteen colors available in Intellivision. The colors available on Intellivision are:

Color number	Name	#RRGGBB	(R,G,B)
0	Black	#000000	(0,0,0)
1	Blue	#002dff	(0,45,255)
2	Red	#ff3d10	(255,61,16)
3	Tan	#c9cfab	(201,207,171)
4	Dark green	#386b3f	(56,107,63)
5	Green	#00a756	(0,167,86)
6	Yellow	#faea50	(250,234,80)
7	White	#ffffff	(255,255,255)
8	Gray	#bdacc8	(189,172,200)
9	Cyan	#24b8ff	(36,184,255)
10	Orange	#ffb41f	(255,180,31)
11	Brown	#546e00	(84,110,0)
12	Pink	#ff4e57	(255,78,87)
13	Light blue	#a496ff	(164,150,255)
14	Yellow green	#75cc80	(117,204,128)
15	Purple	#b51a58	(181,26,88)

Your paint program should be able to modify your current pen color using RGB values (red, green, blue). Some programs allow you to directly enter the RGB hexadecimal value shown, but others require the values 0-255.

To make getting a palette easier, the IntyBASIC distribution includes a file named **colors_reference.bmp** so you don't need to edit palettes or do anything complicated, except copying the required color to your image using the facilities of your paint program.

When drawing your image, you should imagine the 160x96 image being divided into 20x12 cards of 8x8 pixels. And each card should contain only two colors.

1.4 Collision trouble

The behavior of the Intellivision's collision registers sometimes makes it difficult to get a non-repeatable collision. This happens because the collision registers are updated at the end of the video frame.

When the video frame starts (after WAIT), the IntyBASIC program can check for the collision and work accordingly, but the collision will remain flagged in the following frame because the sprite is still visible on the screen (it could be removed in the next frame).

The solution to this problem is to use a variable signaling if the sprite is alive. For example:

```
IF my = 0 THEN       ' Monster inactive
      SPRITE 4,0
ELSE
      SPRITE 4,$0308+mx,$0108+my,$0806 + 12*8
END IF

WAIT                 ' Wait for video frame to complete

IF COL0 AND $0010 THEN  ' Sprite 0 collision vs 4
      IF my <> 0 THEN      ' Monster still alive
            score = score + 5
            my = 0          ' Kill monster in next frame
      END IF
END IF
```

The extra comparison *IF my<>0* will prevent the double collision detection.

1.5 Changes to IntyBASIC

IntyBASIC has continued development over the two years since the publication of "Programming Games for Intellivision". It was at version 1.2.9 and now it is 1.4.2.

Instead of replicating here the whole reference manual for IntyBASIC, I'll only list here the changes to v1.4.

The changes included a complete year of small developments, enhancements, and corrections:

- *VOICE INIT* now stops voice playing in the Intellivoice but doesn't reset it in reality. The reset step is now done invisibly a single time at the start of the IntyBASIC program. Before this, invoking *VOICE INIT* twice caused the Intellivision to stall. You should still invoke *VOICE INIT* at the start of your game, and you can use it now as a way to silence the Intellivoice.

- *FLASH INIT SIZE* allows to specify the space required by the IntyBASIC program in Flash memory, and *FLASH INIT* now selects a 16-sector size by default. You should use *FLASH INIT SIZE* if you want to save more than 16 sectors of data in Flash memory (JLP cartridges).

- *DATA PACKED* now also allows two numbers to be packed into a 16-bit word. This is useful to save memory when you have many values in the range 0-255, at the cost of having to separate them manually in your game.

- Tracker allows to play 8 channels of music (using the extra PSG available in the ECS expansion module). It is sufficient to use a *MUSIC* sentence with another four parameters, so another three voices and drum are played in the extra PSG. But you cannot mix single-PSG music tracks with double-PSG music tracks in a game. All tracks must be single PSG (*MUSIC* sentences with 4 parameters) or double PSG (*MUSIC* sentences with more than 4 parameters).

- Added *ON expr FAST* to avoid generating two instructions (at the risk of crashing your game). If your game requires extra speed, this removes a comparison instruction for limits, so if your input value isn't in the range handled by the **ON** sentence, then your game will crash.

- Added *MUSIC GOSUB* and *MUSIC RETURN*. The usage is *MUSIC GOSUB label*, where *label* is a normal label pointing to another *MUSIC* statement. There is a single stack level, so no nested *MUSIC GOSUB* statements should be used. At the end of the music subroutine, you should use *MUSIC RETURN*.

- The statement *MUSIC VOLUME val* allows to change the volume of the song from 0 to 15, same as the sentence *PLAY VOLUME* but instead it can change the volume inside the music data.

- The statement *MUSIC SPEED val* allows to change the speed of the music. Before you could only depend on the fixed speed signaled by the *DATA* statement at the start of a song. This is very useful in the context of music that plays at a speed, and then has a part that plays faster or slower. Also it is pretty useful for triplets, this is when three musical notes are together with a line; it means these notes are played in the time of two musical notes (for example, if the *MUSIC SPEED* is 8, it means the three notes should be played at *MUSIC SPEED* 5 because 3 x 5 = 15, and yet missing one tick to be 16)

- The direct use of *CONT1*, *CONT2*, *CONT3*, and *CONT4* returns an 8-bit result. It makes it easier to do comparisons with controller values for special things like pressing 1+9 for Pause in a game (it returns $a5, so you can use *IF CONT1=$A5*).

- Name mangling for assembler now uses original names, easing assembler language interfacing. This allows you to interface assembler routines directly to IntyBASIC programs using the known instructions *USR* and *CALL*.

- Support for local labels (using the period character before a label, and it uses the last global label as a prefix). This enables you to have multiple *GOTO* labels inside a *PROCEDURE*, or even data tables without polluting the labels namespace.

- Added *ECS.AVAILABLE* flag, so IntyBASIC can report if it is running with an ECS.

- Added *BITMAP NORMAL*, *BITMAP INVERSE*, and *BITMAP MIRROR_X* for adjusting the interpretation of the following *BITMAP* statements (respectively normal, negation of bits, and mirroring of bits).

- Added *SCREEN ENABLE/DISABLE* for enabling and disabling video using the Intellivision hardware capability. This is useful for drawing complicated screens, or game rooms, and then turn on the screen elegantly to show it instantaneously.

- Added escape sequence \\ to include backslash inside text strings.

- Optimizes *POKE* to direct address with a single MVO instruction.

- Allows the --cc3 option to change the address of RAM memory (for compatibility with the Keyboard Component).

Also the following bugs were detected and solved:

- Solved bug where *IF CONT.B0* wouldn't work.

- Solved bug in optimization of *ABS*.

- Solved bug in optimization of *SGN*.

- Solved bug in *PLAY SIMPLE* (always was processed as *NO DRUMS*)

- Solved bug in compilation of a *VARPTR* expression minus another *VAPRTR* expression.

- Solved bug where the generated metavariable jlp wasn't 3 when using Flash memory.

- Limited numeric escape sequences to 3 digits. This is useful in *PRINT* statements combined with text.

- The manual didn't show the priority bit for sprites in the color parameter: bit 13 = Priority (0= Show over background cards, 1= Show under background cards)

Chapter 2

All about sound

Developing music and sound for a game can be a truly herculean task, but the task can be simplified with the help of a few useful principles.

In this chapter we will talk about how to create reasonable sound effects and convert music sheets.

I'm not a musician, but I hope this helps other non-musicians like me to put sound and music into their games.

2.1 Sound effects

The Intellivision sound processor is the AY-3-8914. It has three voices. Each voice can play an independent tone. Often your game will be playing music in the first and second voice, so we will concentrate on effects playing only in the third voice.

You have two options when developing sound effects in this way: using the noise channel, or not using the noise channel (because your music has a drum pattern; see the IntyBASIC manual or my previous book).

If you are going to use the noise channel because you need explosions in your game, sea effects, or something similar, then you need to put this line in your program before playing music:

```
PLAY SIMPLE NO DRUMS
```

If you are not going to need the noise channel for your sound effects, then the correct line in your program would be:

```
PLAY SIMPLE
```

Furthermore, these settings are on-the-fly, so you can disable your sound effects playing code and command IntyBASIC to play music on all three voice channels by using *PLAY FULL*.

Now to the complicated matters: My recommended sound effect generation is based on the *ON FRAME GOSUB* sentence of IntyBASIC. This sentence calls a procedure when a video frame is going to start. This happens 60 times per second on an NTSC Intellivision, or 50 times per second on a PAL Intellivision.

```
    '
    ' Sound effect tester
    ' by Oscar Toledo G.
    ' Creation date: Dec/30/2020.
    '
    ON FRAME GOSUB play_effects

    FOR c = 0 to 30
        WAIT
    NEXT c

    PRINT AT 0 COLOR 7,"Play effect?"
wait_for_next:
    FOR c = 0 to 15: WAIT: NEXT c

    DO
        WAIT
        c = CONT.key
    LOOP WHILE c = 12

    sound_effect = c: sound_state = 0

    DO
        WAIT
        c = CONT.key
    LOOP WHILE c <> 12

    GOTO wait_for_next
```

```
'
' Play sound effects
'
play_effects: PROCEDURE
    ON sound_effect GOSUB sound_none, sound_tone
    END

sound_none:   PROCEDURE
    SOUND 2,,0          ' Disable tone (volume to zero)
    SOUND 4,,$38        ' Disable noise for third voice
    END

    ' key 1
sound_tone:   PROCEDURE
    SOUND 2,254,12      ' Tone 440hz, volume 12
    sound_state = sound_state + 1
    IF sound_state = 8 THEN sound_effect = 0
    END
```

This simple program will serve us to test any sound effect created in this chapter. You only need to press key 1 to trigger the sound effect. It includes two sound effects: silence, and tone. The silence (*sound_effect = 0*) simply mutes the volume. The tone effect (*sound_effect = 1*) starts a sound effect for four video frames, and then removes it by changing to the silence effect.

When setting a sound effect with this method, we should always assign the sound effect number to the variable *sound_effect*, and reset *sound_state* to zero, because *sound_state* is the way to know the current duration of the sound effect.

If you need an exact frequency for a tone, there is an easy formula:

$$\text{value} = 3579545 \, / \, 32 \, / \, \text{frequency} \qquad (\text{NTSC})$$
$$\text{value} = 4000000 \, / \, 32 \, / \, \text{frequency} \qquad (\text{PAL})$$

Typically the player doesn't note the difference in pitch, and you can forget the fact there are NTSC and PAL Intellivision and just work with the values you want. But if you require it, you can access the *NTSC* variable; it will be non-zero when running over an NTSC Intellivision.

Each sound channel can have a tone value from 0 to 4095, and a volume value from 0 (silence) to 15 (highest volume). Notice that the highest volume is capped around 13, so 14 and 15 aren't noticeably higher in volume.

Now let us create a new procedure based on the *sound_tone* procedure:

```
    ' key 2
sound_ping:   PROCEDURE
    SOUND 2,254,12-sound_state        ' Decrease vol. progressively
    SOUND 4,,$38
    sound_state = sound_state + 1
    IF sound_state = 8 THEN sound_effect = 0
    END
```

Add *sound_ping* to the *ON GOSUB* sentence in the *play_effects* procedure. Because of the order, it will be key 2. After testing it, you can hear that the tone has become a kind of ping. This could be useful for a radar ping.

Now let us test the reverse, creating this procedure:

```
    ' key 3
sound_electronic: PROCEDURE
    SOUND 2,254,4+sound_state         ' Increase vol. progressively
    SOUND 4,,$38
    sound_state = sound_state + 1
    IF sound_state = 8 THEN sound_effect = 0
    END
```

Don't forget to add *sound_electronic* to the *play_effects* procedure. It will be key 3. This sounds more like an electronic music effect.

Let us experiment with a shooting effect by increasing the frequency progressively (i.e. lowering the frequency value in the *SOUND* sentence):

```
     ' key 4
sound_shoot: PROCEDURE
    SOUND 2,127-sound_state*8,12
    SOUND 4,,$38
    sound_state = sound_state + 1
    IF sound_state = 12 THEN sound_effect = 0
    END
```

The *sound_shoot* effect should be key 4. Notice how the increasing value of *sound_state* is used multiplied by 8 for the frequency value.

And we could implement an error (fail) sound by decreasing the output frequency (i.e. increasing the value in the *SOUND* sentence):

```
     ' key 5
sound_fail:   PROCEDURE
    SOUND 2,127+sound_state*64,12
    SOUND 4,,$38
    sound_state = sound_state + 1
    IF sound_state = 12 THEN sound_effect = 0
    END
```

We also multiplied the *sound_state* value but this time by 64.

And now we have a total of 5 sound effects! Just by playing with the frequency and volume individually.

Now let us try a more complicated sound effect moving the two values at the same time:

```
     ' key 6
sound_extra_live: PROCEDURE
    SOUND 2,100-sound_state*4,12-(sound_state % 4)*2
    SOUND 4,,$38
    sound_state = sound_state + 1
    IF sound_state = 16 THEN sound_effect = 0
    END
```

In this example we decrease the frequency value for the sound chip (has the effect of increasing the real frequency in the speaker). And we lower the volume using the modulo operator, creating in each frame a different volume that goes up again: 12, 10, 8, 6, 12, 10, 8, 6, 12, 10, 8, 6.

19

Let us try the same example but increasing frequency, and increasing the volume and returning back to a low volume:

```
' key 7
sound_bird:    PROCEDURE
    SOUND 2,50-sound_state*2,6+(sound_state % 4)*2
    SOUND 4,,$38
    sound_state = sound_state + 1
    IF sound_state = 16 THEN sound_effect = 0
    END
```

It is simply amazing what you can achieve with a single voice, so imagine what you can achieve with two voices.

Let us try an explosion sound:

```
' key 8
sound_explosion:   PROCEDURE
    SOUND 2,,12-sound_state/4
    SOUND 4,28-sound_state/2,$1C ' Mix noise, but turn off tone
    sound_state = sound_state + 1
    IF sound_state = 32 THEN sound_effect = 0
    END
```

It uses only the channel volume, but not the frequency because the mixer setting to $1c (see the IntyBASIC manual) also tunes the noise register frequency (it accepts a value between 0-31; we use the range 13-28).

This procedure is the reason that every other sound effect procedure has the sentence *SOUND 4,,$38* because the explosion sound effect could be interrupted with another sound effect, and the mix register would still be connected to the noise register.

Another try with the noise register but keeping the tone active:

```
' key 9
sound_metal:  PROCEDURE
    SOUND 2,12,12-sound_state/2
    SOUND 4,8-sound_state/4,$18 ' Mix noise and tone
    sound_state = sound_state + 1
    IF sound_state = 16 THEN sound_effect = 0
    END
```

This sound effect is like a hammer in a forge. The sound effect keeps a very high-frequency tone that decreases volume slowly, while mixing the noise register increasing its frequency, so the noise starts kind of deep and turns acute[3].

There is an infinite number of sound effects that you can create using only a single channel, and in fact the following four games include sound effects in the same style and format shown here. So you can explore the other sound effects, and try to discover what makes them sound like that. See appendix D for a bonus program playing digitized sound!

2.2 Introducing and creating music

The music sheets can be converted relatively easily to the IntyBASIC music format. You don't need to be an expert in music (or have enough ear), but you'll need a few principles about music sheets.

By the way, you should be careful about music sheets. There are many freely available on the Internet, and others are per payment, but there is an important warning: not every music sheet is free for your use, or distribution with your game.

The classical music from before 1920 is public domain. This means it can be used without worrying about receiving a letter from a lawyer. Maybe no lawyer will ever hear about your Shakira cover, but why risk a hefty fee? Anyway, this is enough warning.

There are a few things you need to know about music: tempo, notes, duration, and silences[4].

The tempo is the speed used to play the music sheet (the Time Signature 4:4 shown). It's not necessarily an exact indication of the playing

---

[3] A similar effect was used in my game Princess Quest for Intellivision for the metallic walking effect of the beheaded armored knight boss in world 3.

[4] By the way, all the music sheets shown in these pages have been created with MuseScore 3. This beautiful, free, and open-source program is available from http://musescore.org/

speed, so sometimes you can see a musical note ♩ = 120 at the top right of the music sheet, indicating that 120 quarter notes are played each minute.

IntyBASIC sample

nanochess

The notes in a music sheet are presented in a positional way. If you remember your school music lessons then you'll know about C, D, E, F, G, A, and B.[5] These are the musical notes (signaling the pitch of the musical tone). The first seven shown are in octave 2, the following seven are in octave 3, and the remaining groups of seven (pictured in the right hand) are in octave 4, 5 and 6; this is the full range of octaves available in IntyBASIC. Notice there are two bars of notes, and are joined with lines at left and right. The top bar has the treble clef to the left, while the bottom bar has the bass clef to the left. Both technically signal the covered octave range. The small "6" at the beginning of the second line indicates the measure number.

If you read a music sheet, and it has the same arabesque-like symbol at the left, then you can convert the notes pretty easily.

---

[5] In case you are curious, in Spanish these are DO, RE, MI, FA, SOL, LA, and SI. These are also used in U.S. music classes. The only difference is that "SI" is "TI".

How can we convert this to IntyBASIC source code? It is pretty easy actually:

```
'
' Play the first music sheet
' by Oscar Toledo G.
' Creation date: Dec/30/2020.
'

    FOR c = 0 TO 30
         WAIT
    NEXT c

    CLS
    MODE 0,0,0,0,0
    WAIT

    PRINT AT 0 COLOR 7,"Playing"

    PLAY SIMPLE
    PLAY first_music_sheet

    WHILE 1: WEND
first_music_sheet:
    DATA 8
    MUSIC C2,-,-,-
    MUSIC D2,-,-,-
    MUSIC E2,-,-,-
    MUSIC F2,-,-,-
    MUSIC G2,-,-,-
    MUSIC A2,-,-,-
    MUSIC B2,-,-,-
    MUSIC C3,-,-,-
    MUSIC D3,-,-,-
    MUSIC E3,-,-,-
    MUSIC F3,-,-,-
    MUSIC G3,-,-,-
    MUSIC A3,-,-,-
    MUSIC B3,-,-,-
    MUSIC C4,-,-,-
    MUSIC D4,-,-,-
    MUSIC E4,-,-,-
    MUSIC F4,-,-,-
    MUSIC G4,-,-,-
    MUSIC A4,-,-,-
    MUSIC B4,-,-,-
    MUSIC C5,-,-,-
```

```
MUSIC D5,-,-,-
MUSIC E5,-,-,-
MUSIC F5,-,-,-
MUSIC G5,-,-,-
MUSIC A5,-,-,-
MUSIC B5,-,-,-
MUSIC C6,-,-,-
MUSIC D6,-,-,-
MUSIC E6,-,-,-
MUSIC F6,-,-,-
MUSIC G6,-,-,-
MUSIC A6,-,-,-
MUSIC B6,-,-,-
MUSIC STOP
```

The *DATA* statement after the music label is the timing that IntyBASIC will use when playing this melody. The *8* means each note will have a duration of 8 video frames (or 8/50 secs, because the music player for IntyBASIC has an internal timing of 50 hz.)

Then in each *MUSIC* statement the note is put into voice 0, along with an indication of the octave. So it is always a letter and a number for each note. The hyphen symbol is used to mark a rest. If you need to extend a previous note then you use the letter S.

This is enough to do an extremely rudimentary conversion of a music sheet, because we are ignoring the duration of notes, the key notation, and the flat and sharp notes, plus the repetitions.

Duration table	Note	Rest	Relative time
Whole note	𝅝	—	1/1
Half note	𝅗𝅥	—	1/2
Quarter note	𝅘𝅥	𝄽	1/4
Eighth note	𝅘𝅥𝅮	𝄾	1/8
Sixteenth note	𝅘𝅥𝅯	𝄿	1/16

Table of note and rest durations. There are further divisions: 1/32, 1/64, and so on, and these can be easily distinguished by an extra curve (notice the sixteenth note already has two curves).

If you see a dot at the right of a note, it means it has the normal duration **plus half the duration**. So a quarter note with a dot along it has a duration of 1/4+1/8.

It is not so easy to integrate different duration notes in the music. In our previous case we would need to accelerate the music using *DATA 4* instead of *DATA 8*. Now the first four notes would be like this:

```
MUSIC C2,-,-,-
MUSIC S,-,-,-
MUSIC D2,-,-,-
MUSIC S,-,-,-
MUSIC E2,-,-,-
MUSIC S,-,-,-
MUSIC F2,-,-,-
MUSIC S,-,-,-
```

And this allows us now to integrate eighth notes. Remember to extend correctly with *S* the notes that have a longer duration. Otherwise these would sound too short (like staccato).

This little discussion means we should take a look at the music sheet first in order to see the shortest note duration and plan accordingly the timing to be used.

Now let us see the sharp and flat notes.

The left note with the sharp means the musical note is raised by one semitone, while the right note with the flat is lowered by one semitone.

By the way, once a sharp or a flat is used in a note, it remains in effect for the remainder of the measure (until the next vertical line) for our manual interpretation purposes. This can be reset to the normal note if the natural symbol appears:

IntyBASIC allows for some note combinations with the sharp (indicated by the letter S). In the following table, octave 4 is used as our example, but it could be any octave in the range 2 to 6. What is shown are the corresponding IntyBASIC notes for sharp and flat notes used in music sheets.

IntyBASIC note	Sharp note	Flat note
C4	B#	
C4S	C#	Db
D4		
D4S	D#	Eb
E4		Fb
F4	E#	
F4S	F#	Gb
G4		
G4S	G#	Ab
A4		
A4S	A#	Bb
B4		Cb

Finally, we need to know about repetitions. These are marks that mean that some bars are repeated once. Sometimes also there are numeric marks indicating notes that are played the first time, and notes that are played the second time. Like this:

This would be represented in IntyBASIC like this:

```
music_repetition:
    DATA 8
    MUSIC C5,-,-,-
    MUSIC D5,-,-,-
    MUSIC E5,-,-,-
    MUSIC F5,-,-,-

    MUSIC C5,-,-,-
    MUSIC C5,-,-,-
    MUSIC C5,-,-,-
    MUSIC C5,-,-,-

    MUSIC C5,-,-,-
    MUSIC D5,-,-,-
    MUSIC E5,-,-,-
    MUSIC F5,-,-,-

    MUSIC A4,-,-,-
    MUSIC S,-,-,-
    MUSIC S,-,-,-
    MUSIC S,-,-,-

    MUSIC STOP
```

There is a further indication for some melodies: if you see some flat or sharp symbols just to the right of the clef drawing, this is the Key Signature, and it means all the notes marked in these lines for the whole music sheet have that flat or sharp attribute. It also means that if a note with a sharp key has another sharp symbol, it goes up by a further semitone because of the accumulative effect.

Essentially the translation is seamless.

2.3 Invention 8

Can you follow the conversion of the notes to the IntyBASIC notation in the following music sheet? It will help you a lot to learn.

Invention 8 (fragment)

Bach

```
        '                                    MUSIC C5,F3
      ' Play a Bach invention               MUSIC A4#,S
        '                                    MUSIC A4,C4
      FOR c = 0 TO 30                        MUSIC A4#,S
          WAIT                               MUSIC A4,F3
      NEXT c                                 MUSIC G4,S

      CLS                                    MUSIC F4,F4
      MODE 0,0,0,0,0                         MUSIC S,S
      WAIT                                   MUSIC A4,E4
                                             MUSIC S,D4
      PRINT AT 0 COLOR 7,"Bach"              MUSIC C5,C4
                                             MUSIC S,D4
      PLAY SIMPLE                            MUSIC A4,C4
      PLAY tune_1                            MUSIC S,A3#
                                             MUSIC F5,A3
      WHILE 1: WEND                          MUSIC S,A3#
                                             MUSIC C5,A3
        ' Bach Invention 8 (BWV779)          MUSIC S,G3
        ' Fragment
  tune_1:   DATA 7                           MUSIC A5,F3
      MUSIC F4,-                             MUSIC C6,S
      MUSIC S,-                              MUSIC A5#,A3
      MUSIC A4,-                             MUSIC C6,S
      MUSIC S,-                              MUSIC A5,C4
      MUSIC F4,-                             MUSIC C6,S
      MUSIC S,-                              MUSIC A5#,A3
      MUSIC C5,-                             MUSIC C6,S
      MUSIC S,-                              MUSIC A5,F4
      MUSIC F4,-                             MUSIC C6,S
      MUSIC S,-                              MUSIC A5#,C4
                                             MUSIC C6,S
      MUSIC F5,-
      MUSIC S,-                              MUSIC F5,A3
      MUSIC E5,F3                            MUSIC A5,C4
      MUSIC D5,S                             MUSIC G5,A3#
      MUSIC C5,A3                            MUSIC A5,C4
      MUSIC D5,S                             MUSIC F5,A3
```

```
MUSIC A5,C4
MUSIC G5,A3#
MUSIC A5,C4
MUSIC F5,A3
MUSIC A5,C4
MUSIC G5,A3#
MUSIC A5,C4

MUSIC D5,F3
MUSIC F5,A3
MUSIC E5,G3
MUSIC F5,A3
MUSIC D5,F3
MUSIC F5,A3
MUSIC E5,G3
MUSIC F5,A3
MUSIC D5,F3
MUSIC F5,A3
MUSIC E5,G3
MUSIC F5,A3

MUSIC B4,D3
MUSIC S,F3
MUSIC G4,E3
MUSIC S,F3
MUSIC D5,D3
MUSIC S,F3
MUSIC B4,E3
MUSIC S,F3
MUSIC F5,D3
MUSIC S,F3
MUSIC D5,E3
MUSIC S,F3

MUSIC G5,B3
MUSIC A5,S
MUSIC G5,G3
MUSIC F5,S
MUSIC E5,C4
MUSIC F5,S
MUSIC E5,G3
MUSIC D5,S
MUSIC C5,E4
MUSIC D5,S
MUSIC C5,C4
MUSIC A4#,S

MUSIC A4,F4
MUSIC S,G4
MUSIC D5,F4
MUSIC C5,E4
MUSIC B4,D4
MUSIC C5,E4
MUSIC B4,D4
MUSIC A4,C4
MUSIC G4,B3
MUSIC A4,C4
MUSIC G4,B3
MUSIC F4,A3

MUSIC E4,G3
MUSIC F4,S
MUSIC E4,C4
MUSIC D4,B3
MUSIC C4,A3
MUSIC S,B3
MUSIC C5,A3
MUSIC B4,G3
MUSIC C5,F3
MUSIC S,G3
MUSIC E4,F3
MUSIC S,E3

MUSIC F4,D3
MUSIC S,E3
MUSIC C5,D3
MUSIC S,C3
MUSIC E4,G3
MUSIC S,F3
MUSIC C5,E3
MUSIC S,F3
MUSIC D4,G3
MUSIC S,S
MUSIC B4,G2
MUSIC S,S

MUSIC C5,C4
MUSIC S,S
MUSIC S,S
MUSIC S,S
MUSIC STOP
```

Also you can change the instrument used to play the melody or combine them. Change the line *MUSIC F4,-* to *MUSIC F4Y,-* where you can replace the Y with W (the default piano), X (clarinet), Y (flute), Z (bass). Also change the first appearance of the second voice (the line saying *MUSIC E5,F3*, where it could be *MUSIC E5,F3Y*).

This is not by any means a complete guide to music sheets. There are lots of resources that you can find on the Internet with a simple search.

Chapter 3

Oh Mummy!

Oh Mummy! is a game developed by Gem Software in 1984. It was included freely with Amstrad computers. These computers were very popular in Europe.

I knew of the existence of Oh Mummy! through 80's computer magazines, but never played it. This all changed when I went to a meeting of MSX users in Barcelona, Spain, and the featured platform was Amstrad. They allowed me to play some games on their Amstrad computers[6] and one of the games was Oh Mummy!

Amstrad CPC 464 computer. Picture by Bill Bertram (Wikipedia CC-by 2.5)

---

[6] Nice computers by the way. I should have bought one!

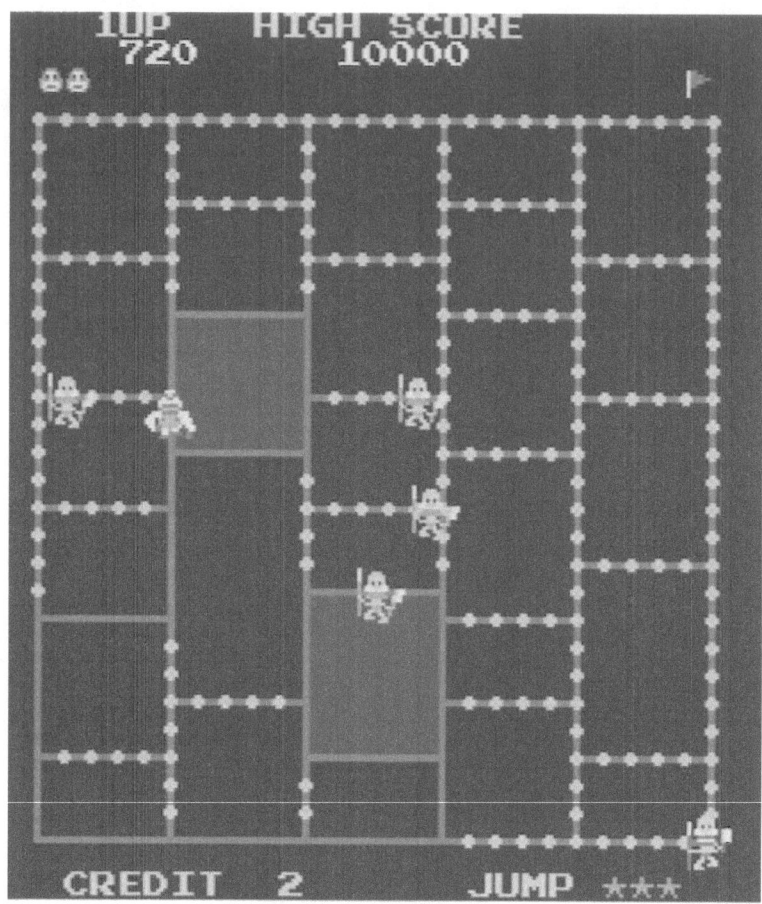

Amidar arcade game by Konami.

The game resembles Amidar, an arcade game by the Japanese company Konami, and distributed in the USA by Stern. In this game the player walks around a maze. Every time a square is completed, the inside is filled. Once all squares on the screen are filled, then the game goes to the next level. Enemies go after the player.

Oh Mummy! changes the theme to an explorer trapped inside a pyramid where it is being pursued by mummies. You do not need to complete all the squares; you only need to find the key and the real sarcophagus to win the level.

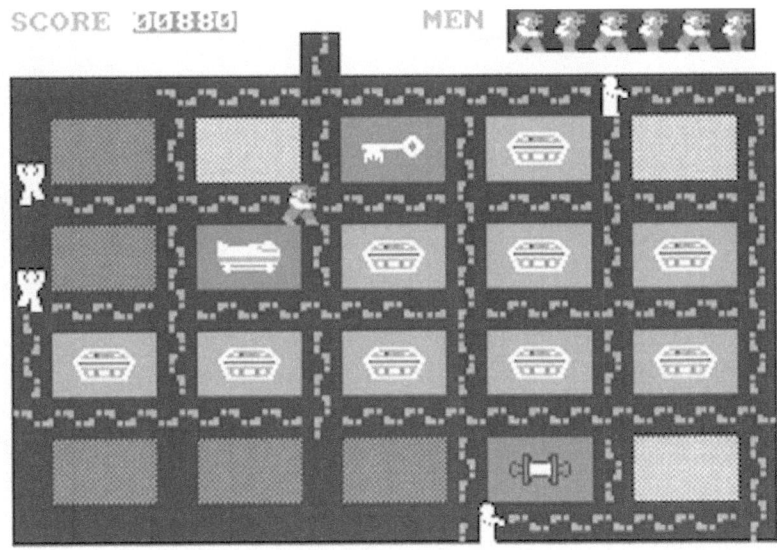

Oh Mummy! original version for Amstrad.

The Intellivision version of this game that appears in this book was published by Intellivision Revolution in the game compilation IntyBASIC Showcase Vol. 2.

3.1 Design

The game engine needs to randomize the items at the start of the board, initialize the mummies at the bottom of the board, and keep track of the player walking on the board to determine when a cell is opened.

This code starts the game:

```
'
' Oh Mummy!
'
' by Oscar Toledo G. (nanochess)
' Inspired on simple game with same name included with Amstrad
'
' Creation date: Dec/13/2016.
' Revision date: Jan/14/2018.
'

'
```

```
' Player and mummies displayed -1,-1 from real
' position (added 8 for final value).
'
CONST DEPTH_X = 7
CONST DEPTH_Y = 7

' Size of bitmap to contain visited cards on screen.
CONST board_size = 16 * 9 / 8

DIM board(20)        ' Content of each tomb
DIM surround(20)     ' Squared surround of each tomb
DIM visit(board_size)   ' Visited cards (bitmap)

DIM x(6)         ' X-coordinate array (player+mummies)
DIM y(6)         ' Y-coordinate array (player+mummies)
DIM t(6)         ' Direction array (player+mummies)

PLAY SIMPLE
WAIT
feature = 0          ' Easy difficulty
```

The constants *DEPTH_X* and *DEPTH_Y* allow the player and mummies to be up and left by one pixel, so they appear to have some depth.

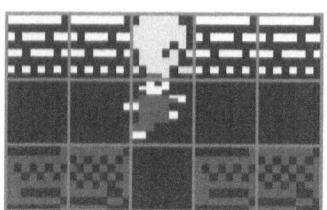 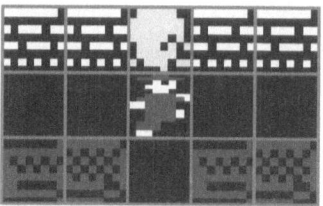

Left side image shows the player offset up and left by one pixel, giving him an appearance of pseudo-3D or depth. Right side image shows the player without any correction, making it look more plain.

The game area measures 16 columns by 9 rows, and this is represented by *board_size* but divided by 8 to get the number of bytes required to save the "visited" state (contained in array *visit*).

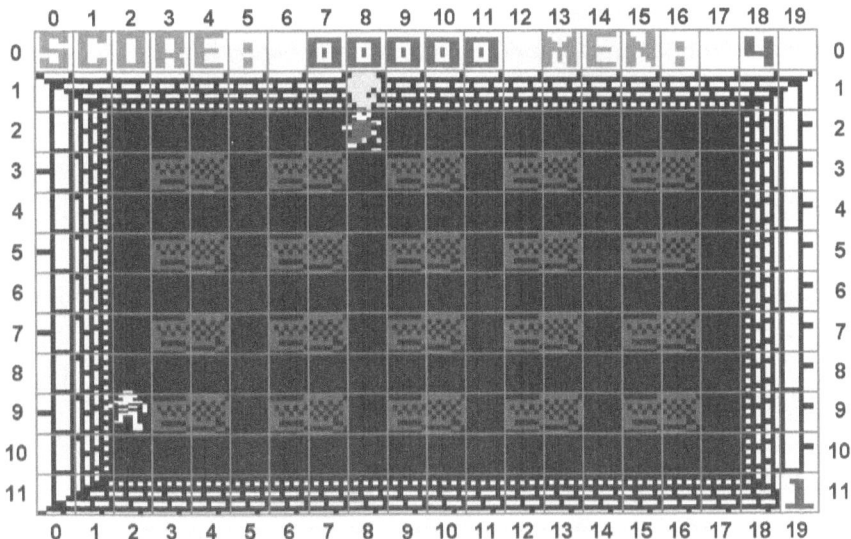

Game area cards on screen. Notice how the playground is 16x9, the size of the array *visit*.

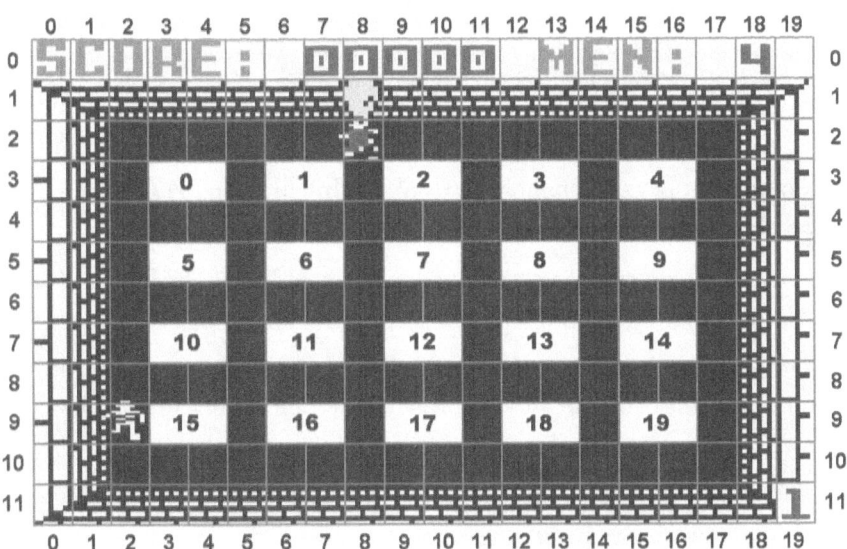

The number of each tomb to be used as index into the array *surround*.

Inside the game area are shown 20 tombs, arranged in a matrix of 5x4 tombs. The "thing" inside each tomb is contained in the array *board*, while the array *surround* contains a count of the cards filled around the tomb, and when it reaches a value of 10 it means it is open.

3.2 Graphics for the game

This game uses two colors for the player main character: yellow and blue. Yellow is for the face, hands and feet, and blue for the suit.

The player and mummies use 8x16 sprites with double Y-resolution. This means the player and mummies have the same size as a standard character cell, but have double detail.

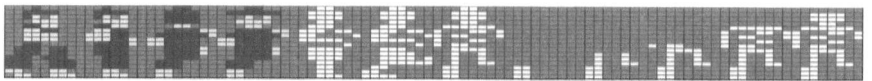

Sprites for Oh Mummy! Notice how the grid is 8x16 because the double Y-resolution mode is being used, so horizontal pixels are "fat". Also notice how the player uses two colors. This is achieved by using two separate sprites: one containing only the blue pixels, and another containing only the yellow pixels.

All the combined graphics for the game don't fit within the maximum number of definable cards of the Intellivision (64 **GRAM** cards), so the player sprite is redefined dynamically to make it animated.

Notice how multicolored sprites are created easily in Intellivision by over-imposing two or more separate sprites in different colors. Although all sprites could be the same scale, the X and Y scale in certain cases can also be used to transform two sprites into a single one, giving the higher detail with an over-imposed sprite.

Of course the eight sprite limitation of Intellivision applies, but with a little ingenuity it can be used to your advantage[7].

---

[7] In the game Sydney Hunter and the Sacred Tribe for Intellivision, the main character uses six sprites to create a multicolored player. The game trick is that only one enemy of 16x16 pixels appears per room and only uses two sprites (two sprites of 8x16), keeping it within the eight-sprite limitation of Intellivision.

The *ASM ORG $F000* line is required because the graphics make the game too big for the standard ROM segment available for Intellivision cartridges. The following data should be put at the end of the "mummy.bas" file:

```
    ASM ORG $F000

    '

    ' Adventurer
    '
sprites_player:
    BITMAP "...X...."   ' 32
    BITMAP "..XXXX.."
    BITMAP "..X....."
    BITMAP "........"
    BITMAP "..XX...."
    BITMAP "....XX.."
    BITMAP "........"
    BITMAP "........"
    BITMAP "..XX...."
    BITMAP ".XXX.XX."
    BITMAP ".XXX.XX."
    BITMAP "XXX.XXX."
    BITMAP "XXX..XXX"
    BITMAP "XXX..XXX"
    BITMAP "........"
    BITMAP "........"

    BITMAP "........"   ' 34
    BITMAP "........"
    BITMAP "...X.X.."
    BITMAP "...XXX.."
    BITMAP "....XX.."
    BITMAP "..XX...."
    BITMAP "..XXXXX."
    BITMAP "..XXXXX."
    BITMAP "........"
    BITMAP "........"
    BITMAP "........"
    BITMAP "........"
    BITMAP "........"
    BITMAP "........"
    BITMAP "XX...XX."
    BITMAP ".XX..XXX"

    BITMAP "...X...."   ' 36
    BITMAP "..XXXX.."
```

```
    BITMAP "..X....."
    BITMAP "........"
    BITMAP "..XX...."
    BITMAP "....XX.."
    BITMAP "....XX.."
    BITMAP "....XX.."
    BITMAP "..XXXX.."
    BITMAP "..XXXX.."
    BITMAP "..XXXX.."
    BITMAP "...XXX.."
    BITMAP "...XXX.."
    BITMAP "...XXX.."
    BITMAP "........"
    BITMAP "........"

    BITMAP "........"   ' 38
    BITMAP "........"
    BITMAP "...X.X.."
    BITMAP "...XXX.."
    BITMAP "....XX.."
    BITMAP "..XX...."
    BITMAP ".XXX...."
    BITMAP ".XXX..X."
    BITMAP "......X."
    BITMAP "........"
    BITMAP "........"
    BITMAP "........"
    BITMAP "........"
    BITMAP "........"
    BITMAP "...XX..."
    BITMAP "...XXX.."

    BITMAP "...XX..."   ' 40
    BITMAP "..XXXX.."
    BITMAP "..XXXX.."
    BITMAP "..XXXX.."
    BITMAP "........"
    BITMAP "..XXXX.."
    BITMAP ".XXXXXX."
    BITMAP "..XXXX.."
    BITMAP "..XXXX.."
    BITMAP "..XXXX.."
```

```
      BITMAP "..XXXX.."              BITMAP "XX......"
      BITMAP "..XXXX.."              BITMAP "XX......"
      BITMAP ".XXX...."              BITMAP "......X."
      BITMAP ".XXX...."              BITMAP "......X."
      BITMAP "........"              BITMAP "........"
      BITMAP "........"              BITMAP "........"
                                     BITMAP "........"
      BITMAP "........"  ' 42        BITMAP ".XX....."
      BITMAP "........"              BITMAP ".XX....."
      BITMAP "........"
      BITMAP "........"
      BITMAP "...XX..."              '
      BITMAP "......XX"              ' Mommy
      BITMAP ".......X"              '
      BITMAP "XX......"         sprites_mummy:
      BITMAP "XX......"              BITMAP "...XX..."  ' 48
      BITMAP "......X."              BITMAP "..XXXX.."
      BITMAP "......X."              BITMAP "..XXXX.."
      BITMAP "........"              BITMAP "...XX..."
      BITMAP "........"              BITMAP "..XXX..."
      BITMAP "........"              BITMAP ".XXX.XX."
      BITMAP ".XX....."              BITMAP ".XX....X"
      BITMAP ".XX....."              BITMAP ".XXXXX.."
                                     BITMAP "......X."
      BITMAP "...XX..."  ' 44        BITMAP "..XXXX.."
      BITMAP ".XXXXXX."              BITMAP "..XXXX.."
      BITMAP "........"              BITMAP "..XXXX.."
      BITMAP "........"              BITMAP "...XX..."
      BITMAP "........"              BITMAP "...XX..."
      BITMAP "..XXXX.."              BITMAP "...XX..."
      BITMAP ".XXXXXX."              BITMAP "...XXXX."
      BITMAP "..XXXX.."
      BITMAP "..XXXX.."              BITMAP "...XX..."  ' 50
      BITMAP "..XXXX.."              BITMAP "..XXXX.."
      BITMAP "..XXXX.."              BITMAP "..XXXX.."
      BITMAP "..XXXX.."              BITMAP "...XX..."
      BITMAP ".XXX...."              BITMAP "..XXX..."
      BITMAP ".XXX...."              BITMAP ".XXX.XX."
      BITMAP "........"              BITMAP ".XX....X"
      BITMAP "........"              BITMAP ".XXXXX.."
                                     BITMAP "......X."
      BITMAP "........"  ' 46        BITMAP "..XXX..."
      BITMAP "........"              BITMAP "..XXXX.."
      BITMAP "...X.X.."              BITMAP "..XXXX.X"
      BITMAP "..XXXX.."              BITMAP "..XXXXXX"
      BITMAP "...XX..."              BITMAP ".XX....."
      BITMAP "......XX"              BITMAP "XX......"
      BITMAP ".......X"              BITMAP "XXXX...."
```

```
BITMAP "...XX..."    ' 52
BITMAP "..XXXX.."
BITMAP "..XXXX.."
BITMAP "...XX..."
BITMAP ".XXXXXX."
BITMAP "X...XX.X"
BITMAP "X.XX...X"
BITMAP "X...XX.."
BITMAP "X.XX...."
BITMAP "..XXXX.."
BITMAP "..X..X.."
BITMAP "..X..X.."
BITMAP "..X..XX."
BITMAP ".XX....."
BITMAP ".XX....."
BITMAP ".XX....."

BITMAP "........"    ' 54
BITMAP "........"
BITMAP "........"
BITMAP "........"
BITMAP "........"
BITMAP "........"
BITMAP "........"
BITMAP "........"
BITMAP "........"
BITMAP "........"
BITMAP "........"
BITMAP "........"
BITMAP "........"
BITMAP ".XX....."
BITMAP ".XX....."
BITMAP ".XX....."

BITMAP "........"    ' 56
BITMAP "........"
BITMAP "........"
BITMAP "........"
BITMAP "........"
BITMAP "........"
BITMAP "........"
BITMAP "........"
BITMAP "........"
BITMAP "........"
BITMAP "..X..X.."
BITMAP "..X..X.."
BITMAP "..X..XX."
BITMAP ".XX....."
```

```
BITMAP ".XX....."
BITMAP ".XX....."

BITMAP "........"    ' 58
BITMAP "........"
BITMAP "........"
BITMAP "........"
BITMAP "........"
BITMAP "........"
BITMAP "........"
BITMAP "X...XX.."
BITMAP "X.XX...."
BITMAP "..XXXX.."
BITMAP "..X..X.."
BITMAP "..X..X.."
BITMAP "..X..XX."
BITMAP ".XX....."
BITMAP ".XX....."
BITMAP ".XX....."

BITMAP "........"    ' 60
BITMAP "........"
BITMAP "........"
BITMAP "........"
BITMAP ".XXXXXX."
BITMAP "X...XX.X"
BITMAP "X.XX...X"
BITMAP "X...XX.."
BITMAP "X.XX...."
BITMAP "..XXXX.."
BITMAP "..X..X.."
BITMAP "..X..X.."
BITMAP "..X..XX."
BITMAP ".XX....."
BITMAP ".XX....."
BITMAP ".XX....."

BITMAP "........"    ' 62
BITMAP "..XXXX.."
BITMAP "..XXXX.."
BITMAP "...XX..."
BITMAP ".XXXXXX."
BITMAP "X...XX.X"
BITMAP "X.XX...X"
BITMAP "X...XX.."
BITMAP "X.XX...."
BITMAP "..XXXX.."
BITMAP "..X..X.."
```

```
    BITMAP "..X..X.."                    BITMAP ".XX....."
    BITMAP "..X..XX."
    BITMAP ".XX....."
    BITMAP ".XX....."
```

Notice the mummies include graphics for the mummy emerging from a tomb (numbers 54 to 62 in **GRAM**).

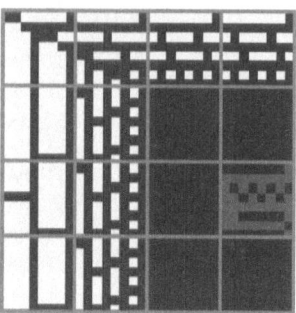

Detail of corner walls for pseudo-3D: The inner bricks are smaller than the outer ones to give an impression of depth.

The game area is composed of walls giving it a pseudo-3D appearance:

```
walls_bitmaps:                           BITMAP "XXXXXXXX"
    BITMAP "XX.....X"   ' 20              BITMAP ".X...X.."
    BITMAP "..XXXXXX"                     BITMAP "XXXXXXXX"
    BITMAP "...XXX.."                     BITMAP "..X...X."
    BITMAP "...X..XX"                     BITMAP "XXXXXXXX"
    BITMAP "...X...X"                     BITMAP ".X.X.X.X"
    BITMAP "...X...X"                     BITMAP "XXXXXXXX"
    BITMAP "...X...X"
    BITMAP "...X...X"                     BITMAP ".......X"   ' 23
                                         BITMAP "XXXXXXXX"
    BITMAP ".......X"   ' 21              BITMAP "...X...."
    BITMAP "XXXXXXXX"                     BITMAP "XXXXXXXX"
    BITMAP "...X...."                     BITMAP "..X...XX"
    BITMAP "XXXXXXXX"                     BITMAP "XXXXXXX."
    BITMAP "XX...X.."                     BITMAP ".XXXX.X."
    BITMAP ".XXXXXXX"                     BITMAP "XXX.X.X."
    BITMAP ".X.XXX.X"
    BITMAP ".X.X.XXX"                     BITMAP "......XX"   ' 24
                                         BITMAP "XXXXXX.."
    BITMAP ".......X"   ' 22              BITMAP "..XXX..."
```

42

```
BITMAP "XX..X..."            BITMAP "XXXXXXXX"
BITMAP "X...X..."            BITMAP ".....X.."
BITMAP "X...X..."
BITMAP "X...X..."            BITMAP "XXX.X.X."   ' 30
BITMAP "X...X..."            BITMAP "X.XXX.X."
                            BITMAP "XXXXXXX."
BITMAP "XX.X.X.X"   ' 25    BITMAP "..X...XX"
BITMAP ".X.X.XXX"            BITMAP "XXXXXXXX"
BITMAP ".X.XXX.X"            BITMAP "...X...X"
BITMAP ".XXX.XXX"            BITMAP "XXXXXXXX"
BITMAP ".X.X.X.X"            BITMAP ".....X.."
BITMAP ".X.X.XXX"
BITMAP ".X.XXX.X"            BITMAP "X...X..."   ' 31
BITMAP ".XXX.XXX"            BITMAP "X...X..."
                            BITMAP "X...X..."
BITMAP "XXX.X.X."   ' 26    BITMAP "X...X..."
BITMAP "X.X.XXX."            BITMAP "XX..X..."
BITMAP "XXXXX.X."            BITMAP "..XXX..."
BITMAP "X.X.X.X."            BITMAP "XXXXXX.."
BITMAP "XXX.X.X."            BITMAP ".....XXX"
BITMAP "X.X.XXX."
BITMAP "XXXXX.X."            BITMAP "...X...X"   ' 32
BITMAP "X.X.X.XX"            BITMAP "...X...X"
                            BITMAP "...X...X"
BITMAP "...X...X"   ' 27    BITMAP "...X...X"
BITMAP "...X...X"            BITMAP "...X...X"
BITMAP "...X...X"            BITMAP "...X...X"
BITMAP "...X...X"            BITMAP "...X...X"
BITMAP "...X..XX"            BITMAP "...XXXXX"
BITMAP "...XXX.."
BITMAP "..XXXXXX"            BITMAP "...X...X"   ' 33
BITMAP "XX...X.."            BITMAP "...X...X"
                            BITMAP "...X...X"
BITMAP ".X.X.XXX"   ' 28    BITMAP "XXXX...X"
BITMAP ".X.XXXX."            BITMAP "...X...X"
BITMAP ".XXXXXXX"            BITMAP "...X...X"
BITMAP "XXX...X."            BITMAP "...X...X"
BITMAP "XXXXXXXX"            BITMAP "...XXXXX"
BITMAP "...X...X"
BITMAP "XXXXXXXX"            BITMAP "X...X..."   ' 34
BITMAP ".....X.."            BITMAP "X...X..."
                            BITMAP "X...XXXX"
BITMAP "XXXXXXXX"   ' 29    BITMAP "X...X..."
BITMAP "X.X.X.X."            BITMAP "X...X..."
BITMAP "XXXXXXXX"            BITMAP "X...X..."
BITMAP "..X...X."            BITMAP "X...X..."
BITMAP "XXXXXXXX"            BITMAP "XXXXX..."
BITMAP "...X...X"
```

```
BITMAP "X...X..."  ' 35          BITMAP "X...X..."
BITMAP "X...X..."                BITMAP "X...X..."
BITMAP "X...XXXX"                BITMAP "X...X..."
BITMAP "X...X..."                BITMAP "X...X..."
```

Finally, the main game screen has several fixed items, although the unopened tombs change graphics and colors with five different schemes, along five levels.

Each tomb has a size of 2x1 cards, so there is a card for the left side, and another for the right side.

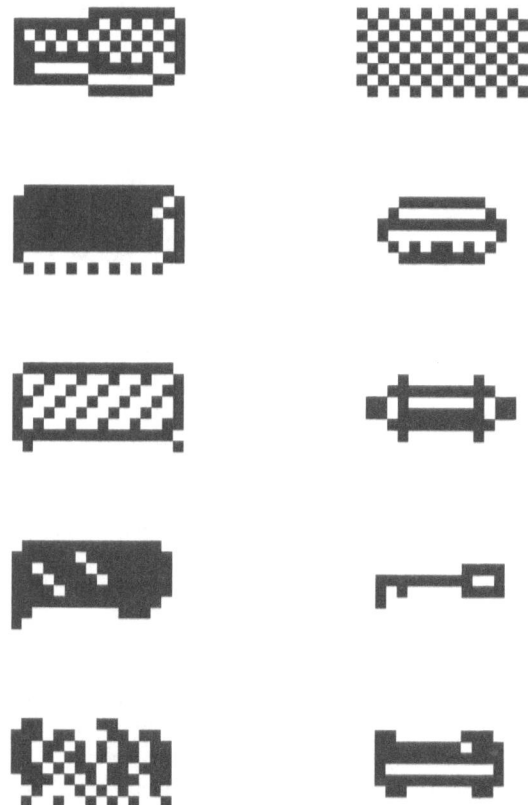

The different tomb graphics for each level. Also the possible contents of each tomb (empy, sarcophagus, scroll, key, real sarcophagus, mummy).

The content of each tomb also has a width of two cards to simplify
the design of the game.

```
        '
        ' Buried graphics
        '
buried_bitmaps:
    BITMAP ".......X"  ' 4 - Left side (lev.1)
    BITMAP "XXXXXXXX"
    BITMAP "X.X.X.X."
    BITMAP "XX.X.X.X"
    BITMAP "XXXXXXXX"
    BITMAP "XX.....X"
    BITMAP "XXXXXX."
    BITMAP ".......X"

    BITMAP "XXXXXXX."  ' 5 - Right side (lev.1)
    BITMAP ".X.X.X.X"
    BITMAP "X.X.X.XX"
    BITMAP ".X.X.X.X"
    BITMAP "X.X.X.XX"
    BITMAP "XXXXX..X"
    BITMAP ".....XX."
    BITMAP "XXXXX..."

    BITMAP ".XXXXXXX"  ' 4 - Left side (lev.2)
    BITMAP "XXXXXXXX"
    BITMAP "XXXXXXXX"
    BITMAP "XXXXXXXX"
    BITMAP "XXXXXXXX"
    BITMAP "XXXXXXXX"
    BITMAP "X......."
    BITMAP ".X.X.X.X"

    BITMAP "XXXXXXX."  ' 5 - Right side (lev.2)
    BITMAP "XXXXXX.X"
    BITMAP "XXXX.XX"
    BITMAP "XXXXX.X"
    BITMAP "XXXXX.X"
    BITMAP "XXXXX.X"
    BITMAP "......XX"
    BITMAP ".X.X.X.."

    BITMAP ".XXXXXXX"  ' 4 - Left side (lev.3)
    BITMAP "X..X..X."
    BITMAP "X.X..X.."
    BITMAP "XX..X..X"
    BITMAP "X..X..X."
```

```
BITMAP "X.X..X.."
BITMAP "XXXXXXXX"
BITMAP ".X......"

BITMAP "XXXXXXX."   ' 5 - Right side (lev.3)
BITMAP ".X..X..X"
BITMAP "X..X..XX"
BITMAP "..X..X.X"
BITMAP ".X..X..X"
BITMAP "X..X..XX"
BITMAP "XXXXXXX."
BITMAP ".......X"

BITMAP ".XXXXXXX"   ' 4 - Left side (lev.4)
BITMAP "XXXXXX.X"
BITMAP "XX.XXXX."
BITMAP "XXX.XXXX"
BITMAP "XXXX.XXX"
BITMAP "XXXXXXXX"
BITMAP "XX......"
BITMAP "X......."

BITMAP "XXXXXX.."   ' 5 - Right side (lev.4)
BITMAP "XXXXXXX."
BITMAP "XXXXXXX."
BITMAP ".XXXXXX."
BITMAP "XXXXXXX."
BITMAP "XXXXXX.."
BITMAP "..XXX..."
BITMAP "........"

BITMAP ".XX....."   ' 4 - Left side (lev.5)
BITMAP "XXX.XX.."
BITMAP "XX.XX.X."
BITMAP "XX.X.XX."
BITMAP "XXX.X.XX"
BITMAP ".XXX.X.X"
BITMAP "..X...X."
BITMAP ".X..X..X"

BITMAP "XX......"   ' 5 - Right side (lev.5)
BITMAP ".XX.XX.."
BITMAP "X.XX.XX."
BITMAP "X.XX.XX."
BITMAP ".XX.XXX."
BITMAP ".XXX.XX."
BITMAP "X.X..X.."
BITMAP ".X.X..X."
```

```
     '
     ' Backgrounds
     '
background_bitmaps_0:
     BITMAP "........"  ' 0 - Steps down
     BITMAP "........"
     BITMAP "........"
     BITMAP "..X....."
     BITMAP "........"
     BITMAP "..XX..X."
     BITMAP "........"
     BITMAP ".....XX."

     BITMAP "........"  ' 1 - Steps up
     BITMAP "........"
     BITMAP "........"
     BITMAP "..XX...."
     BITMAP "........"
     BITMAP "..X..XX."
     BITMAP "........"
     BITMAP "......X."

     BITMAP "........"  ' 2 - Steps left
     BITMAP "........"
     BITMAP "........"
     BITMAP "........"
     BITMAP ".....X.X"
     BITMAP ".....X.."
     BITMAP "..X....."
     BITMAP "..X.X..."

     BITMAP "........"  ' 3 - Steps right
     BITMAP "........"
     BITMAP "........"
     BITMAP "..X.X..."
     BITMAP "....X..."
     BITMAP "........"
     BITMAP ".......X"
     BITMAP ".....X.X"

     BITMAP "X.X.X.X."  ' 4 - Buried
     BITMAP ".X.X.X.X"
     BITMAP "X.X.X.X."
     BITMAP ".X.X.X.X"
     BITMAP "X.X.X.X."
     BITMAP ".X.X.X.X"
     BITMAP "X.X.X.X."
```

47

```
BITMAP ".X.X.X.X"

BITMAP "X.X.X.X."   ' 5 -
BITMAP ".X.X.X.X"
BITMAP "X.X.X.X."
BITMAP ".X.X.X.X"
BITMAP "X.X.X.X."
BITMAP ".X.X.X.X"
BITMAP "X.X.X.X."
BITMAP ".X.X.X.X"

BITMAP "........"   ' 6 - Sarcophagus
BITMAP "....XXXX"
BITMAP "...X...."
BITMAP "..XXXXXX"
BITMAP "..X....."
BITMAP "...X.X.X"
BITMAP "....XXXX"
BITMAP "........"

BITMAP "........"   ' 7
BITMAP "XXXX...."
BITMAP "....X..."
BITMAP "XXXXXX.."
BITMAP ".....X.."
BITMAP "X.X.X..."
BITMAP "XXXX...."
BITMAP "........"

BITMAP "........"   ' 8 - Scroll
BITMAP "....X..."
BITMAP "...XXXXX"
BITMAP ".XX.X..."
BITMAP ".XX.XXXX"
BITMAP "...XXXXX"
BITMAP "....X..."
BITMAP "........"

BITMAP "........"   ' 9
BITMAP "...X...."
BITMAP "XXXX...."
BITMAP "...X.XX."
BITMAP "XXXX.XX."
BITMAP "XXXX...."
BITMAP "...X...."
BITMAP "........"

BITMAP "........"   ' 10 - Key
```

```
BITMAP "........"
BITMAP "........"
BITMAP "..XXXXXX"
BITMAP "..X.X..."
BITMAP "..X....."
BITMAP "........"
BITMAP "........"

BITMAP "........"   ' 11
BITMAP "........"
BITMAP "..XXXX.."
BITMAP "XXX..X.."
BITMAP "..XXXX.."
BITMAP "........"
BITMAP "........"
BITMAP "........"

BITMAP "........"   ' 12 - Real sarcophagus (50 points)
BITMAP "..XX...."
BITMAP "..XXXXXX"
BITMAP "..XXXXXX"
BITMAP "..X....."
BITMAP "..XXXXXX"
BITMAP "...XX..."
BITMAP "........"

BITMAP "........"   ' 13
BITMAP "..XXX..."
BITMAP "XX.XXX.."
BITMAP "XXXXXX.."
BITMAP ".....X.."
BITMAP "XXXXXX.."
BITMAP "...XX..."
BITMAP "........"

BITMAP "........"   ' 14 - Mummy
BITMAP ".X......"
BITMAP ".X......"
BITMAP "..X.X..."
BITMAP "....X..."
BITMAP ".....X.."
BITMAP "........"
BITMAP "........"

BITMAP "........"   ' 15
BITMAP "........"
BITMAP "..X....."
BITMAP "..X....."
```

```
        BITMAP "...X.X.."
        BITMAP ".....X.."
        BITMAP "......X."
        BITMAP "........"

background_bitmaps_1:
        BITMAP "........"   ' 16
        BITMAP ".X.X.X.X"
        BITMAP "........"
        BITMAP ".X......"
        BITMAP ".....X.."
        BITMAP ".X......"
        BITMAP "........"
        BITMAP ".X......"

        BITMAP "........"   ' 17
        BITMAP ".X.X.X.X"
        BITMAP "........"
        BITMAP "........"
        BITMAP "........"
        BITMAP "........"
        BITMAP ".....X.."
        BITMAP "........"

        BITMAP ".XXXXX.."   ' 18 - Door closed
        BITMAP "XXXXXXX."
        BITMAP "XXXXXXX."
        BITMAP "XXXXX.X."
        BITMAP ".XXX.X.X"
        BITMAP ".XXXXX.."
        BITMAP "X.XXX.XX"
        BITMAP "..XXX..."

        BITMAP ".XXXXX.."   ' 19 - Door half-open
        BITMAP "XXXXX.X."
        BITMAP "XXXXX.X."
        BITMAP ".XXXXX.."
        BITMAP ".XXXXX.X"
        BITMAP "........"
        BITMAP ".......X"
        BITMAP "........"
```

3.3 Title screen and difficulty selection

The title screen is an important part of a game. It can be made in several ways, some of which can be very creative. In this case I opted for a standard static screen showing an Egyptian-like woman image, with big letters for the game title.

The graphic goes before the line reading *ASM ORG $F000*.

```
'
' Graphics for title screen
'
INCLUDE "title.bas"
```

The title screen is generated from a BMP graphics file, which is translated by the IntyColor utility.

You can get the original BMP file at the webpage indicated in my preface. And if using the IntyColor utility, you can generate the "title.bas" file using this command line:

```
intycolor -b -n -s0707 title.bmp title.bas mummy_title
```

The option -b means to generate an IntyBASIC source code file. The option -n means to generate only the data (otherwise it makes it a compilable source file). The option -s0707 means to generate graphics for the Color Stack mode (as per sentence *MODE 0,0,7,0,7*). The name of the source graphics file, the name of the target source code, and the name to be used as prefix for the data labels, are all required.

The "title.bas" file should contain the following data (listed here in case you want to enter it by yourself):

```
    REM IntyColor v1.1.5 Jul/25/2017
    REM ./intycolor -b -n -s0707 title.bmp title.bas mummy_title
    REM Created: Sat Jan  6 17:45:08 2018

    ' 64 bitmaps
mummy_title_bitmaps_0:
    DATA $FFFF,$FFFF,$FFFF,$FFFF
    DATA $7777,$0F6F,$0F0F,$9F9F
    DATA $FFFF,$FFFF,$FCFF,$00C0
    DATA $FFFF,$FFFF,$1FFF,$0000
    DATA $FFFF,$FFFF,$FFFF,$3FFF
    DATA $F7F7,$F7F7,$F7F7,$F7F7
    DATA $FFFF,$FCFE,$FFFF,$FFFF
    DATA $4C8E,$4040,$8000,$C280
    DATA $0000,$0000,$0000,$0800
    DATA $0000,$1280,$0000,$2600
    DATA $2006,$0607,$0004,$7F3C
    DATA $BF3F,$3FBF,$3F3F,$BF3F
    DATA $0000,$0000,$0300,$0607
    DATA $0000,$0000,$FCF8,$060E
    DATA $0000,$C000,$C0C0,$C0C0
    DATA $0000,$0000,$E361,$E3E3
mummy_title_bitmaps_1:
    DATA $0000,$0000,$8000,$8080
    DATA $0000,$0C00,$0C0C,$0C0C
    DATA $E9EE,$DFEF,$C7D0,$B5D8
    DATA $C461,$E238,$C43A,$4C34
    DATA $4000,$0000,$0000,$1000
    DATA $7F7F,$3F3F,$3F3F,$1F3F
    DATA $BFBF,$DFDF,$EFEF,$F7EF
    DATA $0C0E,$0C0C,$060C,$0107
    DATA $0606,$0E06,$1C0C,$E0F8
    DATA $FEDC,$C6E6,$C6C6,$C6C6
    DATA $0100,$0101,$0301,$0303
    DATA $B6A2,$B6B6,$3C36,$1C1C
    DATA $CC8C,$CCCC,$CCCC,$676F
```

```
        DATA $6F6D,$6C6E,$6C6C,$ECEC
        DATA $FDD9,$CDED,$CDCD,$CDCD
        DATA $FFBB,$99DD,$9999,$9999
mummy_title_bitmaps_2:
        DATA $B830,$9D98,$8F8D,$8687
        DATA $CCCC,$8CCC,$0C8C,$0C00
        DATA $FFFF,$FEFE,$FFFE,$FFFF
        DATA $7EB0,$FF7F,$3FFF,$1FBF
        DATA $FD04,$FFFD,$FCFE,$FCFC
        DATA $5012,$5040,$A030,$F8C1
        DATA $1F1F,$1FDF,$0F1F,$2FCF
        DATA $FBF7,$FBFB,$FDFB,$FDFD
        DATA $0C06,$180C,$0018,$0000
        DATA $000C,$0000,$0000,$0000
        DATA $9F87,$BFDF,$9FBF,$FFE0
        DATA $FDFE,$FDFD,$FDFD,$BD7D
        DATA $B033,$A08F,$9387,$B6A8
        DATA $0FEF,$EFEF,$EF0F,$4FEF
        DATA $FEFE,$FFFE,$FFFF,$FFFF
        DATA $FFFF,$7FFF,$7F7F,$BFBF
mummy_title_bitmaps_3:
        DATA $DDDD,$DDDD,$DDDD,$DBDB
        DATA $D5CB,$C5CA,$D0D5,$E7D1
        DATA $1F8F,$3F9F,$FF7F,$FFFF
        DATA $DFBF,$DFDF,$EFEF,$EFEF
        DATA $80FC,$FAFA,$FDFD,$FEFE
        DATA $4E00,$8788,$A144,$90A8
        DATA $5B1B,$234B,$0B13,$4783
        DATA $9FFF,$8081,$0886,$3118
        DATA $FFFF,$1FFF,$A041,$4B93
        DATA $F7F7,$FBF7,$1BFB,$FFE3
        DATA $A448,$E9D2,$FBF4,$FFFC
        DATA $0737,$0707,$17E7,$00E7
        DATA $FFFF,$FFFF,$F8FE,$7F87
        DATA $0241,$0104,$7F0F,$FFFF
        DATA $8727,$FF3F,$FFFF,$FFFF
        DATA $FFFF,$FFFF,$FF00,$FFFF


        REM 20x12 cards
mummy_title_cards:
        DATA $0800,$1802,$1802,$180A,$1812,$181A,$1822,$1802,$1802,$182A
        DATA $0800,$0800,$0800,$0800,$0800,$0800,$0800,$0800,$0800,$0800
        DATA $0800,$1802,$1832,$183A,$1842,$184A,$1852,$185A,$2861,$0869
        DATA $0871,$0807,$0879,$0881,$0807,$0807,$0807,$0807,$0889,$0807
        DATA $2000,$1802,$1802,$1892,$189A,$18A2,$18AA,$18B2,$28B9,$08C1
        DATA $08C9,$08D1,$08D9,$08E1,$08E9,$08F1,$08F9,$0901,$0909,$0807
        DATA $2000,$1802,$1912,$191A,$1922,$192A,$1932,$193A,$2000,$0807
        DATA $0807,$0807,$0807,$0807,$0807,$0807,$0807,$0941,$0949,$0807
```

```
DATA $2000,$1802,$1802,$1952,$195A,$1962,$196A,$1972,$197A,$182A
DATA $0800,$0800,$0800,$0800,$0800,$0800,$0800,$0800,$0800,$0800
DATA $0800,$1802,$1802,$1802,$1982,$198A,$1992,$1802,$199A,$182A
DATA $0800,$0800,$0800,$0800,$0800,$0800,$0800,$0800,$0800,$0800
DATA $0800,$1802,$19A2,$19AA,$19B2,$1802,$19BA,$19C2,$19CA,$182A
DATA $0800,$0800,$0800,$0800,$0800,$0800,$0800,$0800,$0800,$0800
DATA $0800,$1802,$1802,$19D2,$19DA,$19E2,$19EA,$19F2,$1802,$182A
DATA $0800,$0800,$0800,$0800,$0800,$0800,$0800,$0800,$0800,$0800
DATA $0800,$19FA,$19FA,$19FA,$19FA,$19FA,$19FA,$19FA,$19FA
DATA $0800,$0800,$0800,$0800,$0800,$0800,$0800,$0800,$0800,$0800
DATA $0800,$0800,$0800,$0800,$0800,$0800,$0800,$0800,$0800,$0800
DATA $0800,$0800,$0800,$0800,$0800,$0800,$0800,$0800,$0800,$0800
DATA $0800,$0800,$0800,$0800,$0800,$0800,$0800,$0800,$0800,$0800
DATA $0800,$0800,$0800,$0800,$0800,$0800,$0800,$0800,$0800,$0800
DATA $0800,$0800,$0800,$0800,$0800,$0800,$0800,$0800,$0800,$0800
DATA $0800,$0800,$0800,$0800,$0800,$0800,$0800,$0800,$0800,$0800
```

The code to show the title screen goes after the line saying "feature = 0" in the file "mummy.bas":

```
      '
      ' Show title screen
      '
mummy_title_screen:
      CLS
      PLAY OFF
      GOSUB sound_silent
      MODE 0,0,7,0,7
      BORDER 0
      FOR c = 0 TO 7
          SPRITE c,0
      NEXT c
      WAIT
      DEFINE 0,16,mummy_title_bitmaps_0
      WAIT
      DEFINE 16,16,mummy_title_bitmaps_1
      WAIT
      DEFINE 32,16,mummy_title_bitmaps_2
      WAIT
      DEFINE 48,16,mummy_title_bitmaps_3
      WAIT
      SCREEN mummy_title_cards

      '
      ' Difficulty selection
```

```
         '
     PRINT AT 200 COLOR 5,"Press Enter to start"

     debounce = 20
select_1:
     WAIT
     PRINT AT 151 COLOR 2,"1> Mode:"
     PRINT AT 173 COLOR 3
     IF feature = 0 THEN PRINT " Easy "
     IF feature = 1 THEN PRINT "Medium"
     IF feature = 2 THEN PRINT " Hard "

     IF debounce <> 0 THEN    ' Can accept another key?
         debounce = debounce - 1 ' No
         GOTO select_1
     END IF

     IF cont.key = 1 THEN    ' Next difficulty
         feature = (feature + 1) % 3
         debounce = 15
     END IF

     IF cont.key <> 11 THEN GOTO select_1

         '
         ' Game started
         '
     e = 5:GOSUB effect
     FOR d = 1 TO 10
         PRINT AT 200 COLOR 5,"Press Enter to start"
         WAIT
         PRINT AT 200 COLOR 7,"Press Enter to start"
         WAIT
         PRINT AT 200,"                        "
         WAIT
         WAIT
     NEXT d

stuck:   GOTO stuck

     '
     ' Get silent
     '
sound_silent: PROCEDURE
     sound_effect = 0
     sound_state = 0
     END
```

55

```
'
' Start a sound effect with priority checking
'
effect: PROCEDURE
    IF e < sound_effect THEN RETURN
    sound_effect = e
    sound_state = 0
    END
```

It turns off the music (if playing), and then sets up the Color Stack mode exactly as the setup for the converted image was requested for IntyColor. It defines the bitmaps being used, and then blasts the graphics to the screen by means of *SCREEN mummy_title_cards*.

It adds a message saying "Press Enter to start". Notice we are using lowercase. This is possible because we are using the Color Stack mode, and it isn't possible in the Foreground/Background mode (*MODE 1*).

Inside a small loop, it updates the display with the current difficulty mode, and waits for *CONT.KEY* to be 11 (pressing the Enter key). Or if it detects key 1 is pressed then it changes the difficulty. To prevent a bouncing of the key, it sets the *debounce* variable to 15 once a key is pressed. The *debounce* variable is decreased on each frame until it is zero, and this is the moment when the loop accepts another key.

The *sound_silent* and *effect* procedures are working code that turns off the sound effects, and enables sound effects. Currently these don't do anything because the game currently doesn't play any sound effect. We will talk about that soon.

3.4 Game start and level setup.

The game starts by redefining the bitmaps to the graphics needed for the levels of the game.

The default speed of the game is adjusted per the difficulty chosen (calculated by *feature * 6 + $30*).

Also the mummies alive at the start of the game are 1, 2 or 3, also per the difficulty. Notice it assigns 0, 1, or 2, but this number is increased immediately at the start of the level.

The score is reset to zero, and the level to zero (it is increased immediately by one). Finally the volume is set up to a middle level using *PLAY VOLUME 12*, and then *PLAY streets_of_cairo* to get the background theme music started.

The following code replaces the line "stuck: goto stuck".

```
'
' Start of game
'
CLS
MODE 1
DEFINE 0,16,background_bitmaps_0
WAIT
DEFINE 16,4,background_bitmaps_1
WAIT
DEFINE ALTERNATE 20,16,walls_bitmaps
WAIT
DEFINE 48,16,sprites_mummy
WAIT

' Game is faster per difficulty
speed = feature * 6 + $30

' Start enemies are more per difficulty
enemies_alive = 0 + feature

#score = 0      ' Reset score
men = 4         ' Lives
level = 0 ' Start level

PLAY VOLUME 12
PLAY streets_of_cairo
```

Now to set up the next level, it increases the number of mummies alive by one (but not exceeding 6). It also increases the level number.

It clears the screen, and then fills the board with random empty cells or tomb cells (to be discovered by the player). Also each cell is marked as non-visited by resetting *surround(c)* to zero indicating that zero cards around each tomb are visited.

```
next_level:

    '

    ' On each level increase number of enemies
    '
    IF enemies_alive < 6 THEN
        enemies_alive = enemies_alive + 1
    END IF

    '
    ' Increase level number
    '
    level = level + 1
    IF level = 11 THEN level = 1

    CLS

    ' Fill board
    FOR c = 0 TO 19
        board(c) = RANDOM(2)    ' Empty or tomb
        surround(c) = 0
    NEXT c
```

Then a scroll (to kill mummies) is put randomly inside the board. It adds one extra scroll if there are many mummies.

```
    c = RANDOM(20)      ' Random cell
    board(c) = 2        ' Put scroll

    ' Add a further scroll if there are more than 5 mummies
    IF enemies_alive >= 5 THEN
        '
        ' Choose a non-used cell
        '
        DO
            c = RANDOM(20)
        LOOP WHILE board(c) >= 2
        board(c) = 2  ' Put a scroll
    END IF
```

The game has a trick under the hood: Sometimes opening a tomb brings an extra mummy to the game!

```
DO
      c = RANDOM(20)
LOOP WHILE board(c) >= 2
board(c) = 3   ' Put a mummy
```

Finally the key and the sarcophagus are added to the board. Both are needed to win the level. The visited status of all cards are set to zero, and it sets the variable *has_scroll*, *has_key*, and *has_tomb* to zero.

```
DO
      c = RANDOM(20)
LOOP WHILE board(c) >= 2
board(c) = 4   ' Put a key

DO
      c = RANDOM(20)
LOOP WHILE board(c) >= 2
board(c) = 5   ' Put a sarcophagus

FOR c = 0 TO board_size - 1
      visit(c) = 0
NEXT c
has_scroll = 0
has_key = 0
has_tomb = 0
```

Each level has a different color theme for the pyramid, and also some special graphics for yet uncovered tombs.

As the Intellivision has few 16-bit variables, the variable *#mirror_x* is reused.

```
      '
      ' Select graphics and color scheme for level
      '
      c = level % 5
      IF c = 1 THEN
            #mirror_x = 1        ' Blue tombs
            #color = $2400       ' Yellow walls
            BORDER 6
      ELSEIF c = 2 THEN
```

```
        #mirror_x = 2        ' Red tombs
        #color = $2400       ' Yellow walls
        BORDER 6
ELSEIF c = 3 THEN
        #mirror_x = 6        ' Yellow tombs
        #color = $2400       ' Yellow walls
        BORDER 6
ELSEIF c = 4 THEN
        #mirror_x = $0207    ' Purple tombs
        #color = $2600       ' White walls
        BORDER 7
ELSE
        #mirror_x = 5        ' Green tombs
        #color = $2400       ' Yellow walls
        BORDER 6
END IF

' Draw top row, keep door open
PRINT AT 20 COLOR #color
PRINT "\276\277\278\278\278\278\278\278"
PRINT COLOR 3," "
PRINT COLOR #color
PRINT "\278\278\278\278\278\278\278\278\278\279\280"

' Draw alternate rows
FOR y = 2 TO 10 STEP 2
    ' Walking row
    PRINT AT y * 20 COLOR #color,"\288\281"
    PRINT COLOR 3, "                 "
    PRINT COLOR #color,"\282\290"
    ' Tombs row
    IF y <> 10 THEN
        PRINT AT y * 20 + 20 COLOR #color,"\289\281"
        PRINT 0,#mirror_x XOR $0820,#mirror_x XOR $0828
        PRINT 0,#mirror_x XOR $0820,#mirror_x XOR $0828
        PRINT 0,#mirror_x XOR $0820,#mirror_x XOR $0828
        PRINT 0,#mirror_x XOR $0820,#mirror_x XOR $0828
        PRINT 0,#mirror_x XOR $0820,#mirror_x XOR $0828,0
        PRINT COLOR #color,"\282\291"
    END IF
NEXT y

' Draw bottom row along the level number
PRINT AT 220 COLOR #color
PRINT "\283\284\285\285\285\285\285\285\285\285"
PRINT "\285\285\285\285\285\285\285\285\286\287"
IF level < 10 THEN
    PRINT AT 239 COLOR #color + 1,<>level
```

```
ELSEIF level < 100 THEN
     PRINT AT 238 COLOR #color + 1,<>level
ELSE
     PRINT AT 237 COLOR #color + 1,<>level
END IF

' Define graphics for tombs
DEFINE 4,2,VARPTR buried_bitmaps((level - 1) % 5 * 8)

WAIT
```

Notice how the level is drawn by using the *PRINT* statements and the escape feature to insert **GRAM** cards. The values in the range 256-319 are translated to **GRAM** card numbers 0-63, easily referred to the **BITMAP** definition shown previously (page 42, *walls_bitmaps*).

Once the level is drawn, this display state is reused when the player dies. But still some things need to be reset, like clearing all the sprites (**MOB**) on screen.

Mummies also are repopulated, clearing all mummies, and then putting them at the bottom of the screen, alternating a mummy to the left, and then one to the right. By default all mummies try to go up at start.

```
    ' Repeat level
repeat_level:
    FOR c = 0 TO 7
         SPRITE c,0
    NEXT c

    ' Populate mummies
    FOR c = 0 TO 5
         y(c) = 0
    NEXT c
    FOR c = 0 TO enemies_alive - 1
         IF (c AND 1) = 0 THEN
              x(c) = 16 + 24 * (c / 2)     ' Left
         ELSE
              x(c) = 136 - 24 * (c / 2)    ' Right
         END IF
         y(c) = 80 ' At bottom
         t(c) = 0  ' Going up
    NEXT c

    WAIT
```

61

The last things that are done are: updating the current score, and showing the number of men remaining. Also the tile corresponding to the pyramid's door is cleared (to make it open) using *#backtab(28) = 0*, and then the player is put directly over that tile (*x=64, y=8*), and also the direction is marked as going down so there is a little animation of the player entering the pyramid.

```
        PRINT AT 0 COLOR #color + 2,"SCORE: "
        PRINT COLOR #color + 1,<5>#score
        PRINT COLOR #color + 2," MEN: "
        PRINT COLOR #color + 1,<>men," "
        current_speed = 0
        #backtab(28) = 0

        '
        ' Player start and movement to enter through the door
        '
        x = 64
        y = 8
        dir = 4

        animation = 0
        shield = 0
stuck:    GOTO stuck
```

Finally the background music should be added to make this partial game able to be compiled by IntyBASIC.

```
        '                              MUSIC S,S,-
        ' Background music             MUSIC E4,E3,-
        '                              MUSIC S,S,-
streets_of_cairo:                      MUSIC S,B3,-
        DATA 7                         MUSIC S,S,-
        MUSIC E4,-,-                   MUSIC E4,B2,-
        MUSIC S,-,-                    MUSIC S,S,-
        MUSIC F4#,-,-                  MUSIC F4#,B3,-
        MUSIC S,-,-                    MUSIC S,S,-

        MUSIC G4,E3,-                  MUSIC G4,E3,-
        MUSIC S,S,-                    MUSIC S,S,-
        MUSIC S,B3,-                   MUSIC B4,B3,-
        MUSIC S,S,-                    MUSIC S,S,-
        MUSIC F4#,B2,-                 MUSIC F4#,B2,-
        MUSIC S,S,-                    MUSIC S,S,-
        MUSIC S,B3,-                   MUSIC G4,B3,-
```

```
MUSIC S,S,-                    MUSIC F3#,A3,-
MUSIC E4,E3,-                  MUSIC S,S,-
MUSIC S,S,-                    MUSIC S,S,-
MUSIC S,B3,-                   MUSIC S,S,-
MUSIC S,S,-                    MUSIC E3,G3,-
MUSIC G4,B2,-                  MUSIC S,S,-
MUSIC S,S,-                    MUSIC S,S,-
MUSIC A4,B3,-                  MUSIC S,S,-
MUSIC S,S,-                    MUSIC E3,-,-
                               MUSIC S,-,-
MUSIC B4,E3,-                  MUSIC F3#,-,-
MUSIC B4,S,-                   MUSIC S,-,-
MUSIC B4,B3,-
MUSIC B4,S,-                   MUSIC G3,E3,-
MUSIC B4,E3,-                  MUSIC S,S,-
MUSIC S,S,-                    MUSIC B3,S,-
MUSIC C5,B3,-                  MUSIC S,S,-
MUSIC S,S,-                    MUSIC F3#,B2,-
MUSIC B4,C3,-                  MUSIC S,S,-
MUSIC S,S,-                    MUSIC G3,S,-
MUSIC A4,A3,-                  MUSIC S,S,-
MUSIC S,S,-                    MUSIC E3,E2,-
MUSIC G4,C3,-                  MUSIC S,S,-
MUSIC S,S,-                    MUSIC S,S,-
MUSIC A4,A3,-                  MUSIC S,S,-
MUSIC S,S,-                    MUSIC E3,-,-
                               MUSIC S,-,-
MUSIC B4,E3,-                  MUSIC F3#,-,-
MUSIC S,S,-                    MUSIC S,-,-
MUSIC -,-,-
MUSIC -,-,-                    MUSIC G3,B3,-
MUSIC F5#,B2,-                 MUSIC S,S,-
MUSIC S,S,-                    MUSIC S,S,-
MUSIC S,S,-                    MUSIC S,S,-
MUSIC G5,S,-                   MUSIC F3#,A3,-
MUSIC E5,E2,-                  MUSIC S,S,-
MUSIC S,S,-                    MUSIC S,S,-
MUSIC -,-,-                    MUSIC S,S,-
MUSIC -,-,-                    MUSIC E3,G3,-
MUSIC E3,-,-                   MUSIC S,S,-
MUSIC S,-,-                    MUSIC S,S,-
MUSIC F3#,-,-                  MUSIC S,S,-
MUSIC S,-,-                    MUSIC E3,-,-
                               MUSIC S,-,-
MUSIC G3,B3,-                  MUSIC F3#,-,-
MUSIC S,S,-                    MUSIC S,-,-
MUSIC S,S,-
MUSIC S,S,-                    MUSIC G3,E3,-
```

```
MUSIC S,S,-           MUSIC E3,E2,-
MUSIC B3,S,-          MUSIC S,S,-
MUSIC S,S,-           MUSIC S,S,-
MUSIC F3#,B2,-        MUSIC S,S,-
MUSIC S,S,-
MUSIC G3,S,-          MUSIC REPEAT
MUSIC S,S,-
```

3.5 Main game loop

The main game loop replaces the line "stuck: goto stuck".

It starts by calculating the sprite number required for the player, and whether it is going to use the X-mirror feature provided by the STIC (display hardware). The sprite number in the variable *spr* is used to define the new bitmaps for the player in the same card number (44).

The blue sprite of the player is set up using *SPRITE 0* with the current coordinates in *x* and *y* variable. If the player has the scroll, the color is changed to green (*has_scroll * 4 + 1 = 5* = green color).

The yellow sprite of the player is sct up using *SPRITE 1;* nothing special about the color in this one.

```
main_loop:
    ' Select sprite per animation frame
    IF animation = 0 THEN spr = 40:#mirror_x = $0080 + DEPTH_Y
    IF animation = 1 THEN spr = 40:#mirror_x = $0480 + DEPTH_Y
    IF animation = 2 THEN spr = 32:#mirror_x = $0080 + DEPTH_Y
    IF animation = 3 THEN spr = 36:#mirror_x = $0080 + DEPTH_Y
    IF animation = 4 THEN spr = 44:#mirror_x = $0080 + DEPTH_Y
    IF animation = 5 THEN spr = 44:#mirror_x = $0480 + DEPTH_Y
    IF animation = 6 THEN spr = 32:#mirror_x = $0480 + DEPTH_Y
    IF animation = 7 THEN spr = 36:#mirror_x = $0480 + DEPTH_Y

    ' The player graphics are redefined
    DEFINE 44,4,VARPTR sprites_player((spr - 32) * 4)

    ' Player color blue
    SPRITE 0,x + $0300 + DEPTH_X, y + #mirror_x
    SPRITE 0, , , 44 * 8 + $0801 + has_scroll * 4
```

```
' Player color yellow
SPRITE 1,x + $0300 + DEPTH_X, y + #mirror_x
SPRITE 1, , , 44 * 8 + $0816
```

The mummies use the remaining sprites 2-7. Each sprite corresponds in order to the mummy 0 to 5 from arrays *x*, *y*, and the animation is inferred from the direction data contained in array *t*.

Whenever the *y* position of a mummy is zero, it means the mummy is inactive, and the sprite is disabled by means of *SPRITE 2 + c, 0*.

Notice the *t(c)* array offers the following information about a mummy:

- 0 = Going up.
- 1 = Going down.
- 2 = Going left.
- 3 = Going right.
- >= 4 the mummy is appearing inside an opened tomb.

Finally the game waits for the video frame to complete by using the sentence *WAIT*.

```
' Show mummies
FOR c = 0 TO 5
    IF y(c) = 0 THEN
        SPRITE 2 + c,0
    ELSE
        d = t(c)
        IF d >= 4 THEN      ' Mummy appearing
            spr = 54 + ((d - 16) / 48) * 2
            #mirror_x = $0088
            d = d + 2
            IF d >= 254 THEN d = d AND 1
            t(c) = d
        ELSEIF d < 2 THEN   ' Going up/down
            spr = 52
            IF FRAME AND 16 THEN
                #mirror_x = $0480 + DEPTH_Y
            ELSE
                #mirror_x = $0080 + DEPTH_Y
            END IF
```

```
              ELSEIF d = 3 THEN  ' Going right
                   #mirror_x = $0080 + DEPTH_Y
                   spr = 48
                   IF FRAME AND 16 THEN spr = 50
              ELSE 'IF d = 2 THEN      ' Going left
                   #mirror_x = $0480 + DEPTH_Y
                   spr = 48
                   IF FRAME AND 16 THEN spr = 50
              END IF
              SPRITE 2 + c,x(c) + $0300 + DEPTH_X, y(c) + #mirror_x
              SPRITE 2 + c, , , spr * 8 + $0807
         END IF
    NEXT c
    WAIT
    ' Here goes the collision code

    ' Here goes the victory code

    ' Here goes the mummies movement code

    ' Here goes the player movement code

    GOTO main_loop
```

3.6 Player movement

This code replaces the comment reading "Here goes the player movement
code":

```
IF (FRAME AND 1)<>0 THEN
   ' Player in crossroad
   IF (x AND 7)=0 THEN
        IF (y AND 7)=0 THEN
          ' Draw footprints
          a = y / 8
          b = x / 8 - 2
          PRINT AT a * 20 + (b + 2)
          IF dir = 4 THEN PRINT $0803+0*8
          IF dir = 1 THEN PRINT $0803+1*8
          IF dir = 8 THEN PRINT $0803+2*8
          IF dir = 2 THEN PRINT $0803+3*8

          ' Take note of visited card
          IF a >= 2 THEN
             a = a - 2
```

```
                IF (visit(a * 2 + b / 8) AND bit(b AND 7)) = 0 THEN
                    visit(a*2+b/8) = visit(a*2+b/8) + bit(b AND 7)
                    ' Add counts of visits to each tomb
                    #c = (a * 16 + b) * 4
                    IF reference_board(#c) <> -1 THEN
                        c = reference_board(#c)
                        GOSUB increase
                    END IF
                    #c = #c + 1
                    IF reference_board(#c) <> -1 THEN
                        c = reference_board(#c)
                        GOSUB increase
                    END IF
                    #c = #c + 1
                    IF reference_board(#c) <> -1 THEN
                        c = reference_board(#c)
                        GOSUB increase
                    END IF
                    #c = #c + 1
                    IF reference_board(#c) <> -1 THEN
                        c = reference_board(#c)
                        GOSUB increase
                    END IF
                END IF
            END IF
        END IF
END IF
IF y < 16 THEN
    c = dir
    IF dir = 4 THEN       ' Entering dungeon
        IF y = 15 THEN
            IF has_key + has_tomb = 2 THEN
                #backtab(28) = 0
            ELSEIF has_key + has_tomb THEN
                #backtab(28) = $0803+19*8
            ELSE
                #backtab(28) = $0803+18*8
            END IF
        END IF
    END IF
ELSE
    c = cont
    IF c = $48 THEN GOTO mummy_title_screen
    IF (c AND $E0) THEN
        c = 0
    ELSE
        c = mummy_controller_direction(c AND $1f)
    END IF
```

```
        END IF
        IF c <> 255 THEN
            ' Check if can change direction
            IF (c = 1 OR c = 4) THEN        ' Up/down
                    IF (x AND 7) <> 0 THEN
                    ELSEIF x % 24 < 16 THEN
                    ELSE
                        dir = c
                    END IF
            ELSEIF (c = 2 OR c = 8) THEN' Left/right
                    IF (y AND 7) <> 0 THEN
                    ELSEIF (y - 16) % 16 >= 8 THEN
                    ELSE
                        dir = c
                    END IF
            ELSE
                dir = c
            END IF
            IF dir = 1 THEN        ' Up
                animation = 0 + (FRAME AND 8) / 8
                IF y <= 16 THEN
                    IF x = 64 THEN
                        IF has_key=1 AND has_tomb=1 THEN y = y - 1
                    END IF
                END IF
                IF y > 16 THEN y = y - 1
            END IF
            IF dir = 2 THEN        ' Right
                animation = 2 + (FRAME AND 8) / 8
                IF x < 136 THEN x = x + 1
            END IF
            IF dir = 4 THEN        ' Down
                animation = 4 + (FRAME AND 8) / 8
                IF y < 80 THEN y = y + 1
            END IF
            IF dir = 8 THEN        ' Left
                animation = 6 + (FRAME AND 8) / 8
                IF x > 16 THEN x = x - 1
            END IF
        END IF
    END IF
END IF
```

The player only moves once every two frames.

The code first checks if the player is on a "crossroad". This is a place aligned to the 8x8 grid of cards, so it draws the footsteps of the player, and also takes note of the visited card. The variable a contains the screen row (a value between 0 and 11), and the variable *b* contains the screen column (a value between 0 and 19).

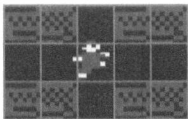

Player at crossroad. It's the equidistant intersection between four tombs where the player can change movement direction. Or put another way: the place where X and Y modulo 8 is equal to zero.

When the row is greater than or equal to 2, it calculates the bit on the *visit* array using the following expression: *visit(a * 2 + b / 8) AND bit(b AND 7)*. As each row contains 16 cards, *a* is multiplied by 2 (2 bytes = 16 bits), and added to the value of *b* divided by 8 (to select byte 0 or byte 1). Then it checks if the bit is already set using the *AND* operator, along the *bit* data table.

If the card wasn't already visited, it then increases the visit count for each of the surrounding cells. The table *reference_board* indicates which cells are surrounding a card on screen (this table was generated automatically by the program in appendix A). And for each cell, the *increase* subroutine is called to increase the visit count. Notice this is **easier** and **faster** than doing a loop of the twenty cells counting the ten cards surrounding each one – 20*10 = 200 operations per frame!!! It would be too much for the Intellivision processor and the game wouldn't run smoothly.

If the Y-coordinate of the player is less than 16, it means the player is entering the pyramid, and only checks whether the entry is complete and closes the door per availability of the key or real sarcophagus.

It reads the controller and extracts the direction (0 for no movement, 1=up, 2=right, 4=down, 8=left) using the *mummy_controller_direction* table with the lower 5 bits of the controller input.

As the tombs map is fixed and repetitive, it is easy to check if the player can go up or down without crashing into a tomb, or left and right.

The *animation* variable is set up according to the direction of movement. Also the extra special case is the player exiting through the door, but only is possible if the player has the key and the sarcophagus.

The code for the *increase* procedure needs to be added after the line saying *GOTO main_loop*:

```
    '
    ' Increase count of visits to a given square
    '
increase:    PROCEDURE
    surround(c) = surround(c) + 1
    IF surround(c) <> 10 THEN RETURN

    ' Tomb opened!
    a = (c / 5 * 2 + 3) * 20 + c % 5 * 3 + 3
    PRINT AT a
    d = board(c)    ' What it contains?
    IF d = 0 THEN ' Nothing
        e = 1
        GOSUB effect
        PRINT $1880,$1888
    END IF
    IF d = 1 THEN ' Sarcophagus
        e = 2
        GOSUB effect
        #score = #score + 5
        PRINT $0C06+6*8,$0C06+7*8
    END IF
    IF d = 2 THEN ' Scroll
        e = 3
        GOSUB effect
        has_scroll = 1
        PRINT $0A07+8*8,$0A07+9*8
    END IF
    IF d = 3 THEN ' Mummy
        e = 4: GOSUB effect
        PRINT $0806+15*8,$1806+15*8
        IF enemies_alive < 6 THEN    ' Only if there is space
            x(enemies_alive) = c % 5 * 24 + 24
            y(enemies_alive) = c / 5 * 16 + 24
            IF y > y(enemies_alive) THEN
                y(enemies_alive) = y(enemies_alive) - 1
                t(enemies_alive) = 0 + 16
            ELSE
                y(enemies_alive) = y(enemies_alive) + 1
                t(enemies_alive) = 1 + 16
```

```
                END IF
                ' And carried to next level
                enemies_alive = enemies_alive + 1
            END IF
        END IF
        IF d = 4 THEN ' Key
            e = 5
            GOSUB effect
            has_key = 1
            #score = #score + 20
            PRINT $0A06+10*8,$0A06+11*8
            IF has_tomb = 0 THEN
                #backtab(28) = $0803+19*8
            ELSE
                #backtab(28) = 0
            END IF
        END IF
        IF d = 5 THEN ' Real sarcophagus
            e = 6
            GOSUB effect
            has_tomb = 1
            #score = #score + 50
            PRINT $0A06+12*8,$0A06+13*8
            IF has_key = 0 THEN
                #backtab(28) = $0803+19*8
            ELSE
                #backtab(28) = 0
            END IF
        END IF
        GOSUB update_score
        END

        '
        ' Update score
        '
update_score: PROCEDURE
        PRINT AT 7
        IF has_scroll THEN
            PRINT COLOR $0206
        ELSE
            PRINT AT 7 COLOR #color + 1
        END IF
        PRINT <5>#score
        END
```

It first increases the *surround(c)* value (*c* is the number of the tomb). If it doesn't reach 10 (tomb still not opened), it returns to the main loop.

If the tomb has been opened, it reads the *board(c)* value to discover what is hidden inside the tomb.

Each type of content has a different sound effect (variable *e* is loaded with the effect number and *gosub effect* starts the sound effect).

The *#score* variable is increased per the discovery, and then the *PRINT* statement is used to reveal the content of the tomb.

Finding the key or the real sarcophagus also opens the door. It becomes fully open if both are found. Finding the scroll, key, or real sarcophagus updates the respective variables *has_scroll*, *has_key*, and *has_tomb*.

Finally opening a tomb containing a mummy starts a new mummy using the *enemies_alive* value as index into the array of mummies. The mummy tries to go up or down per the current player Y position. And the value of *enemies_alive* is increased by one.

Updating the score on screen is done in the procedure *update_score*. It changes the color of the score digits if the player has a scroll, or else it uses the current color scheme for the level.

These data tables follow the code:

```
'

' Table to convert controller direction
' to a usable value.
'

' 1 - Up
' 2 - Right
' 4 - Down
' 8 - Left
'
mummy_controller_direction:
    DATA -1, 4, 2, 4, 1,-1, 2,-1
    DATA  8, 8,-1,-1, 1,-1,-1,-1
    DATA -1, 4, 2,-1,-1,-1,-1,-1
    DATA  8,-1,-1,-1, 1,-1,-1,-1


    '

    ' For the visited cards array.
    '
bit:
    DATA $80,$40,$20,$10,$08,$04,$02,$01
```

```
'
' Reference board of which tombs are
' touched by which card.
'
reference_board:
    DATA 0,-1,-1,-1
    DATA 0,-1,-1,-1
    DATA 0,-1,-1,-1
    DATA 0,1,-1,-1
    DATA 1,-1,-1,-1
    DATA 1,-1,-1,-1
    DATA 1,2,-1,-1
    DATA 2,-1,-1,-1
    DATA 2,-1,-1,-1
    DATA 2,3,-1,-1
    DATA 3,-1,-1,-1
    DATA 3,-1,-1,-1
    DATA 3,4,-1,-1
    DATA 4,-1,-1,-1
    DATA 4,-1,-1,-1
    DATA 4,-1,-1,-1
    DATA 0,-1,-1,-1
    DATA -1,-1,-1,-1
    DATA -1,-1,-1,-1
    DATA 0,1,-1,-1
    DATA -1,-1,-1,-1
    DATA -1,-1,-1,-1
    DATA 1,2,-1,-1
    DATA -1,-1,-1,-1
    DATA -1,-1,-1,-1
    DATA 2,3,-1,-1
    DATA -1,-1,-1,-1
    DATA -1,-1,-1,-1
    DATA 3,4,-1,-1
    DATA -1,-1,-1,-1
    DATA -1,-1,-1,-1
    DATA 4,-1,-1,-1
    DATA 0,5,-1,-1
    DATA 0,5,-1,-1
    DATA 0,5,-1,-1
    DATA 0,1,5,6
    DATA 1,6,-1,-1
    DATA 1,6,-1,-1
    DATA 1,2,6,7
    DATA 2,7,-1,-1
    DATA 2,7,-1,-1
    DATA 2,3,7,8
```

```
DATA 3,8,-1,-1
DATA 3,8,-1,-1
DATA 3,4,8,9
DATA 4,9,-1,-1
DATA 4,9,-1,-1
DATA 4,9,-1,-1
DATA 5,-1,-1,-1
DATA -1,-1,-1,-1
DATA -1,-1,-1,-1
DATA 5,6,-1,-1
DATA -1,-1,-1,-1
DATA -1,-1,-1,-1
DATA 6,7,-1,-1
DATA -1,-1,-1,-1
DATA -1,-1,-1,-1
DATA 7,8,-1,-1
DATA -1,-1,-1,-1
DATA -1,-1,-1,-1
DATA 8,9,-1,-1
DATA -1,-1,-1,-1
DATA -1,-1,-1,-1
DATA 9,-1,-1,-1
DATA 5,10,-1,-1
DATA 5,10,-1,-1
DATA 5,10,-1,-1
DATA 5,6,10,11
DATA 6,11,-1,-1
DATA 6,11,-1,-1
DATA 6,7,11,12
DATA 7,12,-1,-1
DATA 7,12,-1,-1
DATA 7,8,12,13
DATA 8,13,-1,-1
DATA 8,13,-1,-1
DATA 8,9,13,14
DATA 9,14,-1,-1
DATA 9,14,-1,-1
DATA 9,14,-1,-1
DATA 10,-1,-1,-1
DATA -1,-1,-1,-1
DATA -1,-1,-1,-1
DATA 10,11,-1,-1
DATA -1,-1,-1,-1
DATA -1,-1,-1,-1
DATA 11,12,-1,-1
DATA -1,-1,-1,-1
DATA -1,-1,-1,-1
DATA 12,13,-1,-1
```

```
DATA -1,-1,-1,-1
DATA -1,-1,-1,-1
DATA 13,14,-1,-1
DATA -1,-1,-1,-1
DATA -1,-1,-1,-1
DATA 14,-1,-1,-1
DATA 10,15,-1,-1
DATA 10,15,-1,-1
DATA 10,15,-1,-1
DATA 10,11,15,16
DATA 11,16,-1,-1
DATA 11,16,-1,-1
DATA 11,12,16,17
DATA 12,17,-1,-1
DATA 12,17,-1,-1
DATA 12,13,17,18
DATA 13,18,-1,-1
DATA 13,18,-1,-1
DATA 13,14,18,19
DATA 14,19,-1,-1
DATA 14,19,-1,-1
DATA 14,19,-1,-1
DATA 15,-1,-1,-1
DATA -1,-1,-1,-1
DATA -1,-1,-1,-1
DATA 15,16,-1,-1
DATA -1,-1,-1,-1
DATA -1,-1,-1,-1
DATA 16,17,-1,-1
DATA -1,-1,-1,-1
DATA -1,-1,-1,-1
DATA 17,18,-1,-1
DATA -1,-1,-1,-1
DATA -1,-1,-1,-1
DATA 18,19,-1,-1
DATA -1,-1,-1,-1
DATA -1,-1,-1,-1
DATA 19,-1,-1,-1
DATA 15,-1,-1,-1
DATA 15,-1,-1,-1
DATA 15,-1,-1,-1
DATA 15,16,-1,-1
DATA 16,-1,-1,-1
DATA 16,-1,-1,-1
DATA 16,17,-1,-1
DATA 17,-1,-1,-1
DATA 17,-1,-1,-1
DATA 17,18,-1,-1
```

```
DATA 18,-1,-1,-1
DATA 18,-1,-1,-1
DATA 18,19,-1,-1
DATA 19,-1,-1,-1
DATA 19,-1,-1,-1
DATA 19,-1,-1,-1
```

The *reference_board* data is ordered in such a way that each row corresponds to a tile of the game board (16x9 tiles). There are invalid tiles because they correspond to a location over a tomb (the player cannot walk over tombs).

The table is generated automatically by a utility program that is shown in Appendix A.

3.7 Collision with mummies

Once the display is resolved by the hardware, the collision flags are updated and can be checked for the benefit of our game.

The following code replaces the line reading "Here goes the collision code":

```
    '
    ' Check for collision of player vs mummy
    ' 'shield' exists because of frame delay in COL0
    '
    IF shield THEN
        shield = shield - 1
    ELSEIF COL0 AND $00FC THEN

        '
        ' Check what mummy
        '
        IF COL0 AND $0004 THEN c = 0
        IF COL0 AND $0008 THEN c = 1
        IF COL0 AND $0010 THEN c = 2
        IF COL0 AND $0020 THEN c = 3
        IF COL0 AND $0040 THEN c = 4
        IF COL0 AND $0080 THEN c = 5
        shield = 2
```

```
          '
          ' If player has scroll then remove a mummy
          '
      IF has_scroll THEN
          WHILE c + 1 < enemies_alive
              x(c) = x(c + 1)
              y(c) = y(c + 1)
              t(c) = t(c + 1)
              c = c + 1
          WEND
          y(c) = 0
          has_scroll = 0
          e = 7
          GOSUB effect
          GOSUB update_score

          ' Deduct from next level
          enemies_alive = enemies_alive - 1

      ELSEIF y(c) <> 0 THEN    ' Alive mummy
          PLAY OFF
          e = 8
          GOSUB effect
          FOR c = 0 TO 60
              WAIT
          NEXT c
          ' All men wasted?
          IF men = 0 THEN
              FOR c = 0 TO 255
                  WAIT
                  WAIT
                  PRINT AT 225 COLOR #color,"GAME OVER"
              NEXT c
              GOTO mummy_title_screen
          END IF
          men = men - 1
          PLAY streets_of_cairo
          GOTO repeat_level
      END IF
  END IF
```

The *shield* variable "protects" the player from unfair death. If it is active then collisions are ignored (while decreasing it until it reaches zero).

Checking the individual bits of *COL0* allows to know which mummy touched the player, and puts his number into the variable *c*, and also sets *shield* to 2.

If the player has a scroll (signaled by the variable *has_scroll*), it needs to remove a mummy, set to zero the *has_scroll* variable, update the score (because it changes color), and decrease the variable *enemies_alive*. Notice the mummy removal is done by displacing the data over the old mummy. This is required because adding a mummy is done by using the variable *enemies_alive* to get the free index of the mummies array, instead of looking for free slots (it would be slower).

If the player doesn't have a scroll, and the mummy is alive, then a death sound effect is played, and one man is subtracted, restarting the music, and repeating the level.

If no man remains then the "GAME OVER" message is shown prominently over the game area, and the game returns to the title screen after a delay.

3.8 Victory

The player's victory becomes reality when his x,y coordinates reach the position of the pyramid's door and he is going up (*dir = 1*).

Once every 5 levels, it will show an intermediate bonus screen giving an extra man to the player.

It jumps to *next_level* to show another level.

This code replaces the line reading "Here goes the victory code":

```
'
' If player gets to entry door
'
IF x = 64 THEN
    IF y = 8 THEN
        IF dir = 1 THEN          ' Going up
            IF level % 5 = 0 THEN    ' Each 5 levels
                FOR c = 0 TO 7
                    SPRITE c,0
```

```
                        NEXT c
                        CLS
                        MODE 0,0,0,0,0
                        BORDER 0
                        WAIT
                        PRINT AT 2 COLOR 2,"!! STOP PRESS !!"
                        PRINT AT 43 COLOR 6," British Museum"
                        PRINT AT 61,"today announced"
                        PRINT AT 81,"successful"
                        PRINT AT 101,"excavation of"
                        PRINT AT 121,"ancient Egyptian"
                        PRINT AT 141,"pyramid."

                        ' Extra life!
                        IF men < 9 THEN
                            men = men + 1
                        PRINT AT 183 COLOR 1,"Leader of team"
                        PRINT AT 201,"given extra man"
                        PRINT AT 221,"for next dig."
                        END IF
                        FOR c = 0 TO 255
                            WAIT
                            WAIT
                            WAIT
                            WAIT
                        NEXT c
                        CLS
                        MODE 1
                    END IF
                    GOTO next_level
                END IF
            END IF
    END IF
END IF
```

3.9 Mummies alive

The game is working but the mummies are still static inside the pyramid.
The mummies don't have a fixed speed, but instead move with a fractional
speed depending on difficulty.

The trick is adding the *speed* variable to the *current_speed* variable.
Once *current_speed* becomes greater than 64 ($40) it moves the mummies by
a pixel. On some frames the mummies won't move.

This code replaces the line reading "Here goes the mummies movement code":

```
IF (FRAME AND 1) = 0 THEN
' Fractional speed
current_speed = current_speed + speed
WHILE current_speed > $40
    FOR m = 0 TO enemies_alive - 1
        x1 = x(m)
        y1 = y(m)
        IF y1 <> 0 THEN
            d1 = t(m)
            IF d1 >= 16 THEN GOTO hack
            IF (x1 AND 7) = 0 AND (y1 AND 7) = 0 THEN
                ' Mummy getting out of tomb
                IF d1 < 2 THEN
                    IF (x1 % 24) < 16 THEN t(m) = 2
                END IF
                ' Mummy in crossroad
                IF x1 % 24 >= 16 THEN
                    IF y1 % 16 < 8 THEN
                        ' Random chance of
                        ' following player.
                        c = RANDOM(12)
                        IF c <= level THEN
                            IF y < y1 THEN
                                d1 = 0
                            ELSEIF y > y1 THEN
                                d1 = 1
                            ELSEIF x < x1 THEN
                                d1 = 2
                            ELSEIF x > x1 THEN
                                d1 = 3
                            END IF
                        ELSEIF c <> level + 1 THEN
                            d1 = RANDOM(4)
                        ELSE
                            ' No change
                        END IF
                        t(m) = d1
                    END IF
                END IF
            END IF
        END IF

        ' Move mummy in current direction
        d1 = t(m)
        IF d1 = 0 THEN
            IF y1 > 16 THEN y1 = y1 - 1
```

```
                        END IF
                        IF d1 = 1 THEN
                                IF y1 < 80 THEN y1 = y1 + 1
                        END IF
                        IF d1 = 2 THEN
                                IF x1 > 16 THEN x1 = x1 - 1
                        END IF
                        IF d1 = 3 THEN
                                IF x1 < 136 THEN x1 = x1 + 1
                        END IF
                        x(m) = x1
                        y(m) = y1
hack:
                    END IF
            NEXT m
            current_speed = current_speed - $40
        WEND
        END IF
```

For each mummy, the game moves the mummy in his current direction being careful to not get outside the screen. The mummy only changes his direction when the mummy is aligned in the 8x8 grid, and aligned between 4 tombs: either the direction to get closer to the player, a random direction (per the current level; advanced levels make mummies go after the player more often), or to keep going in the same direction.

3.10 Sound effects

The sound effects are one of the most important parts of a game. IntyBASIC eases the sound generation during a game by making the programmer able to run a parallel process with the game engine.

This task is called every frame by using the *ON FRAME GOSUB* statement. This should be added at the start of the game:

```
ON FRAME GOSUB generate_effect
```

And now this should be added to the game just before the line saying *ASM ORG $F000.*

```
      '
      ' Generate sound effects
      '
generate_effect:   PROCEDURE
      ON sound_effect GOSUB
sound_0,sound_1,sound_2,sound_3,sound_4,sound_5,sound_6,sound_7,soun
d_8
      END


      '
      ' No sound effect
      '
sound_0: PROCEDURE
      SOUND 2,,0
      END


      '
      ' Empty tomb discovered
      '
sound_1: PROCEDURE
      SOUND 2,(FRAME AND 1)*500+3000
      SOUND 2,,15-sound_state / 4-(sound_state AND 1)
      sound_state = sound_state + 1
      IF sound_state = 16 THEN GOSUB sound_silent
      END


      '
      ' Sarcophagus found
      '
sound_2: PROCEDURE
      SOUND 2,200 - sound_state * 12
      SOUND 2,,13-sound_state / 2+(sound_state AND 2)
      sound_state = sound_state + 1
      IF sound_state = 16 THEN GOSUB sound_silent
      END


      '
      ' Scroll found
      '
sound_3: PROCEDURE
      SOUND 2,(FRAME AND 3)*50+50,15
      sound_state = sound_state + 1
      IF sound_state = 16 THEN GOSUB sound_silent
      END


      '
      ' Mummy found
```

```
'
sound_4: PROCEDURE
    IF sound_state AND 4 THEN
        IF sound_state AND 2 THEN
            SOUND 2,1000 + sound_state * 64,15
        ELSE
            SOUND 2,1000 - sound_state * 64,15
        END IF
    ELSE
        SOUND 2,,0
    END IF
    sound_state = sound_state + 1
    IF sound_state = 100 THEN GOSUB sound_silent
    END


    '
    ' Key found
    '
sound_5: PROCEDURE
    IF sound_state AND 1 THEN
        SOUND 2,400 - sound_state * 5,15
    ELSE
        SOUND 2,200 - sound_state * 3,15
    END IF
    sound_state = sound_state + 1
    IF sound_state = 25 THEN GOSUB sound_silent
    END


    '
    ' Real sarcophagus found
    '
sound_6: PROCEDURE
    IF sound_state AND 1 THEN
        SOUND 2,320 - sound_state * 5,15
    ELSE
        SOUND 2,160 - sound_state * 3,15
    END IF
    sound_state = sound_state + 1
    IF sound_state = 25 THEN GOSUB sound_silent
    END


    '
    ' Eaten mummy (with scroll)
    '
sound_7: PROCEDURE
    IF sound_state AND 2 THEN
        SOUND 2,212 - sound_state * 5,15
    ELSE
```

```
        SOUND 2,200 - sound_state * 5,15
    END IF

    sound_state = sound_state + 1
    IF sound_state = 40 THEN GOSUB sound_silent
    END


    '
    ' Eaten by mummy
    '
sound_8: PROCEDURE
    IF sound_state AND 2 THEN
        SOUND 2,385 + sound_state * 10,15
    ELSE
        SOUND 2,400 + sound_state * 10,15
    END IF

    sound_state = sound_state + 1
    IF sound_state = 40 THEN GOSUB sound_silent
    END
```

On each video frame, the procedure *generate_effect* is called, and based on the value of the variable *sound_effect* it decides what it is going to put into channel 2 of the audio.

The *PLAY* statement is already using the channels 0 and 1 to generate the background music.

If no sound effect is being generated (*sound_effect* equals zero), the *sound_0* procedure is called and sets the volume of channel 2 to zero, making it silent. The frequency of channel 2 isn't changed because its value isn't important.

Chapter 4

Pumpkin Master

Pumpkin Master is a SHMUP game (Shoot'em Up all the enemies). Your enemies are the evil pumpkins commanded by the horrid Pumpkin Master.

It is Halloween and you have a problem: there is an on-going invasion of evil pumpkins, and you ask the neighbors for help. They refuse to help after discovering the invitation isn't for eating pumpkin cake!

This game was published by 2600 Connection.

4.1 Design of the game

The game is a shooter where the player is located at the bottom, and can move to the left and right. The player can shoot one bullet at a time, and the bullet disappears once it reaches the top of the screen (or hits an enemy).

The enemies are pumpkins coming out in random waves, and each wave has a different shape. Occasionally a pumpkin can throw a projectile to the player. Due to the lack of enough sprites (remember the Intellivision only has 8 sprites, or MOB, able to be displayed at the same time), the bullets are created using cards with two different bitmaps (one for the bullet at the top of the card, and one for the bullet at the bottom of the card).

After defeating a predetermined number of enemy waves, a boss screen appears where the evil pumpkin master throws tons of bullets, and the player has to destroy it tile by tile.

The start of the game "pumpkin.bas" is like this:

```
'
' Pumpkin master
'
' by Oscar Toledo G. (nanochess)
' http://nanochess.org
'
' Creation date: Oct/28/2018.
'


ON FRAME GOSUB play_sound

' Number of pumpkins at same time, maximum of 6
CONST PUMPKINS = 6

CONST VOLUME_TITLE = 12      ' Volume of music during title
CONST VOLUME_GAME = 10       ' Volume of music inside the game
CONST VOLUME_BOSS = 14       ' Volume of music during boss

UNSIGNED #score, #record

DIM x(PUMPKINS)              ' X-coordinate of pumpkin or boss bullet
DIM y(PUMPKINS)              ' Y-coordinate of pumpkin or boss bullet
DIM s(PUMPKINS)              ' State of pumpkin (in current wave)
DIM z(PUMPKINS)              ' Timing of pumpkin explosion
DIM b(PUMPKINS)              ' Pumpkin bullet

#record = 25                 ' Setup a default record

FOR c = 0 TO 60
     WAIT
NEXT c
```

The maximum number of pumpkins is denoted by the constant *PUMPKINS*, and it cannot be higher than 6, because there are only 8 sprites supported by the Intellivision display, and to avoid flickering.

There are different volume levels for the title background music (*VOLUME_TITLE*), the game background music (*VOLUME_GAME*), and the boss background music (*VOLUME_BOSS*).

We also have two unsigned 16-bit variables: *#score* and *#record*, to keep respectively the current score of the player, and the record (or highest score reached).

The current X position, Y position, state of the pumpkin, and timing of pumpkin explosion are saved for each pumpkin (arrays x, y, s, and z). Also there is an array b for the bullets shot by pumpkins.

4.2 Title screen

The title screen is composed of an initial screen showing a welcome message, because this game originally was released for free at the Atariage forums in the Intellivision subforum. After it comes the proper title screen.

The title screen bitmap was based on an image downloaded from Pixabay (the URL is listed in the source code), then edited with Paint.NET, and further processed with IntyColor to create the IntyBASIC source code with all the bitmaps and color.

The Pumpkin Master title graphics, not including ornaments (added later with IntyBASIC code). Notice how the title letters fit in the grid in order to use the fewest possible GRAM cards. Also the pumpkin is centered in the grid as even one pixel in excess would make it use another GRAM card.

You can get the original BMP file at the webpage indicated in my preface. And if using the IntyColor utility, you can generate the "pumpkin_title.bas" file using this command line:

```
intycolor -b -n -s0000 pumpkin.bmp pumpkin_title.bas pumpkin
```

The option -b means to generate an IntyBASIC source code file.
The option -n means to generate only the data (otherwise it makes it a
compilable source file). The option -s0000 means to generate graphics for
the Color Stack mode (as per sentence *MODE 0,0,0,0,0*). The name of the
source graphics file, the name of the target source code, and the name to
be used as prefix for the data labels are all required.

The "pumpkin_title.bas" file should contain the following data (listed
here in case you want to enter it by yourself):

```
    REM IntyColor v1.1.5 Jul/25/2017
    REM intycolor -b -n -s0000 pumpkin.bmp pumpkin_title.bas pumpkin
    REM Created: Sun Oct 28 21:28:30 2018

    ' 59 bitmaps
pumpkin_bitmaps_0:
    DATA $0000,$0000,$0000,$0600
    DATA $667C,$6666,$607C,$6060
    DATA $0000,$6666,$6666,$3E66
    DATA $0000,$667D,$6666,$6666
    DATA $0000,$66C7,$6666,$6766
    DATA $0606,$66C6,$6767,$C666
    DATA $0006,$C666,$8686,$66C6
    DATA $0000,$667C,$6666,$6666
    DATA $0706,$0507,$0404,$0404
    DATA $1808,$D8B8,$1998,$1819
    DATA $0000,$19F0,$98F9,$F998
    DATA $0303,$83F7,$F3E3,$E133
    DATA $0000,$19CF,$181F,$CF18
    DATA $0000,$9F1B,$1898,$1898
    DATA $0606,$0000,$0000,$0000
    DATA $0100,$0003,$0300,$0101
pumpkin_bitmaps_1:
    DATA $E000,$1810,$FC68,$B868
    DATA $60C0,$1830,$070C,$0303
    DATA $0000,$1800,$F8F0,$CEFB
    DATA $0000,$0000,$0000,$70F0
    DATA $0100,$0301,$0101,$0000
    DATA $83FE,$B0E0,$F0D0,$3F6F
    DATA $8000,$3CE0,$0007,$9FE7
    DATA $0706,$0F0F,$6100,$BFDE
```

```
        DATA $D18C,$6071,$C020,$7EF9
        DATA $F8F8,$00E0,$0000,$7CE0
        DATA $0100,$0303,$0707,$1F0F
        DATA $FEFF,$FBFD,$EFF7,$DFDF
        DATA $FE7F,$FEFE,$FDFD,$FBFD
        DATA $FF7F,$FFFF,$FFFF,$FFFF
        DATA $BFBF,$DFDF,$EFEF,$F7EF
        DATA $DFBF,$F7EF,$FDFB,$FEFE
pumpkin_bitmaps_2:
        DATA $C000,$F0E0,$F8F0,$FCFC
        DATA $1F1F,$3F3F,$3F3F,$3E3E
        DATA $BFBF,$7F7F,$7F7F,$FFFF
        DATA $9BBB,$838B,$8081,$E0C0
        DATA $FFFF,$FFFF,$7FFF,$FF3F
        DATA $F6F7,$F0F4,$00C0,$C080
        DATA $3FFF,$3F3F,$7F7F,$FF7F
        DATA $7E7E,$BEBE,$DEBE,$DEDE
        DATA $3E3E,$1E3E,$1E1E,$0F1E
        DATA $FFFF,$FFFF,$FFFF,$78F9
        DATA $F7F7,$F7F7,$F7F7,$F7F7
        DATA $FFFF,$F7F7,$E3E3,$FFFF
        DATA $FBFB,$FBFB,$FBFB,$FBFB
        DATA $FFFF,$FFFF,$FFFF,$CFEF
        DATA $DEDE,$DEDE,$DCDC,$BCDC
        DATA $070F,$0707,$0103,$0001
pumpkin_bitmaps_3:
        DATA $7C7C,$BEBC,$DFDE,$F7EF
        DATA $3737,$3839,$0018,$E080
        DATA $FFFF,$00FF,$0000,$1E00
        DATA $F8FB,$00C0,$0000,$6F28
        DATA $0F0F,$1F1F,$7E3E,$FBFD
        DATA $B8B8,$7070,$E0E0,$80C0
        DATA $3D7B,$0F1E,$0003,$0000
        DATA $FDFC,$7EFE,$E79F,$0118
        DATA $9F1E,$FFFF,$BF7F,$00DE
        DATA $DF6F,$DFDF,$79BE,$20C6
        DATA $EEF7,$B8DC,$8060,$0000


        REM 20x12 cards
pumpkin_cards:
        DATA $0000,$0000,$0000,$0000,$0000,$0000,$0000,$1806,$0000,$0000
        DATA $0000,$0000,$0000,$0000,$0000,$0000,$0000,$0000,$0000,$0000
        DATA $0000,$0000,$0000,$180E,$1816,$181E,$1826,$182E,$1836,$183E
        DATA $1846,$184E,$1856,$185E,$1866,$186E,$0000,$0000,$0000,$0000
        DATA $0000,$0000,$0000,$0000,$0000,$0000,$1876,$0000,$087D,$0885
        DATA $0000,$0000,$0000,$0000,$0000,$0000,$0000,$0000,$0000,$0000
        DATA $0000,$0000,$0000,$0000,$0000,$0000,$0000,$0000,$0000,$088D
        DATA $0895,$089D,$0000,$0000,$0000,$0000,$0000,$0000,$0000,$0000
```

```
DATA $0000,$0000,$0000,$0000,$0000,$0000,$08A5,$08AD,$08B5,$08BD
DATA $08C5,$08CD,$0000,$0000,$0000,$0000,$0000,$0000,$0000,$0000
DATA $0000,$0000,$0000,$0000,$0000,$0000,$18D2,$18DA,$18E2,$18EA
DATA $18F2,$18FA,$1902,$0000,$0000,$0000,$0000,$0000,$0000,$0000
DATA $0000,$0000,$0000,$0000,$0000,$0000,$190A,$1912,$191A,$1922
DATA $192A,$1932,$193A,$0000,$0000,$0000,$0000,$0000,$0000,$0000
DATA $0000,$0000,$0000,$0000,$0000,$0000,$1942,$194A,$1952,$195A
DATA $1962,$196A,$1972,$0000,$0000,$0000,$0000,$0000,$0000,$0000
DATA $0000,$0000,$0000,$0000,$0000,$0000,$197A,$1982,$198A,$1992
DATA $199A,$19A2,$19AA,$0000,$0000,$0000,$0000,$0000,$0000,$0000
DATA $0000,$0000,$0000,$0000,$0000,$0000,$0000,$19B2,$19BA,$19C2
DATA $19CA,$19D2,$0000,$0000,$0000,$0000,$0000,$0000,$0000,$0000
DATA $0000,$0000,$0000,$0000,$0000,$0000,$0000,$0000,$0000,$0000
DATA $0000,$0000,$0000,$0000,$0000,$0000,$0000,$0000,$0000,$0000
DATA $0000,$0000,$0000,$0000,$0000,$0000,$0000,$0000,$0000,$0000
DATA $0000,$0000,$0000,$0000,$0000,$0000,$0000,$0000,$0000,$0000
```

Now let us add this code to the main file "pumpkin.bas" in order to show the title screen:

```
' For the good guys :)
'
PRINT AT 61 COLOR 5,"For all my friends"
PRINT AT 81 COLOR 5,"   at Atariage!"
GOSUB wait_and_clean

PRINT AT 102 COLOR 5,"Is it already"
PRINT AT 122 COLOR 2,"Halloween 2018?"
PRINT AT 216 COLOR 3,";)"
GOSUB wait_and_clean

PLAY SIMPLE


'
' Title screen
'
title_screen:
    PLAY music_game
    PLAY VOLUME VOLUME_TITLE
title_screen_2:
    CLS
    MODE 0,0,1,0,0
    WAIT
    FOR c = 0 TO 7
        SPRITE c, 0
```

```
NEXT c
WAIT
DEFINE 0,16,pumpkin_bitmaps_0
WAIT
DEFINE 16,16,pumpkin_bitmaps_1
WAIT
DEFINE 32,16,pumpkin_bitmaps_2
WAIT
DEFINE 48,11,pumpkin_bitmaps_3
DEFINE ALTERNATE 60,4,game_bitmaps_0
WAIT
' Show the Pumpkin Master and the title letters
SCREEN pumpkin_cards,20,0,20,11

' Add some houses
SPRITE 0,$0308 + 8,  $0088 + 64, $1801 + 62 * 8
SPRITE 1,$0308 + 24, $0088 + 64, $1801 + 62 * 8
SPRITE 2,$0308 + 40, $0088 + 64, $1801 + 62 * 8
SPRITE 3,$0308 + 104, $0088 + 64, $1801 + 62 * 8
SPRITE 4,$0308 + 120, $0088 + 64, $1801 + 62 * 8
SPRITE 5,$0308 + 136, $0088 + 64, $1801 + 62 * 8

' Add a pair of pumpkins
SPRITE 6,$0308 + 64, $0088 + 8, $1802 + 60 * 8
SPRITE 7,$0308 + 92, $0088 + 22, $1802 + 60 * 8

' Show the record in a color bar (as ground)
#backtab(180) = $2000
PRINT AT 183 COLOR 5,"Record: ",<5>#record,"0"
#backtab(200) = $2000

PRINT AT 224 COLOR 6,"Press button"

' Wait for controller to be "free"
DO
    WAIT
    c = CONT
LOOP WHILE c

' Now wait for controller press
DO
    WAIT
    c = CONT
LOOP WHILE c = 0

' Minigame 1
' Minigame 2
```

```
stuck:    GOTO stuck

    '
    ' Wait and clean story
    '
wait_and_clean:          PROCEDURE
    FOR c = 0 TO 180
        IF c >= 60 THEN d = CONT: IF d THEN EXIT FOR
        WAIT
    NEXT c
    FOR c = 60 TO 119
        #backtab(c) = 0
    NEXT c
    END

' See https://pixabay.com/es/pumpkin-helloween-witch-bruja-3726795/
    INCLUDE "pumpkin_title.bas"

    '
    ' Pumpkin Boogie
    '
    INCLUDE "pumpkin_music.bas"

    '
    ' Boss "music"
    '
music_beat:
    DATA 6
    MUSIC C2W,-,-
    MUSIC S,-,-
    MUSIC S,-,-
    MUSIC -,-,-
    MUSIC C2#W,-,-
    MUSIC S,-,-
    MUSIC S,-,-
    MUSIC -,-,-
    MUSIC REPEAT

    '
    ' Bitmaps used for the game
    '
game_bitmaps_0:
    BITMAP "........"  ' 0 Pumpkin
    BITMAP "........"
    BITMAP "........"
    BITMAP ".XX....."
    BITMAP "..X....."
    BITMAP "...X...."
```

```
BITMAP ".XX.XXX."
BITMAP "XX.XX.XX"
BITMAP "X..XX..X"
BITMAP "XXXX.XXX"
BITMAP "XXXXXXXX"
BITMAP "X.XXXX.X"
BITMAP "X..X...X"
BITMAP "XX...XXX"
BITMAP ".XXXXXX."
BITMAP "..XXXX.."

BITMAP "...XX..."   ' 2 House
BITMAP "...XX..."
BITMAP "...XX..."
BITMAP "..XXX..."
BITMAP ".X..X..."
BITMAP "X.XX.X.."
BITMAP ".X.XX.X."
BITMAP "XX.XXX.X"
BITMAP "XXXXXXX."
BITMAP "X.XXX.XX"
BITMAP "X.XXX.XX"
BITMAP "XXXXXXXX"
BITMAP "X.XXX.XX"
BITMAP "X.XXX.XX"
BITMAP "XXX.XXXX"
BITMAP "XXX.XXXX"

BITMAP "...X...."   ' 4 Pumpkin bullet 1
BITMAP "...XX..."
BITMAP "...XX..."
BITMAP "...XX..."
BITMAP "....X..."
BITMAP "........"
BITMAP "........"
BITMAP "........"

BITMAP "........"   ' 5 Pumpkin bullet 2
BITMAP "........"
BITMAP "........"
BITMAP "....X..."
BITMAP "...XX..."
BITMAP "...XX..."
BITMAP "...XX..."
BITMAP "...X...."

BITMAP "X......."   ' 6 Pumpkin explosion
BITMAP "X......X"
```

```
      BITMAP ".XX....."
      BITMAP "XX....XX"
      BITMAP ".X....X."
      BITMAP ".X..X.X."
      BITMAP ".X.X...."
      BITMAP "........"
      BITMAP "XX....XX"
      BITMAP ".X...X.."
      BITMAP "........"
      BITMAP "..X..X.."
      BITMAP ".XX..XX."
      BITMAP "X.....X."
      BITMAP ".......X"
      BITMAP ".......X"

      BITMAP "..XXXX.."   ' 8 Nuclear mushroom 1
      BITMAP ".XXXXXX."
      BITMAP "XXXXXXXX"
      BITMAP "XXXXXXXX"
      BITMAP "X.X.XX.X"
      BITMAP "X.XXXX.X"
      BITMAP "..XX.X.."
      BITMAP "..XXXX.."
      BITMAP "..X.XX.."
      BITMAP "..XXXX.."
      BITMAP "..XX.X.."
      BITMAP "..XXXX.."
      BITMAP ".XXXXXX."
      BITMAP ".X.XXXX."
      BITMAP "XXXXX.XX"
      BITMAP "XXXXXXXX"

      BITMAP "..XXXX.."   ' 10 Nuclear mushroom 2
      BITMAP ".XXXXXX."
      BITMAP "XXXXXXXX"
      BITMAP "XXXX.XXX"
      BITMAP "X.XXXX.X"
      BITMAP "X.X.XX.X"
      BITMAP "..XXXX.."
      BITMAP "..XX.X.."
      BITMAP "..XXXX.."
      BITMAP "..X.XX.."
      BITMAP "..XXXX.."
      BITMAP "..XXXX.."
      BITMAP ".XXXX.X."
      BITMAP ".X.XXXX."
      BITMAP "XXXX.XXX"
      BITMAP "XXXXXXXX"
```

```
BITMAP ".X......"  ' 12 Player bullet
BITMAP "XX......"
BITMAP "XX......"
BITMAP "XX......"
BITMAP "XXX....."
BITMAP "XXX....."
BITMAP ".XX....."
BITMAP ".X......"
```

The first two messages are shown with simple *PRINT* sentences, and each one calls the *wait_and_clean* procedure that waits a fixed time (even less if the user presses the controller), and then erases the message.

Then it starts the background music of the title screen (*music_game*), defines the graphics for the title screen, and sends the card data to the screen using the *SCREEN* sentence.

The final title screen. Notice the eight sprites being used, and the extra text. It's easy to calculate the PRINT AT position for "Record" (9*20+3 = 183) and "Press button" (11*20+4 = 224)

Because of some extra ornaments on the title screen, it also defines some of the game graphics at the GRAM locations 60 to 63 (to get houses and pumpkin sprites).

It adds six houses and two pumpkins to the title screen using sprites.

Although not specified when processing the graphics for the title screen, it uses the color blue for the Color Stack mode, allowing to show a blue bar with the highest record.

Finally it waits for the controller to be activated by the player, by pushing the disc or any button.

The title screen invokes background music, and the following music data should be put in the file "pumpkin_music.bas":

```
        ' srand(1540785469)
music_game:
        DATA 6
        MUSIC C3W,C5W,-,-
        MUSIC C3,C4,-,-
        MUSIC S,S,-
        MUSIC D3#,A4,-,-
        MUSIC E3,F4#,-,-
        MUSIC S,S,-
        MUSIC G3,G4,-,-
        MUSIC C3,C4,-,-
        MUSIC S,S,-
        MUSIC A3,-,-,-
        MUSIC G3,-,-,-
        MUSIC S,-,-
        MUSIC F3,F4,-,-
        MUSIC F3,C5,-,-
        MUSIC S,S,-
        MUSIC G3#,D5,-,-
        MUSIC A3,C5,-,-
        MUSIC S,S,-
        MUSIC C4,F4,-,-
        MUSIC F3,-,-,-
        MUSIC S,-,-
        MUSIC D4,-,-,-
        MUSIC C4,-,-,-
        MUSIC S,-,-
        MUSIC G3,B5,-,-
        MUSIC G3,-,-,-
        MUSIC S,-,-
        MUSIC A3#,B5,-,-
        MUSIC B3,-,-,-
        MUSIC S,-,-
        MUSIC D4,B5,-,-
        MUSIC G3,-,-,-
        MUSIC S,-,-
        MUSIC E4,B5,-,-
        MUSIC D4,-,-,-
        MUSIC S,-,-
        MUSIC F3,F5,-,-
        MUSIC F3,F4,-,-
        MUSIC S,S,-
        MUSIC G3#,D5,-,-
        MUSIC A3,B4,-,-
        MUSIC S,S,-
        MUSIC C4,C5,-,-
        MUSIC F3,F4,-,-
        MUSIC S,S,-
        MUSIC D4,-,-,-
        MUSIC C4,-,-,-
        MUSIC S,-,-
        MUSIC C3,C5,-,-
        MUSIC C3,C4,-,-
        MUSIC S,S,-
        MUSIC D3#,A4,-,-
        MUSIC E3,F4#,-,-
        MUSIC S,S,-
        MUSIC G3,G4,-,-
        MUSIC C3,C4,-,-
        MUSIC S,S,-
        MUSIC A3,-,-,-
        MUSIC G3,-,-,-
        MUSIC S,-,-
        MUSIC C3,-,-
        MUSIC C3,-,-
        MUSIC S,-,-
        MUSIC D3#,-,-
        MUSIC E3,-,-
        MUSIC S,-,-
        MUSIC G3,-,-
        MUSIC C3,-,-
        MUSIC S,-,-
```

```
MUSIC A3,-,-              MUSIC A3,-,-,-
MUSIC G3,-,-              MUSIC G3,-,-,-
MUSIC S,-,-              MUSIC S,-,-
MUSIC C3,E5,-,-          MUSIC C3,C5,-,-
MUSIC C3,-,-,-          MUSIC C3,C4,-,-
MUSIC S,-,-              MUSIC S,S,-
MUSIC D3#,E5,-,-          MUSIC D3#,A4,-,-
MUSIC E3,-,-,-          MUSIC E3,F4#,-,-
MUSIC S,-,-              MUSIC S,S,-
MUSIC G3,E5,-,-          MUSIC G3,G4,-,-
MUSIC C3,-,-,-          MUSIC C3,C4,-,-
MUSIC S,-,-              MUSIC S,S,-
MUSIC A3,E5,-,-          MUSIC A3,-,-,-
MUSIC G3,-,-,-          MUSIC G3,-,-,-
MUSIC S,-,-              MUSIC S,-,-
MUSIC C3,-,-              MUSIC C3,C4,-,-
MUSIC C3,-,-              MUSIC C3,G4,-,-
MUSIC S,-,-              MUSIC S,S,-
MUSIC D3#,-,-            MUSIC D3#,C4,-,-
MUSIC E3,-,-            MUSIC E3,A4,-,-
MUSIC S,-,-              MUSIC S,S,-
MUSIC G3,-,-            MUSIC G3,C4,-,-
MUSIC C3,-,-            MUSIC C3,C5,-,-
MUSIC S,-,-              MUSIC S,S,-
MUSIC A3,-,-            MUSIC A3,C4,-,-
MUSIC G3,-,-            MUSIC G3,A4,-,-
MUSIC S,-,-              MUSIC S,S,-
MUSIC C3,C5,-,-          MUSIC C3,C4,-,-
MUSIC C3,C4,-,-          MUSIC C3,G4,-,-
MUSIC S,S,-              MUSIC S,S,-
MUSIC D3#,A4,-,-          MUSIC D3#,C4,-,-
MUSIC E3,F4#,-,-          MUSIC E3,A4,-,-
MUSIC S,S,-              MUSIC S,S,-
MUSIC G3,G4,-,-          MUSIC G3,C4,-,-
MUSIC C3,C4,-,-          MUSIC C3,C5,-,-
MUSIC S,S,-              MUSIC S,S,-
MUSIC A3,-,-,-          MUSIC A3,C4,-,-
MUSIC G3,-,-,-          MUSIC G3,A4,-,-
MUSIC S,-,-              MUSIC S,S,-
MUSIC C3,E5,-,-          MUSIC F3,F5,-,-
MUSIC C3,-,-,-          MUSIC F3,F4,-,-
MUSIC S,-,-              MUSIC S,S,-
MUSIC D3#,-,-,-          MUSIC G3#,D5,-,-
MUSIC E3,-,-,-          MUSIC A3,B4,-,-
MUSIC S,-,-              MUSIC S,S,-
MUSIC G3,E5,-,-          MUSIC C4,C5,-,-
MUSIC C3,-,-,-          MUSIC F3,F4,-,-
MUSIC S,-,-              MUSIC S,S,-
```

```
MUSIC D4,-,-,-          MUSIC A3,-,-,-
MUSIC C4,-,-,-          MUSIC G3,-,-,-
MUSIC S,-,-             MUSIC S,-,-
MUSIC G3,B5,-,-         MUSIC C3,C4,-,-
MUSIC G3,-,-,-          MUSIC C3,G4,-,-
MUSIC S,-,-             MUSIC S,S,-
MUSIC A3#,B5,-,-        MUSIC D3#,A4,-,-
MUSIC B3,-,-,-          MUSIC E3,G4,-,-
MUSIC S,-,-             MUSIC S,S,-
MUSIC D4,B5,-,-         MUSIC G3,C4,-,-
MUSIC G3,-,-,-          MUSIC C3,-,-,-
MUSIC S,-,-             MUSIC S,-,-
MUSIC E4,B5,-,-         MUSIC A3,-,-,-
MUSIC D4,-,-,-          MUSIC G3,-,-,-
MUSIC S,-,-             MUSIC S,-,-
MUSIC F3,F4,-,-         MUSIC C3,C4,-,-
MUSIC F3,C5,-,-         MUSIC C3,G4,-,-
MUSIC S,S,-             MUSIC S,S,-
MUSIC G3#,D5,-,-        MUSIC D3#,C4,-,-
MUSIC A3,C5,-,-         MUSIC E3,A4,-,-
MUSIC S,S,-             MUSIC S,S,-
MUSIC C4,F4,-,-         MUSIC G3,C4,-,-
MUSIC F3,-,-,-          MUSIC C3,C5,-,-
MUSIC S,-,-             MUSIC S,S,-
MUSIC D4,-,-,-          MUSIC A3,C4,-,-
MUSIC C4,-,-,-          MUSIC G3,A4,-,-
MUSIC S,-,-             MUSIC S,S,-
MUSIC C3,C4,-,-         MUSIC C3,C5,-,-
MUSIC C3,G4,-,-         MUSIC C3,C4,-,-
MUSIC S,S,-             MUSIC S,S,-
MUSIC D3#,C4,-,-        MUSIC D3#,A4,-,-
MUSIC E3,A4,-,-         MUSIC E3,F4#,-,-
MUSIC S,S,-             MUSIC S,S,-
MUSIC G3,C4,-,-         MUSIC G3,G4,-,-
MUSIC C3,C5,-,-         MUSIC C3,C4,-,-
MUSIC S,S,-             MUSIC S,S,-
MUSIC A3,C4,-,-         MUSIC A3,-,-,-
MUSIC G3,A4,-,-         MUSIC G3,-,-,-
MUSIC S,S,-             MUSIC S,-,-
MUSIC C3,E5,-,-         MUSIC C3,C5,-,-
MUSIC C3,-,-,-          MUSIC C3,C4,-,-
MUSIC S,-,-             MUSIC S,S,-
MUSIC D3#,-,-,-         MUSIC D3#,A4,-,-
MUSIC E3,-,-,-          MUSIC E3,F4#,-,-
MUSIC S,-,-             MUSIC S,S,-
MUSIC G3,E5,-,-         MUSIC G3,G4,-,-
MUSIC C3,-,-,-          MUSIC C3,C4,-,-
MUSIC S,-,-             MUSIC S,S,-
```

```
MUSIC A3,-,-,-
MUSIC G3,-,-,-
MUSIC S,-,-
MUSIC C3,C4,-,-
MUSIC C3,G4,-,-
MUSIC S,S,-
MUSIC D3#,A4,-,-
MUSIC E3,G4,-,-
MUSIC S,S,-
MUSIC G3,C4,-,-
MUSIC C3,-,-,-
MUSIC S,-,-
MUSIC A3,-,-,-
MUSIC G3,-,-,-
MUSIC S,-,-
MUSIC C3,C5,-,-
MUSIC C3,C4,-,-
MUSIC S,S,-
MUSIC D3#,A4,-,-
MUSIC E3,F4#,-,-
MUSIC S,S,-
MUSIC G3,G4,-,-
MUSIC C3,C4,-,-
MUSIC S,S,-
MUSIC A3,-,-,-
MUSIC G3,-,-,-
MUSIC S,-,-
MUSIC C3,E5,-,-
MUSIC C3,E5,-,-
MUSIC S,S,-
MUSIC D3#,E5,-,-
MUSIC E3,E5,-,-
MUSIC S,S,-
MUSIC G3,E5,-,-
MUSIC C3,E5,-,-
MUSIC S,S,-
MUSIC A3,E5,-,-
MUSIC G3,E5,-,-
MUSIC S,S,-
MUSIC C3,C5,-,-
MUSIC C3,C4,-,-
MUSIC S,S,-
MUSIC D3#,A4,-,-
MUSIC E3,F4#,-,-
MUSIC S,S,-
MUSIC G3,G4,-,-
MUSIC C3,C4,-,-
MUSIC S,S,-

MUSIC A3,-,-,-
MUSIC G3,-,-,-
MUSIC S,-,-
MUSIC F3,A5,-,-
MUSIC F3,-,-,-
MUSIC S,-,-
MUSIC G3#,-,-,-
MUSIC A3,-,-,-
MUSIC S,-,-
MUSIC C4,A5,-,-
MUSIC F3,-,-,-
MUSIC S,-,-
MUSIC D4,-,-,-
MUSIC C4,-,-,-
MUSIC S,-,-
MUSIC F3,F5,-,-
MUSIC F3,F4,-,-
MUSIC S,S,-
MUSIC G3#,D5,-,-
MUSIC A3,B4,-,-
MUSIC S,S,-
MUSIC C4,C5,-,-
MUSIC F3,F4,-,-
MUSIC S,S,-
MUSIC D4,-,-,-
MUSIC C4,-,-,-
MUSIC S,-,-
MUSIC F3,A5,-,-
MUSIC F3,-,-,-
MUSIC S,-,-
MUSIC G3#,A5,-,-
MUSIC A3,-,-,-
MUSIC S,-,-
MUSIC C4,A5,-,-
MUSIC F3,-,-,-
MUSIC S,-,-
MUSIC D4,A5,-,-
MUSIC C4,-,-,-
MUSIC S,-,-
MUSIC F3,F5,-,-
MUSIC F3,F4,-,-
MUSIC S,S,-
MUSIC G3#,D5,-,-
MUSIC A3,B4,-,-
MUSIC S,S,-
MUSIC C4,C5,-,-
MUSIC F3,F4,-,-
MUSIC S,S,-
```

```
MUSIC D4,-,-,-          MUSIC E4,B5,-,-
MUSIC C4,-,-,-          MUSIC D4,B5,-,-
MUSIC S,-,-             MUSIC S,S,-
MUSIC G3,G4,-,-         MUSIC C3,C4,-,-
MUSIC G3,D5,-,-         MUSIC C3,G4,-,-
MUSIC S,S,-             MUSIC S,S,-
MUSIC A3#,G4,-,-        MUSIC D3#,C4,-,-
MUSIC B3,E5,-,-         MUSIC E3,A4,-,-
MUSIC S,S,-             MUSIC S,S,-
MUSIC D4,G4,-,-         MUSIC G3,C4,-,-
MUSIC G3,G5,-,-         MUSIC C3,C5,-,-
MUSIC S,S,-             MUSIC S,S,-
MUSIC E4,G4,-,-         MUSIC A3,C4,-,-
MUSIC D4,E5,-,-         MUSIC G3,A4,-,-
MUSIC S,S,-             MUSIC S,S,-
MUSIC G3,G5,-,-         MUSIC C3,-,-
MUSIC G3,G4,-,-         MUSIC C3,-,-
MUSIC S,S,-             MUSIC S,-,-
MUSIC A3#,E5,-,-        MUSIC D3#,-,-
MUSIC B3,C5#,-,-        MUSIC E3,-,-
MUSIC S,S,-             MUSIC S,-,-
MUSIC D4,D5,-,-         MUSIC G3,-,-
MUSIC G3,G4,-,-         MUSIC C3,-,-
MUSIC S,S,-             MUSIC S,-,-
MUSIC E4,-,-,-          MUSIC A3,-,-
MUSIC D4,-,-,-          MUSIC G3,-,-
MUSIC S,-,-             MUSIC S,-,-
MUSIC G3,G4,-,-         MUSIC C3,E5,-,-
MUSIC G3,D5,-,-         MUSIC C3,E5,-,-
MUSIC S,S,-             MUSIC S,S,-
MUSIC A3#,E5,-,-        MUSIC D3#,E5,-,-
MUSIC B3,D5,-,-         MUSIC E3,E5,-,-
MUSIC S,S,-             MUSIC S,S,-
MUSIC D4,G4,-,-         MUSIC G3,E5,-,-
MUSIC G3,-,-,-          MUSIC C3,E5,-,-
MUSIC S,-,-             MUSIC S,S,-
MUSIC E4,-,-,-          MUSIC A3,E5,-,-
MUSIC D4,-,-,-          MUSIC G3,E5,-,-
MUSIC S,-,-             MUSIC S,S,-
MUSIC G3,B5,-,-         MUSIC C3,-,-
MUSIC G3,B5,-,-         MUSIC C3,-,-
MUSIC S,S,-             MUSIC S,-,-
MUSIC A3#,B5,-,-        MUSIC D3#,-,-
MUSIC B3,B5,-,-         MUSIC E3,-,-
MUSIC S,S,-             MUSIC S,-,-
MUSIC D4,B5,-,-         MUSIC G3,-,-
MUSIC G3,B5,-,-         MUSIC C3,-,-
MUSIC S,S,-             MUSIC S,-,-
```

```
MUSIC A3,-,-
MUSIC G3,-,-
MUSIC S,-,-
MUSIC C3,E5,-,-
MUSIC C3,-,-,-
MUSIC S,-,-
MUSIC D3#,E5,-,-
MUSIC E3,-,-,-
MUSIC S,-,-
MUSIC G3,E5,-,-
MUSIC C3,-,-,-
MUSIC S,-,-
MUSIC A3,E5,-,-
MUSIC G3,-,-,-
MUSIC S,-,-
MUSIC C3,-,-
MUSIC C3,-,-
MUSIC S,-,-
MUSIC D3#,-,-
MUSIC E3,-,-
MUSIC S,-,-
MUSIC G3,-,-
MUSIC C3,-,-
MUSIC S,-,-
MUSIC A3,-,-
MUSIC G3,-,-
MUSIC S,-,-
MUSIC C3,E5,-,-
MUSIC C3,E5,-,-
MUSIC S,S,-
MUSIC D3#,E5,-,-
MUSIC E3,E5,-,-
MUSIC S,S,-
MUSIC G3,E5,-,-
MUSIC C3,E5,-,-
MUSIC S,S,-
MUSIC A3,E5,-,-
MUSIC G3,E5,-,-
MUSIC S,S,-
MUSIC C3,-,-
MUSIC C3,-,-
MUSIC S,-,-
MUSIC D3#,-,-
MUSIC E3,-,-
MUSIC S,-,-
MUSIC G3,-,-
MUSIC C3,-,-
MUSIC S,-,-

MUSIC A3,-,-
MUSIC G3,-,-
MUSIC S,-,-
MUSIC C3,E5,-,-
MUSIC C3,E5,-,-
MUSIC S,S,-
MUSIC D3#,E5,-,-
MUSIC E3,E5,-,-
MUSIC S,S,-
MUSIC G3,E5,-,-
MUSIC C3,E5,-,-
MUSIC S,S,-
MUSIC A3,E5,-,-
MUSIC G3,E5,-,-
MUSIC S,S,-
MUSIC C3,C4,-,-
MUSIC C3,G4,-,-
MUSIC S,S,-
MUSIC D3#,C4,-,-
MUSIC E3,A4,-,-
MUSIC S,S,-
MUSIC G3,C4,-,-
MUSIC C3,C5,-,-
MUSIC S,S,-
MUSIC A3,C4,-,-
MUSIC G3,A4,-,-
MUSIC S,S,-
MUSIC G3,G4,-,-
MUSIC G3,D5,-,-
MUSIC S,S,-
MUSIC A3#,E5,-,-
MUSIC B3,D5,-,-
MUSIC S,S,-
MUSIC D4,G4,-,-
MUSIC G3,-,-,-
MUSIC S,-,-
MUSIC E4,-,-,-
MUSIC D4,-,-,-
MUSIC S,-,-
MUSIC G3,B5,-,-
MUSIC G3,-,-,-
MUSIC S,-,-
MUSIC A3#,B5,-,-
MUSIC B3,-,-,-
MUSIC S,-,-
MUSIC D4,B5,-,-
MUSIC G3,-,-,-
MUSIC S,-,-
```

```
MUSIC E4,B5,-,-          MUSIC A3,-,-
MUSIC D4,-,-,-           MUSIC G3,-,-
MUSIC S,-,-              MUSIC S,-,-
MUSIC C3,C4,-,-          MUSIC C3,E5,-,-
MUSIC C3,G4,-,-          MUSIC C3,E5,-,-
MUSIC S,S,-              MUSIC S,S,-
MUSIC D3#,C4,-,-         MUSIC D3#,E5,-,-
MUSIC E3,A4,-,-          MUSIC E3,E5,-,-
MUSIC S,S,-              MUSIC S,S,-
MUSIC G3,C4,-,-          MUSIC G3,E5,-,-
MUSIC C3,C5,-,-          MUSIC C3,E5,-,-
MUSIC S,S,-              MUSIC S,S,-
MUSIC A3,C4,-,-          MUSIC A3,E5,-,-
MUSIC G3,A4,-,-          MUSIC G3,E5,-,-
MUSIC S,S,-              MUSIC S,S,-
MUSIC C3,-,-             MUSIC C3,C4,-,-
MUSIC C3,-,-             MUSIC C3,G4,-,-
MUSIC S,-,-              MUSIC S,S,-
MUSIC D3#,-,-            MUSIC D3#,A4,-,-
MUSIC E3,-,-             MUSIC E3,G4,-,-
MUSIC S,-,-              MUSIC S,S,-
MUSIC G3,-,-             MUSIC G3,C4,-,-
MUSIC C3,-,-             MUSIC C3,-,-,-
MUSIC S,-,-              MUSIC S,-,-
MUSIC A3,-,-             MUSIC A3,-,-,-
MUSIC G3,-,-             MUSIC G3,-,-,-
MUSIC S,-,-              MUSIC S,-,-
MUSIC C3,E5,-,-          MUSIC F3,F5,-,-
MUSIC C3,-,-,-           MUSIC F3,F4,-,-
MUSIC S,-,-              MUSIC S,S,-
MUSIC D3#,-,-,-          MUSIC G3#,D5,-,-
MUSIC E3,-,-,-           MUSIC A3,B4,-,-
MUSIC S,-,-              MUSIC S,S,-
MUSIC G3,E5,-,-          MUSIC C4,C5,-,-
MUSIC C3,-,-,-           MUSIC F3,F4,-,-
MUSIC S,-,-              MUSIC S,S,-
MUSIC A3,-,-,-           MUSIC D4,-,-,-
MUSIC G3,-,-,-           MUSIC C4,-,-,-
MUSIC S,-,-              MUSIC S,-,-
MUSIC C3,-,-             MUSIC F3,F5,-,-
MUSIC C3,-,-             MUSIC F3,F4,-,-
MUSIC S,-,-              MUSIC S,S,-
MUSIC D3#,-,-            MUSIC G3#,D5,-,-
MUSIC E3,-,-             MUSIC A3,B4,-,-
MUSIC S,-,-              MUSIC S,S,-
MUSIC G3,-,-             MUSIC C4,C5,-,-
MUSIC C3,-,-             MUSIC F3,F4,-,-
MUSIC S,-,-              MUSIC S,S,-
```

```
MUSIC D4,-,-,-            MUSIC S,S,-
MUSIC C4,-,-,-            MUSIC G3,B5,-,-
MUSIC S,-,-              MUSIC G3,-,-,-
MUSIC F3,A5,-,-          MUSIC S,-,-
MUSIC F3,-,-,-           MUSIC A3#,-,-,-
MUSIC S,-,-              MUSIC B3,-,-,-
MUSIC G3#,-,-,-          MUSIC S,-,-
MUSIC A3,-,-,-           MUSIC D4,B5,-,-
MUSIC S,-,-              MUSIC G3,-,-,-
MUSIC C4,A5,-,-          MUSIC S,-,-
MUSIC F3,-,-,-           MUSIC E4,-,-,-
MUSIC S,-,-              MUSIC D4,-,-,-
MUSIC D4,-,-,-           MUSIC S,-,-
MUSIC C4,-,-,-           MUSIC G3,G4,-,-
MUSIC S,-,-              MUSIC G3,D5,-,-
MUSIC F3,F4,-,-          MUSIC S,S,-
MUSIC F3,C5,-,-          MUSIC A3#,G4,-,-
MUSIC S,S,-              MUSIC B3,E5,-,-
MUSIC G3#,D5,-,-         MUSIC S,S,-
MUSIC A3,C5,-,-          MUSIC D4,G4,-,-
MUSIC S,S,-              MUSIC G3,G5,-,-
MUSIC C4,F4,-,-          MUSIC S,S,-
MUSIC F3,-,-,-           MUSIC E4,G4,-,-
MUSIC S,-,-              MUSIC D4,E5,-,-
MUSIC D4,-,-,-           MUSIC S,S,-
MUSIC C4,-,-,-           MUSIC G3,B5,-,-
MUSIC S,-,-              MUSIC G3,-,-,-
MUSIC G3,G4,-,-          MUSIC S,-,-
MUSIC G3,D5,-,-          MUSIC A3#,B5,-,-
MUSIC S,S,-              MUSIC B3,-,-,-
MUSIC A3#,G4,-,-         MUSIC S,-,-
MUSIC B3,E5,-,-          MUSIC D4,B5,-,-
MUSIC S,S,-              MUSIC G3,-,-,-
MUSIC D4,G4,-,-          MUSIC S,-,-
MUSIC G3,G5,-,-          MUSIC E4,B5,-,-
MUSIC S,S,-              MUSIC D4,-,-,-
MUSIC E4,G4,-,-          MUSIC S,-,-
MUSIC D4,E5,-,-          MUSIC REPEAT
```

This music was generated by a small Artificial Intelligence program that appears in Appendix B. Unfortunately the *srand* constant is only guaranteed to work with my Macbook Pro computer, because of differences among C language compilers on various platforms and operating systems.

4.3 Game setup

The game requires the setup of several variables before the proper game starts. First, it clears the screen, sets up the Color Stack mode with black background, removes all sprites, and defines the game bitmaps at the GRAM cards 0-15. This code replaces the "stuck: goto stuck" line and continues from there:

```
'
' Prepare for starting game
'
CLS
MODE 0,0,0,0,0
FOR c = 0 TO 7
    SPRITE c, 0
NEXT c
WAIT
DEFINE 0,16,game_bitmaps_0
WAIT
```

The variable *lives* contains the number of houses remaining for the player, the variable *level* indicates the actual level number, and the variable *sub level* contains the wave number.

At start, the score and the arrays containing the pumpkin enemies' information are reset to zero, and the *start_wave* subroutine is called to start a pumpkin wave.

```
first_time_ever = 1      ' In order to show story
lives = 4       ' Default lives
level = 1       ' Start level
sublevel = 0        ' Sublevel (or wave number)
#score = 0          ' Reset score
FOR c = 0 TO PUMPKINS - 1
    x(c) = 0
    y(c) = 0
    s(c) = 0
    b(c) = 0
NEXT c
GOSUB start_wave     ' Start a pumpkins wave
```

The following part of the code is where the game is restarted when the player loses a house. It removes the player's bullet and redraws the house in the bottom center of the playfield.

It also updates the current score, lives indicator, and level. There is a special consideration if the house was lost inside a boss screen; it stops the execution there to go directly to the *boss_loop*.

```
      '
      ' Restart game after losing a life
      '
restart_game:
      PLAY VOLUME VOLUME_GAME
      by = 0              ' No player bullet
      px = 84             ' Setup player at bottom center
      py = 96

      GOSUB update_score
      GOSUB update_lives
      GOSUB update_level

      ' If restarting inside boss level, go to boss game loop
      IF sublevel = 10 THEN PLAY VOLUME VOLUME_BOSS: GOTO boss_loop
```

Grid showing the positioning for history text. Notice the off-grid position for houses, which is possible because these are sprites.

There is a tiny animated story for the first time that the game is launched. It reuses the pumpkin arrays to show extra tiny houses at the bottom around the player's house. When the time comes, the tiny houses run to the sides of the screen, and the arrays are reset to leave them ready for pumpkins.

```
' Is it the first time the game restarts? show story.
IF first_time_ever = 1 THEN
    first_time_ever = 0

    ' Re-use pumpkin arrays for tiny houses
    FOR c = 0 TO 2
        x(c) = px - 12 * (c + 1)
    NEXT c
    FOR c = 3 TO 5
        x(c) = px + 12 * (c - 2)
    NEXT c
    SPRITE 7, $0300 + px, $0080 + py, $1801 + 2 * 8
    FOR c = 0 TO 6
        SPRITE c, $0300 + x(c), $0080 + py, $1801 + 2 * 8
    NEXT c

    PRINT AT 65 COLOR 6,"Hey guys!"
    PRINT AT 85,"Thanks for"
    PRINT AT 105,"helping me."
    GOSUB wait_and_clean

    PRINT AT 64 COLOR 2,"Of course, we"
    PRINT AT 84,"like to eat"
    PRINT AT 104,"pumpkin."
    GOSUB wait_and_clean

    PRINT AT 62 COLOR 6,"Wait, we aren't"
    PRINT AT 82,"eating pumpkin"
    PRINT AT 102,"but killing them."
    GOSUB wait_and_clean

    PRINT AT 65 COLOR 2,"Killing?"
    GOSUB wait_and_clean

    PRINT AT 61 COLOR 6,"These are witched"
    PRINT AT 81,"pumpkins!"
    GOSUB wait_and_clean

    PRINT AT 65 COLOR 2,"Witched?"
    GOSUB wait_and_clean
```

```
            PRINT AT 63 COLOR 2,"Err... we have"
            PRINT AT 83,"things to do..."
            PRINT AT 103,"See you later!"

            ' Tiny houses run to the sides
            FOR d = 0 TO 120
                ' Houses at left side
                FOR c = 0 TO 2
                    IF x(c) THEN x(c) = x(c) - 1
                NEXT c
                ' House at right side
                FOR c = 3 TO 5
                    IF x(c) < 168 THEN x(c) = x(c) + 1
                NEXT c
                ' Update sprites
                FOR c = 0 TO 6
                    SPRITE c, $0300 + x(c), $0080 + py, $1801 + 2 * 8
                NEXT c
                WAIT
            NEXT d
            GOSUB wait_and_clean

            PRINT AT 63 COLOR 6,"Cowards! I'll"
            PRINT AT 83,"use my homebrew"
            PRINT AT 103,"proton cannon."
            GOSUB wait_and_clean

            ' Clean pumpkins array
            FOR c = 0 TO PUMPKINS - 1
                x(c) = 0
                y(c) = 0
                s(c) = 0
            NEXT c
    END IF

stuck:    GOTO stuck

boss_loop:    GOTO boss_loop
```

The houses "run" to the sides simply by making the first three houses (indexes 0-2) go left $x(c) = x(c) - 1$, and the right three houses (indexes 3-5) go right $x(c) = x(c) + 1$, and then update the sprites in each frame.

We are missing the following required procedures to make it a compilable section of the game:

```
      '
      ' Start a new attack wave
      '
start_wave:   PROCEDURE
      DO
            c = RAND(10)
      LOOP WHILE wave = c
      wave = c
      sublevel = sublevel + 1
      next_wave = 30 + RAND(30)
      IF sublevel = 11 THEN
            sublevel = 0
            level = level + 1
            GOSUB update_level
      END IF
      END


      '
      ' Update current score
      '
update_score: PROCEDURE
      PRINT AT 0 COLOR 4,"1UP "
      PRINT COLOR 5,<5>#score,"0"
      END


      '
      ' Update level
      '
update_level: PROCEDURE
      PRINT AT 12 COLOR 4,"L"
      PRINT COLOR 5,<2>level
      END


      '
      ' Update number of lives
      '
update_lives: PROCEDURE
      PRINT AT 18 COLOR 4,"H"
      PRINT COLOR 5,<>lives
      END
```

4.4 Basic game loop

Now we can start with the main game loop for the game. Once again, this
code replaces the line "stuck: goto stuck".

```
      '
      ' Game loop for pumpkins waves
      '
game_loop:

      '
      ' Update player house and bullet
      '
      GOSUB update_player
      MODE 0,0,0,0,0:BORDER 0

      WAIT

      GOSUB move_player
      GOTO game_loop
```

Basically we'll update the player sprite, wait for a video frame to happen, and then move the player per the controller indications.

The *update_player* procedure also updates the bullet sprite (active if the variable *by* is nonzero).

```
      '
      ' Update player house and bullet
      '
update_player:      PROCEDURE
    IF by THEN
        SPRITE 6, $0300 + bx, $0000 + by, $0805 + 12 * 8
    ELSE
        SPRITE 6, 0
    END IF
    SPRITE 7, $0300 + px, $0080 + py, $1801 + 2 * 8
    END
```

The *move_player* procedure also moves the player's bullet towards the top, 4 pixels each time. It disappears once it touches the score bar.

Both controllers are read using the idiom *CONT* (although *CONT1* or *CONT2* can be used, but it would only accept input from that controller).

The *d* variable contains the state of buttons, and the input is ignored if any key from the pad is pressed (*d* becomes $80, $40 or $20).

When the *d* variable contains $a0, $c0, or $60, it means a side-button has been pressed, and if the *by* variable is zero, it starts a new bullet at the current player position (*bx = px + 2*, and *by = 96*).

Finally it moves the player to the left or the right, limiting it to the border of the screen just by checking if the *px* variable is already touching the border before adding or subtracting 2 pixels.

Notice the usage of operator + in the *IF* statement. It replaces the *OR* operator, and it is faster for the purposes of the game.

```
     '
     ' Move player and bullet
     '
move_player: PROCEDURE
    IF by THEN      ' Active bullet?
        by = by - 4    ' Move towards top
        IF by < 16 THEN by = 0 ' Disappears if touches score bar
    END IF

    c = CONT
    d = c AND $E0
    IF (d = $80) + (d = $40) + (d = $20) THEN ' Ignore keypad
    ELSE
        IF (d = $a0) + (d = $c0) + (d = $60) THEN ' Side-button
            IF by = 0 THEN' Only if no active bullet?
                bx = px + 2    ' Start a bullet
                by = 96
                IF sound_effect < 3 THEN
                    sound_effect = 1
                    sound_state = 0
                END IF
            END IF
        END IF
        c = controller_direction(c AND $1F)
        ' Move to right
        IF c = 2 THEN IF px < 160 THEN px = px + 2
        ' Move to left
        IF c = 4 THEN IF px > 8 THEN px = px - 2
    END IF
    END

    '
    ' Table for converting disc direction to 4-way direction
    '
controller_direction:
    DATA 0,3,2,3,1,0,2,0
```

```
DATA 4,4,0,0,1,0,0,0
DATA 0,3,2,0,0,0,0,0
DATA 4,0,0,0,1,0,0,0
```

4.5 Adding some pumpkins

The following code displays the sprites for the pumpkins, and it goes right after the "game_loop:" line:

```
'
' Check also if no pumpkins are shown
' (in order to trigger another wave)
'
valid = 0
FOR c = 0 TO PUMPKINS - 1
    IF y(c) THEN
        IF s(c) THEN
            SPRITE c, $0300 + x(c),$0080 + y(c),$1802 + 0 * 8
        ELSE
            SPRITE c, $0300 + x(c),$0080 + y(c),$1802 + 6 * 8
            z(c) = z(c) - 1
            IF z(c) = 0 THEN y(c) = 0
        END IF
        valid = 1
        ' Shot if possible
        IF c = d THEN ' Pumpkin can shoot
            IF b(c) = 0 THEN   ' Free space for shot
                IF x(c) > 7 THEN    ' Pumpkin inside screen
                    IF x(c) < 168 THEN
                        b(c) = x(c)/8 + (y(c)/8) * 20 - 21
                        IF sound_effect < 3 THEN
                            sound_effect = 2
                            sound_state = 0
                        END IF
                    END IF
                END IF
            END IF
        END IF
    ELSE
        SPRITE c, 0
    END IF
NEXT c
```

It not only displays the pumpkins, but it also detects if no pumpkins remain to be seen in order to trigger another wave when *valid = 0*.

Now this code goes after the *WAIT* sentence in order to move the pumpkins:

```
'
' Start a new wave of pumpkins, pumpkin boss or move pumpkins
'
IF next_wave THEN  ' Waiting for next wave
    next_wave = next_wave - 1
    IF next_wave = 0 THEN   ' Start it?
        ON wave GOSUB start_0, start_1, start_2, start_3,
start_4, start_5, start_6, start_7, start_8, start_9
    END IF
ELSEIF valid = 0 THEN    ' No pumpkins alive?
    IF sublevel = 9 THEN      ' Last wave?

        '
        ' Start boss wave
        '
        sublevel = 10

        ' Remove pumpkin bullets
        FOR c = 0 TO PUMPKINS - 1
            b(c) = 0
        NEXT c

        ' Bring in the Pumpkin Master and clean screen
        SCREEN pumpkin_cards, 60, 20, 20, 7, 20
        FOR c = 160 TO 239
            #backtab(c) = 0
        NEXT c

        ' Remove all pumpkins
        FOR c = 0 TO PUMPKINS - 1
            y(c) = 0
            s(c) = 0
            SPRITE c, 0
        NEXT c

        ' Count of boss blocks
        blocks = 7 * 7 - 7

        ' Start boss music
        PLAY VOLUME VOLUME_BOSS
        PLAY music_beat
```

```
                    ' Go to boss game loop
                    GOTO boss_loop
            ELSE
                    GOSUB start_wave
            END IF
        ELSE
            ON wave GOSUB move_0, move_1, move_2, move_3, move_4,
move_5, move_6, move_7, move_8, move_9
        END IF
```

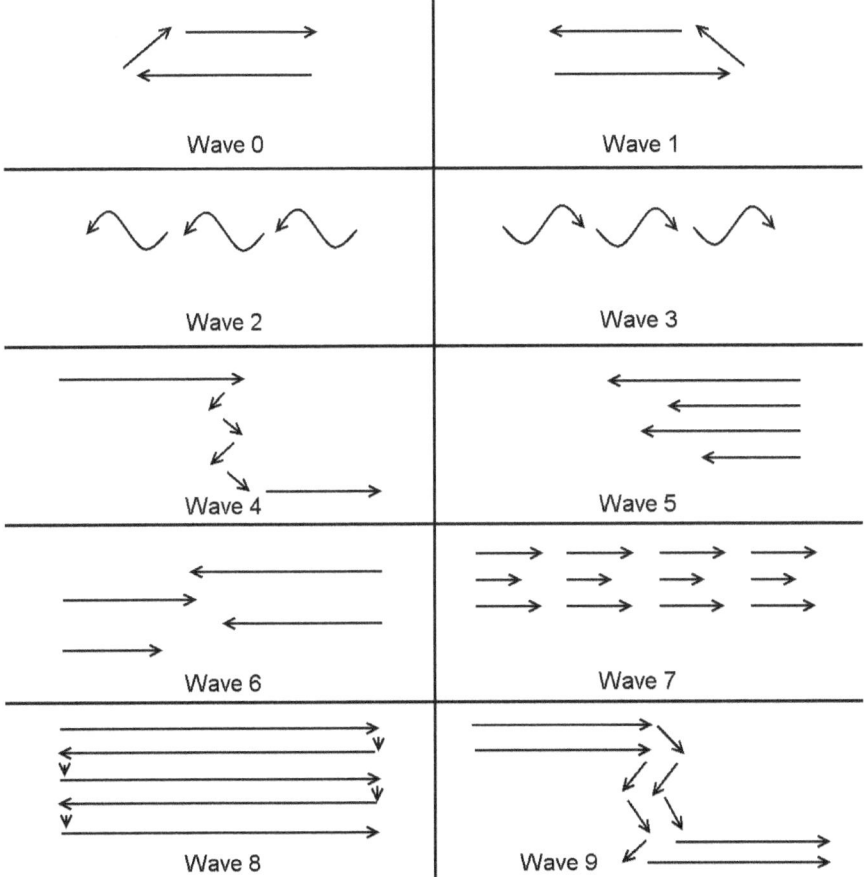

The ten attack waves for pumpkins.

When *next_wave* isn't zero, it counts toward zero, and on becoming zero it starts a pumpkins wave. If *next_wave* was zero, and *valid* also equals zero, then it means no pumpkins are alive, and starts a new wave or a boss wave (if *sublevel=9*). Finally, if *valid* is non-zero (pumpkins alive) it keeps moving the current wave.

Notice the two *ON* sentences break into two lines in this text, but these should be only one line in the source code.

In order for this code to work, we also need the code for each of the 10 waves (*start_0* to *9*, and *move_0* to *9*).

The following code should be added before the *update_player* procedure.

The wave 0 are the pumpkins entering from the right side, going in diagonal up+left, and then retreating to the right side. The *start_0* procedure is in charge of putting the pumpkins in a row **outside** the screen.

The *move_0* procedure then revises the state of each pumpkin to know what to do. In state 1 (*move_01*) it goes to the left and changes to state 2 if it reaches $x = 8$. In state 2 (*move_02*) it goes in diagonal up+left, and if it reaches $y = 24$, it goes to state 3. Finally in state 3 (*move_03*) it goes to the right until it exits the screen. In that moment the pumpkin is removed from the screen (setting $y(c)$ and $s(c)$ to zero).

```
    '
    ' Start wave 0
    '
start_0: PROCEDURE
    FOR c = 0 TO PUMPKINS - 1
        x(c) = 168 + c * 12
        y(c) = 48
        s(c) = 1
    NEXT c
    END


    '
    ' Move wave 0
    '
move_0:  PROCEDURE
    FOR c = 0 TO PUMPKINS - 1
        ON s(c) GOTO move_00, move_01, move_02, move_03

move_01:
        x(c) = x(c) - 2
```

```
                IF x(c) = 8 THEN s(c) = 2
                GOTO move_00

move_02:
                x(c) = x(c) + 1
                y(c) = y(c) - 1
                IF y(c) = 24 THEN s(c) = 3
                GOTO move_00

move_03: x(c) = x(c) + 2
                IF x(c) = 168 THEN y(c) = 0: s(c) = 0
                GOTO move_00

move_00:
        NEXT c
        END
```

Wave 1 is same as the wave 0, except the pumpkins enter the screen from the left, and also exit to the left.

```
        '
        ' Start wave 1
        '
start_1: PROCEDURE
        FOR c = 0 TO PUMPKINS - 1
                x(c) = 0 - c * 12
                y(c) = 48
                s(c) = 1
        NEXT c
        END


        '
        ' Move wave 1
        '
move_1:  PROCEDURE
        FOR c = 0 TO PUMPKINS - 1
                ON s(c) GOTO move_010, move_011, move_012, move_013

move_011:
                x(c) = x(c) + 2
                IF x(c) = 160 THEN s(c) = 2
                GOTO move_010

move_012:
                x(c) = x(c) - 1
                y(c) = y(c) - 1
                IF y(c) = 24 THEN s(c) = 3
```

```
            GOTO move_010

move_013:      x(c) = x(c) - 2
           IF x(c) = 0 THEN y(c) = 0: s(c) = 0
           GOTO move_010

move_010:
    NEXT c
    END
```

In wave 2, the pumpkins enter from the right side of the screen, and go all the way to the left where they disappear. The trick here is that the Y-coordinate undulates using a sine table provided by *sin24*.

Wave 3 is the same, but pumpkins enter from the left side of the screen and go all the way to the right where they disappear.

```
    '
    ' Start wave 2
    '
start_2: PROCEDURE
    FOR c = 0 TO PUMPKINS - 1
        x(c) = 168 + c * 12
        y(c) = 48
        s(c) = 1
    NEXT c
    END


    '
    ' Move wave 2
    '
move_2:  PROCEDURE
    FOR c = 0 TO PUMPKINS - 1
        ON s(c) GOTO move_020, move_021

move_021:
        x(c) = x(c) - 2
        y(c) = 24 + sin24((x(c) AND $3e) / 2)
        IF x(c) = 0 THEN y(c) = 0: s(c) = 0
        GOTO move_020

move_020:
    NEXT c
    END

    '
```

```
      ' Start wave 3
      '
start_3: PROCEDURE
    FOR c = 0 TO PUMPKINS - 1
          x(c) = 0 - c * 12
          y(c) = 48
          s(c) = 1
    NEXT c
    END


      ' Move wave 3
      '
move_3:  PROCEDURE
    FOR c = 0 TO PUMPKINS - 1
          ON s(c) GOTO move_030, move_031

move_031:
          x(c) = x(c) + 2
          y(c) = 24 + sin24((x(c) AND $3e) / 2)
          IF x(c) = 168 THEN y(c) = 0: s(c) = 0
          GOTO move_030

move_030:
    NEXT c
    END


      ' Sine table for curvy movement
      '
sin24:
    DATA 0,2,5,7,9,11,13,15
    DATA 17,19,20,21,22,23,24,24
    DATA 24,24,24,23,22,21,20,19
    DATA 17,15,13,11,9,7,5,2
```

Wave 4 makes the pumpkins enter from the left side of the screen at the top, and go to the center, then descend making a zig-zag pattern (again using the *sin24* table), and once each pumpkin reaches the bottom it exits to the right of the screen.

```
      '
      ' Start wave 4
      '
start_4: PROCEDURE
    FOR c = 0 TO PUMPKINS - 1
```

```
              x(c) = 0 - c * 12
              y(c) = 24
              s(c) = 1
       NEXT c
       END


       '
       ' Move wave 4
       '
move_4:  PROCEDURE
       FOR c = 0 TO PUMPKINS - 1
              ON s(c) GOTO move_040, move_041, move_042, move_043

move_041:
              x(c) = x(c) + 2
              IF x(c) = 90 THEN s(c) = 2
              GOTO move_040

move_042:
              y(c) = y(c) + 1
              x(c) = 72 + sin24(y(c) AND $1f)
              IF y(c) = 80 THEN s(c) = 3
              GOTO move_040

move_043:
              x(c) = (x(c) AND $fe) + 2
              IF x(c) = 168 THEN y(c) = 0: s(c) = 0
              GOTO move_040

move_040:
       NEXT c
       END
```

Wave 5 makes the pumpkins enter from the right of the screen in a random order, and go all the way to the left.

```
       '
       ' Start wave 5
       '
start_5: PROCEDURE
       FOR c = 0 TO PUMPKINS - 1
              x(c) = 168 + RANDOM(32) * 2
              y(c) = 24 + c * 8
              s(c) = 1
       NEXT c
       END
```

```basic
        '
        ' Move wave 5
        '
move_5:  PROCEDURE
    FOR c = 0 TO PUMPKINS - 1
        ON s(c) GOTO move_050, move_051

move_051:
        x(c) = x(c) - 2
        IF x(c) = 0 THEN y(c) = 0: s(c) = 0
        GOTO move_050

move_050:
    NEXT c
    END
```

Wave 6 is similar to wave 5, except that half of the pumpkins enter from the left side of the screen, and the other half enters from the right side.

```basic
        '
        ' Start wave 6
        '
start_6: PROCEDURE
    FOR c = 0 TO PUMPKINS - 1
        IF c AND 1 THEN
            x(c) = 168 + RANDOM(32) * 2
            s(c) = 1
        ELSE
            x(c) = 0 - RANDOM(32) * 2
            s(c) = 2
        END IF
        y(c) = 24 + c * 8
    NEXT c
    END


        '
        ' Move wave 6
        '
move_6:  PROCEDURE
    FOR c = 0 TO PUMPKINS - 1
        ON s(c) GOTO move_060, move_061, move_062

move_061:
        x(c) = x(c) - 2
        IF x(c) = 0 THEN y(c) = 0: s(c) = 0
```

```
            GOTO move_060

move_062:
            x(c) = x(c) + 2
            IF x(c) = 168 THEN y(c) = 0: s(c) = 0
            GOTO move_060

move_060:
    NEXT c
    END
```

Wave 7 makes pumpkins enter from the left in a triangle shape (à la Megamania), and go all the way to the right.

```
    '
    ' Start wave 7
    '
start_7: PROCEDURE
    FOR c = 0 TO PUMPKINS - 1
        d = c % 3
        IF d = 0 THEN x(c) = 0 - c / 3 * 32:y(c) = 24
        IF d = 1 THEN x(c) = 0 - c / 3 * 32:y(c) = 40
        IF d = 2 THEN x(c) = -16 - c / 3 * 32: y(c) = 32
        s(c) = 1
    NEXT c
    END


    '
    ' Move wave 7
    '
move_7:  PROCEDURE
    FOR c = 0 TO PUMPKINS - 1
        ON s(c) GOTO move_70, move_71

move_71:
        x(c) = x(c) + 2
        IF x(c) = 168 THEN y(c) = 0: s(c) = 0
        GOTO move_70

move_70:
    NEXT c
    END
```

In wave 8, pumpkins "scan" each row of the screen from left to right, and then from right to left, descending at each step (à la Centipede, except nothing stops the pumpkins to make them descend faster).

```
    '
    ' Start wave 8
    '
start_8: PROCEDURE
    FOR c = 0 TO PUMPKINS - 1
        x(c) = 0 - c * 12
        y(c) = 24
        s(c) = 1
    NEXT c
    END


    '
    ' Move wave 8
    '
move_8:  PROCEDURE
    FOR c = 0 TO PUMPKINS - 1
        ON s(c) GOTO move_080, move_081, move_082, move_083,
move_084, move_085

move_081:
        x(c) = x(c) + 2
        IF x(c) = 160 THEN s(c) = 2
        GOTO move_080

move_082:
        x(c) = x(c) - 1
        y(c) = y(c) + 1
        IF (y(c) AND 7) = 0 THEN
            IF y(c) = 80 THEN s(c) = 5 ELSE s(c) = 3
        END IF
        GOTO move_080

move_083:    x(c) = x(c) - 2
        IF x(c) = 8 THEN s(c) = 4
        GOTO move_080

move_084:
        x(c) = x(c) + 1
        y(c) = y(c) + 1
        IF (y(c) AND 7) = 0 THEN s(c) = 1
        GOTO move_080

move_085:
        x(c) = x(c) - 2
```

```
            IF x(c) = 0 THEN s(c) = 0: y(c) = 0
            GOTO move_080

move_080:
    NEXT c
    END
```

Wave 9 makes two rows of pumpkins enter from the left side of the screen, and go to the center, then descend making diagonals to the left and right. When the pumpkins reach the bottom, they all exit through the right side of the screen.

```
    '
    ' Start wave 9
    '
start_9: PROCEDURE
    FOR c = 0 TO PUMPKINS - 1
        IF c AND 1 THEN
            x(c) = 0 - c / 2 * 24
            y(c) = 24
        ELSE
            x(c) = 0 - c / 2 * 24
            y(c) = 40
        END IF
        s(c) = 1
        z(c) = 54
    NEXT c
    END


    '
    ' Move wave 9
    '
move_9:  PROCEDURE
    FOR c = 0 TO PUMPKINS - 1
        ON s(c) GOTO move_090, move_091, move_092, move_093

move_091:
        x(c) = x(c) + 2
        z(c) = z(c) - 1
        IF z(c) = 0 THEN s(c) = 2
        GOTO move_090

move_092:
        IF y(c) AND 8 THEN
            x(c) = x(c) - 1
            y(c) = y(c) + 1
```

```
            ELSE
                x(c) = x(c) + 1
                y(c) = y(c) + 1
            END IF
            IF y(c) = 80 THEN s(c) = 3
            GOTO move_090

move_093:
            x(c) = x(c) + 2
            IF x(c) >= 168 THEN s(c) = 0: y(c) = 0
            GOTO move_090

move_090:
        NEXT c
        END
```

4.6 The pumpkins shoot!

All is very nice but the pumpkins aren't even slightly menacing. Let us change that by making them to shoot pumpkin seeds!

Add this code just after the line with the label *game_loop*:

```
    '
    ' Update pumpkins and drop bullets
    '
    IF drop_bullet THEN      ' Not yet time for a bullet?
        drop_bullet = drop_bullet - 1
        d = PUMPKINS
    ELSE
        c = level
        IF c > 10 THEN c = 10
        drop_bullet = 15 - c + RAND(16)   ' Time for next bullet
        d = RAND(PUMPKINS) 'Choose a random pumpkin that will shoot
    END IF
```

The variable *drop_bullet* tells the game if it is time to drop a new bullet from the pumpkins. If that is the case then the variable *d* will have the number of the pumpkin that will shoot. In any other case the variable *d* will be the constant *PUMPKINS* (outside the number of pumpkins) so no bullet is generated. Of course, as the level increases, the bullets are shot

123

more frequently, by means of *15 - level,* where *level* is capped at ten in order to not make it very difficult.

Just after the *WAIT* sentence in the main loop, add this code:

```
' Check if player is touched by background (bullet)
IF COL7 AND $0100 THEN  GOTO player_touched

'
' Move pumpkins bullets in 4px steps.
'
next_bullet = (next_bullet + 1) AND 3
IF next_bullet = 0 THEN
    FOR c = 0 TO PUMPKINS - 1
        d = b(c)
        IF d THEN
            #backtab(d) = $0802 + 5 * 8
        END IF
    NEXT c
ELSEIF next_bullet = 2 THEN
    FOR c = 0 TO PUMPKINS - 1
        d = b(c)
        IF d THEN
            #backtab(d) = 0
            IF d >= 220 THEN
                d = 0
            ELSE
                d = d + 20
                #backtab(d) = $0802 + 4 * 8
            END IF
            b(c) = d
        END IF
    NEXT c
END IF
```

Using hardware collisions, it detects if a bullet touches the player and jumps to *player_touched* in order to make it explode.

For every 4 frames of video, in the first one it updates the pumpkin shots on the screen to be at offset 4px, and in the third one it moves all pumpkin shots 4px down to be at offset 0px on screen.

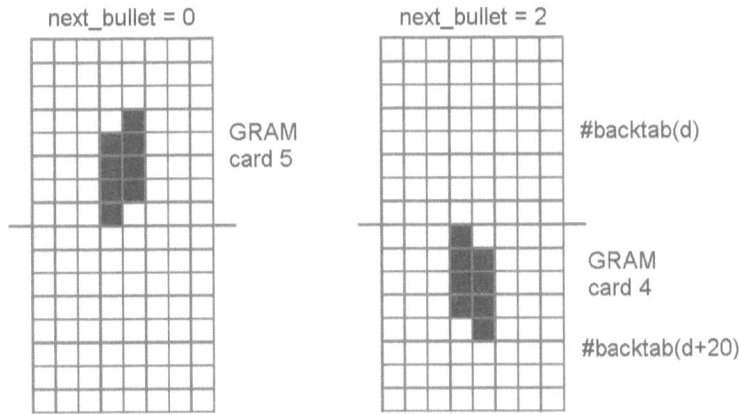

next_bullet = 0

GRAM card 5

next_bullet = 2

#backtab(d)

GRAM card 4

#backtab(d+20)

How the pumpkin bullets have smooth displacement using only **GRAM** cards.

Notice how the bullets' position is preserved as the card number on screen, and also that once a bullet goes off-screen it is removed (it assigns *b(c)* to zero). This means each bullet uses a single memory location! Pretty useful because the base Intellivision is limited in terms of memory.

We need to add further code just after the *GOTO game_loop* line:

```
    '
    ' Player explosion
    '
player_touched:
    PLAY VOLUME 0
    sound_effect = 4: sound_state = 0


    '
    ' Screen cleaning changes if it's pumpkins or boss wave.
    '
    IF sublevel = 10 THEN
        FOR c = 0 TO PUMPKINS - 1
            SPRITE c, 0
            y(c) = 0
            s(c) = 0
        NEXT c
    ELSE
        FOR c = 20 TO 239
            #backtab(c) = 0
        NEXT c
        FOR c = 0 TO PUMPKINS - 1
            b(c) = 0
```

```
        NEXT c
END IF


'
' Player nuclear explosion
' (not really, the pumpkin bullet hit the freezer and
' it was filled with beer :P)
'
SPRITE 6,0
FOR c = 0 TO 127
    IF c = 0 THEN
        SPRITE 7, $0300 + px, $0080 + py
    END IF
    IF c = 32 THEN
        SPRITE 7, $0300 + px, $0180 + py - 8
    END IF
    IF c = 64 THEN
        SPRITE 7, $0700 + px - 4, $0180 + py - 8
    END IF
    IF c = 96 THEN
        SPRITE 7, $0700 + px - 4, $0280 + py - 24
    END IF
    IF C AND 2 THEN
        SPRITE 7,,,$0807 + 10 * 8
    ELSE
        SPRITE 7,,,$0807 + 8 * 8
    END IF
    d = c AND 15
    MODE 0,d,d,d,d
    BORDER d
    WAIT
NEXT c
SPRITE 7,0
MODE 0,0,0,0,0
BORDER 0
FOR c = 0 TO 10
    WAIT
NEXT c

' No more lives = Game over
IF lives = 0 THEN
    FOR c = 0 TO 255
        PRINT AT 105 COLOR C AND 7,"GAME   OVER"
        WAIT
    NEXT c
    IF #score > #record THEN #record = #score
    GOTO title_screen
END IF
```

```
' One life less, restart game
lives = lives - 1
GOTO restart_game
```

When the player is touched, the game immediately invokes the explosion sound effect. Then it clears the screen (in pumpkin screens it only removes all sprites; in boss screens it clears the boss area). It also cleans all the arrays of enemies.

It removes the player's bullet using *SPRITE 6,0*, and then starts a sequence where a kind of thermonuclear explosion is shown[8]. The same two alternating sprites are used but the sprites are scaled on the X and Y axes to be bigger each time: see the $0300 and $0700 value for X scaling, and $0080 (double-Y resolution; an 8x16 sprite is the same size as an 8x8 card), $0180 (one pixel per line), and $0280 (two pixels per line) for Y scaling.

When the animation is complete, the player's house is removed from the screen, and if the variable *lives* is equal to zero then the game is over, and updates the *#record* variable with the highest *#score*. If there are still houses to play, it restarts the game by jumping to *restart_game*.

4.7 Die pumpkin! Die!

The pumpkins cannot be killed, yet. This is going to be solved now! The code uses the collision register to ease the detection.

This code goes after the line reading "*IF COL7*":

---

[8] But not really, it is only the beer in the freezer exploding. Like in The Simpsons' season 4 episode 18, where Bart intends to do an April Fools' prank to Homer using an agitated beer.

```
            ' Check if player bullet touches pumpkin
        IF COL6 AND $003F THEN
            ' Hardware saves us from tedious collision checking
            c = 255
            IF COL6 AND $0001 THEN c = 0
            IF COL6 AND $0002 THEN c = 1
            IF COL6 AND $0004 THEN c = 2
            IF COL6 AND $0008 THEN c = 3
            IF COL6 AND $0010 THEN c = 4
            IF COL6 AND $0020 THEN c = 5
            IF c < 6 THEN  ' Pumpkin touched?
                IF y(c) THEN   ' Pumpkin alive?
                    IF s(c) THEN   ' Pumpkin moving?
                        s(c) = 0  ' Cease movement
                        z(c) = 8  ' Start explosion timing
                        by = 0
                        #score = #score + 1
                        GOSUB update_score
                        sound_effect = 3: sound_state = 0
                    END IF
                END IF
            END IF
        END IF
```

When the bullet sprite touches a pumpkin, the Intellivision hardware tells us which sprite was touched.

Using the *AND* operator we can extract the bit and see what pumpkin was touched. The 6 *IF* sentences do that, and assign the variable c with the pumpkin number.

If the pumpkin was touched, and it is still alive (remember the collision flags are delayed by one video frame), and it is still moving, then it stops the pumpkin, and starts the pumpkin explosion by setting $z(c) = 8$. It also adds one to *#score*, updates the score on screen, and starts a sound effect.

4.8 Sound effects

The sound effects for the game again take advantage of the "multitask" capability of IntyBASIC to call a subroutine on each video frame.

So let us add this to the start of the game:

```
ON FRAME GOSUB play_sound
```

And then add this at the end of the game:

```
'
' Play sound effects
'
play_sound:   PROCEDURE
    ON sound_effect GOSUB play_none, play_fire, play_drop,
play_explosion_1, play_explosion_2
    END

play_none:   PROCEDURE
    SOUND 2,,0
    SOUND 4,,$38
    END

play_fire:   PROCEDURE
    SOUND 2,200 - sound_state * sound_state,12
    SOUND 4,,$38
    sound_state = sound_state + 1
    IF sound_state = 10 THEN sound_effect = 0
    END

play_drop:   PROCEDURE
    SOUND 2,100 + (RAND AND 1) + sound_state * sound_state,12
    SOUND 4,,$38
    sound_state = sound_state + 1
    IF sound_state = 10 THEN sound_effect = 0
    END

play_explosion_1: PROCEDURE
    SOUND 2,1000+sound_state * 16,12 - sound_state / 4
    SOUND 4,,$38
    sound_state = sound_state + 1
    IF sound_state = 24 THEN sound_effect = 0
    END

play_explosion_2: PROCEDURE
    SOUND 2,2000-sound_state*16,12 - sound_state / 8
    SOUND 4,31-sound_state/4,$18
    sound_state = sound_state + 1
    IF sound_state = 96 THEN sound_effect = 0
    END
```

There are only four sound effects in this game:

- *play_fire* (*sound_effect* = *1*), used when the player fires.
- *play_drop* (*sound_effect* = *2*), used when a pumpkin fires.
- *play_explosion_1* (*sound_effect* = *3*), used for pumpkin destroyed.
- *play_explosion_2* (*sound_effect* = *4*), used for player destroyed.

The firing sounds are exponential style, using the *sound_state* * *sound_state* expression, where *sound_state* increases by one in each video frame.

The explosion sound for the player uses the noise channel of the sound processor, changing its frequency with *31-sound_state/4* (starting from a low noise frequency) and also the audio frequency with *2000-sound_state*16* (a low tone becoming slightly higher in frequency).

4.9 Extra fun

One thing I did with this game was to include two extra minigames: Astro Pumpkin, and Pumpkin Catapult.

Astro Pumpkin is a small game where pumpkins come from up, down, left, and right. The player must shoot the pumpkins before touching the house in the center. My little homage to Cosmic Ark.

Pumpkin Catapult is a game where the player needs to adjust his/her catapult in order to hit the Pumpkin Master until destroying it completely.

The games are called by pressing 1 or 2 on the numeric keypad. Replace the comment lines reading "Minigame 1" and "Minigame 2" with these lines:

```
IF c = $41 THEN GOTO astro_pumpkin
IF c = $21 THEN GOTO pumpkin_catapult
```

Now add this to the end of the source code file "pumpkin.bas":

```
    ASM ORG $D000

    '
    ' Astro pumpkin
    '
astro_pumpkin:
    '
    ' Prepare for starting game
    '
    CLS
    MODE 0,0,0,0,0
    FOR c = 0 TO 7
        SPRITE c, 0
    NEXT c
    WAIT
    DEFINE 0,16,game_bitmaps_0
    WAIT

    PRINT AT 83 COLOR 6,"Astro Pumpkin"
    FOR c = 0 TO 60
        WAIT
    NEXT c
    CLS
```

A small title screen so the player knows the key worked. Now it
proceeds to initialize the score, house position, lives, and level. It also resets
the pumpkin arrays.

```
    #score = 0
    px = 84
    py = 52
    lives = 0
    level = 1

    FOR c = 0 TO PUMPKINS - 1
        x(c) = 0
        y(c) = 0
        s(c) = 0
    NEXT c

    c = level
    IF c > 50 THEN c = 50
    next_wave = 60 - c

    GOSUB update_score
```

The main game loop shows the pumpkins and moves them in their respective direction (contained in *s(c)*). It also handles pumpkins exploding.

The sentences *SPRITE 6* and *SPRITE 7* draw respectively the player's bullet, and the house.

```
astro_loop:
    FOR c = 0 TO PUMPKINS - 1
        IF y(c) THEN
            IF s(c) THEN
                SPRITE c, $0300 + x(c), $0080 + y(c), $1802 + 0*8
                ON s(c) GOTO , astro_1, astro_2, astro_3, astro_4
astro_1: y(c) = y(c) - 1: GOTO astro_0     ' up
astro_2: x(c) = x(c) + 1: GOTO astro_0     ' right
astro_3: y(c) = y(c) + 1: GOTO astro_0     ' down
astro_4: x(c) = x(c) - 1: GOTO astro_0     ' left
            ELSE
                SPRITE c, $0300 + x(c), $0080 + y(c), $1802 + 6*8
                z(c) = z(c) - 1
                IF z(c) = 0 THEN y(c) = 0
            END IF
        ELSE
            SPRITE c, 0
        END IF
astro_0:
    NEXT c
    SPRITE 6, $0300 + bx, $0100 + by + 1, $0005 + 10 * 8
    SPRITE 7, $0300 + px, $0080 + py, $1801 + 2 * 8
    WAIT
```

Now it checks if it can throw another pumpkin at the player (*next_wave* becomes zero), and restarts the *next_wave* counter per the current difficulty level. The pumpkin appears randomly at one of four positions (top center, bottom center, center left, and center right).

```
next_wave = next_wave - 1
IF next_wave = 0 THEN
    c = level
    IF c > 50 THEN c = 50
    next_wave = 60 - c

    d = 0
    WHILE y(d)
        d = d + 1
        IF d = PUMPKINS THEN EXIT WHILE
```

132

```
        WEND
        IF d < PUMPKINS THEN      ' Start a pumpkin
            c = RANDOM(4) + 1
            IF c = 1 THEN x(d) = 84: y(d) = 104: s(d) = 1
            IF c = 2 THEN x(d) = 0: y(d) = 52: s(d) = 2
            IF c = 3 THEN x(d) = 84: y(d) = 1: s(d) = 3
            IF c = 4 THEN x(d) = 168: y(d) = 52: s(d) = 4
        END IF
        level = level + 1
    END IF
```

If the player's house is crashed into by a pumpkin, all the screen flashes in red, and the game returns to the title screen.

```
IF COL7 AND $003F THEN
    SPRITE 6, 0
    FOR c = 0 TO 50
        BORDER 2:MODE 0,2,2,2,2 ' Red
        SPRITE 7,,,$0807 + 2 * 8
        WAIT
        BORDER 0:MODE 0,0,0,0,0 ' Black
        SPRITE 7,,,$1801 + 2 * 8
        WAIT
        WAIT
        WAIT
    NEXT c
    GOTO title_screen
END IF
```

If the player's bullet touches a pumpkin, it detects again by hardware bits which pumpkin was destroyed, and increases score (generating sound effect, starting explosion, and so on).

```
    ' Check if player bullet touches pumpkin
IF COL6 AND $003F THEN
    ' Hardware saves us of tedious collision checking
    c = 255
    IF COL6 AND $0001 THEN c = 0
    IF COL6 AND $0002 THEN c = 1
    IF COL6 AND $0004 THEN c = 2
    IF COL6 AND $0008 THEN c = 3
    IF COL6 AND $0010 THEN c = 4
    IF COL6 AND $0020 THEN c = 5
    IF c < 6 THEN ' Pumpkin touched?
        IF y(c) THEN   ' Pumpkin alive?
```

```
                    IF s(c) THEN    ' Pumpkin moving?
                        s(c) = 0  ' Cease movement
                        z(c) = 8  ' Start explosion timing
                        by = 0
                        #score = #score + 1
                        GOSUB update_score
                        sound_effect = 3: sound_state = 0
                    END IF
                END IF
            END IF
        END IF
END IF
```

If there is an active bullet, it should be moved in the requested direction. As the house cannot move in this minigame, the disc directions are used to start bullets.

```
IF by THEN      ' Active bullet?
    IF bz = 1 THEN by = by - 4: IF by < 8 THEN by = 0
    IF bz = 2 THEN bx = bx + 4: IF bx >= 168 THEN by = 0
    IF bz = 3 THEN by = by + 4: IF by >= 104 THEN by = 0
    IF bz = 4 THEN bx = bx - 4: IF bx < 8 THEN by = 0
END IF

c = CONT
d = c AND $E0
IF (d = $80) + (d = $40) + (d = $20) THEN ' Ignore keypad
ELSE
    c = controller_direction(c AND $1F)
    IF c = 1 THEN ' Up
        IF by = 0 THEN
            bx = px
            by = py - 8
            bz = c
            IF sound_effect < 3 THEN
                sound_effect = 1: sound_state = 0
            END IF
        END IF
    END IF
    IF c = 2 THEN ' Right
        IF by = 0 THEN
            bx = px + 8
            by = py
            bz = c
            IF sound_effect < 3 THEN
                sound_effect = 1: sound_state = 0
            END IF
```

```
                     END IF
             END IF
             IF c = 3 THEN ' Down
                     IF by = 0 THEN
                             bx = px
                             by = py + 8
                             bz = c
                             IF sound_effect < 3 THEN
                                     sound_effect = 1: sound_state = 0
                             END IF
                     END IF
             END IF
             IF c = 4 THEN ' Left
                     IF by = 0 THEN
                             bx = px - 8
                             by = py
                             bz = c
                             IF sound_effect < 3 THEN
                                     sound_effect = 1: sound_state = 0
                             END IF
                     END IF
             END IF
     END IF
     GOTO astro_loop
```

This completes the Astro Pumpkin mini game.

And now we go to see the Pumpkin Catapult game. There are no enemies in this game. It is only the player against the Pumpkin Master using a catapult and some physics-like effects!

Again we start with a minimum title screen:

```
     '
     ' Pumpkin catapult
     '
pumpkin_catapult:
     '
     ' Prepare for starting game
     '
     CLS
     MODE 0,0,0,0,0
     FOR c = 0 TO 7
         SPRITE c, 0
     NEXT c
     WAIT
     DEFINE 0,16,game_bitmaps_0
```

```
    WAIT

    PRINT AT 82 COLOR 6,"Pumpkin Catapult"
    FOR c = 0 TO 60
        WAIT
    NEXT c
```

Now the screen is cleared and the Pumpkin Master is drawn on the screen. Also the position for the house is set up and the angle and speed for the bullet. A starting count of blocks is prepared.

```
    CLS

    SCREEN pumpkin_cards, 66, 113, 7, 7, 20

    px = 8
    py = 96

    angle = 0
    speed = 1

    ' Count of boss blocks
    blocks = 7 * 7 - 7

    debounce = 0
```

The current angle and speed are shown, and the bullet and house are drawn. The *gronk* variable is turned on when the enemy is hit, so the screen flashes briefly.

```
catapult_loop:
    PRINT AT 0 COLOR 5,"Pumpkangle: ",<2>angle, " S:",<2>speed

    SPRITE 6, $0300 + bx, $0100 + by + 1, $0005 + 10 * 8
    SPRITE 7, $0300 + px, $0080 + py, $1801 + 2 * 8
    '
    ' If boss hit then flash screen
    '
    IF gronk THEN
        MODE 0,7,7,7,7:BORDER 7:gronk = 0
    ELSE
        MODE 0,0,0,0,0:BORDER 0
    END IF
    WAIT
```

If there is an active bullet, it checks if the bullet hits the Pumpkin Master. If there is a hit, a block is removed from the screen (and *blocks = blocks - 1*), the *gronk* variable is set to one, and the score increased.

When the Pumpkin Master is completely destroyed, the minigame returns to the main title screen.

```
IF by THEN      ' Active bullet?
    c = (bx + 3) / 8 + ((by + 3) / 8) * 20 - 21
    IF c >= 20 AND c < 240 AND #backtab(c) <> 0 THEN ' Crashes?
        #backtab(c) = 0        ' Remove block
        gronk = 1       ' Signal flash requested
        by = 0            ' Remove bullet
        #score = #score + 2
        sound_effect = 3: sound_state = 0
        blocks = blocks - 1      ' One block less
        GOSUB update_score
        IF blocks = 0 THEN ' All blocks completed?
            '
            ' Return to pumpkins waves
            '
            sound_effect = 4:sound_state = 0
            FOR c = 0 TO PUMPKINS - 1
                y(c) = 0
                s(c) = 0
                SPRITE c, 0
            NEXT c
            GOTO title_screen
        END IF
    END IF
END IF
```

If the player's bullet is active, it moves in displacements of *#sx* and *#sy* fractional (8 integer bits and 8 bits of fraction). The bullet can exit through the top or bottom of the screen. The speed of the bullet is reduced, and some gravity is applied. If *#sy* is positive it increases by 1/17 each time, and otherwise it decreases by 1/16 if *#sy* is negative because the division operator of IntyBASIC doesn't handle negative numbers. This code for physics looks complicated but it creates a beautiful cannon bullet effect.

```
IF by THEN
    #bx = #bx + #sx          ' Move bullet in x
    bx = #bx / 256           ' Get pixel for screen
    #by = #by + #sy          ' Move bullet in y
    IF bx > 164 THEN by = 0 ' Remove if touches right border
    IF #by < $0200 THEN by = 1 ELSE by = #by / 256
    IF #by > $6400 THEN by = 0   ' Remove if touches bottom
    #sx = #sx * 15 / 16      ' Reduce x speed
    IF #sy < 0 THEN          ' Going upwards
        #sy = -(-#sy * 15 / 16) + 16
    ELSE                     ' Gravity
        #sy = #sy * 17 / 16 + 16
    END IF
END IF
```

The *debounce* variable allows the debouncing of the disc controller directions; otherwise the controls would be impossible to adjust.

Moving up and down adjusts the angle, while moving left and right adjusts the speed.

Pressing any side button starts a bullet launch using *cos* and *sin* fractional tables in the indicated angle multiplied by the selected speed, and also starts a firing sound effect.

```
IF debounce THEN debounce = debounce - 1

c = CONT
d = c AND $E0
IF (d = $80) + (d = $40) + (d = $20) THEN ' Ignore keypad
ELSE
    IF (d = $c0) + (d = $a0) + (d = $60) THEN
        IF by = 0 THEN
            #bx = px * 256
            #by = py * 256
            bx = #bx / 256
            by = #by / 256
            #sx = cos(angle) * speed
            #sy = -sin(angle) * speed
            IF sound_effect < 3 THEN
                sound_effect = 1: sound_state = 0
            END IF
        END IF
    END IF
    c = controller_direction(c AND $1F)
```

```
          IF debounce THEN c = 0
          IF c = 3 THEN IF angle > 0 THEN angle = angle - 1
          IF c = 1 THEN IF angle < 89 THEN angle = angle + 1
          IF c = 2 THEN IF speed < 12 THEN speed = speed + 1
          IF c = 4 THEN IF speed > 1 THEN speed = speed - 1
          IF c THEN debounce = 5
      END IF
      GOTO catapult_loop

sin:
      DATA 0,4,9,13,18,22,27,31,36,40
      DATA 44,49,53,58,62,66,71,75,79,83
      DATA 88,92,96,100,104,108,112,116,120,124
      DATA 128,132,136,139,143,147,150,154,158,161
      DATA 165,168,171,175,178,181,184,187,190,193
      DATA 196,199,202,204,207,210,212,215,217,219
      DATA 222,224,226,228,230,232,234,236,237,239
      DATA 241,242,243,245,246,247,248,249,250,251
      DATA 252,253,254,254,255,255,255,256,256,256

cos:
      DATA 256,256,256,256,255,255,255,254,254,253
      DATA 252,251,250,249,248,247,246,245,243,242
      DATA 241,239,237,236,234,232,230,228,226,224
      DATA 222,219,217,215,212,210,207,204,202,199
      DATA 196,193,190,187,184,181,178,175,171,168
      DATA 165,161,158,154,150,147,143,139,136,132
      DATA 128,124,120,116,112,108,104,100,96,92
      DATA 88,83,79,75,71,66,62,58,53,49
      DATA 44,40,36,31,27,22,18,13,9,4
```

Chapter 5

Meteor Storm

The Earth's colonies are in need of supplies, but the spacial routes are polluted with asteroids and aliens. Your mission is to fight in these routes until you reach each colony and deliver the supplies.

The game shows the cockpit of your spaceship[9], and in a pseudo-3D fashion you can see the aliens approaching your ship, and their missiles, also the asteroids.

 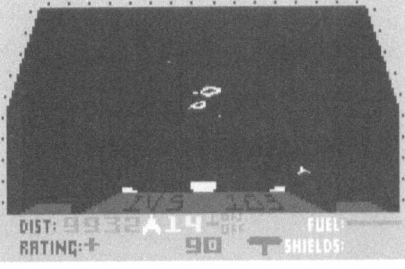

Sega Subroc for Colecovision, and Blockade Runner for Intellivision.

---

[9] The first time I saw a spaceship cockpit was in a game called The Last Warrior, published in the Compute! Magazine issue 64 from September, 1985. I was age 7, and these were the most amazing graphics I had ever seen. I was very disappointed once I typed the program, and saw the primitive gameplay, basically moving a crosshair over enemies displacing slowly, but watching the cockpit was worth it. See more at: https://www.atarimagazines.com/compute/issue64/last_warrior.php

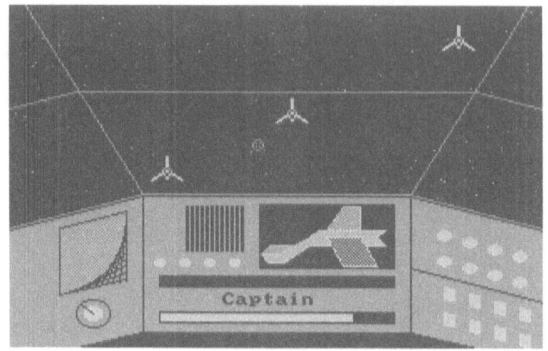

The Last Warrior. Game published in the Compute! Magazine.

Other similar games were the arcade game SubRoc by Sega, which was also very popular with its Colecovision port. The Intellivision had one similar game: Blockade Runner, but it suffered from collision problems.

In Meteor Storm you move your spaceship using the controller directions, until the enemy is in the center of your crosshair, then pressing any of the side buttons launches twin lasers.

When something hits your spaceship, the cockpit gets broken, making it harder to see what's happening.

This game was published by Intellivision Revolution in the game compilation IntyBASIC Showcase Vol. 2.

5.1 Game design

The game shows up to six aliens, asteroids, or enemy bullets as sprites, plus two sprites to show the player's twin lasers.

```
'
' Meteor Storm
'
' by Oscar Toledo G. (nanochess)
'
' Creation date: Mar/18/2018.
'

CONST COCKPIT_COLOR2 = 8      ' Cockpit color
CONST MAX = 6
```

```
UNSIGNED #score, #record

DIM fx(MAX)
DIM fy(MAX)
DIM t(MAX)
DIM dx(MAX)
DIM dy(MAX)
DIM pp(MAX)

DIM #star(4)   ' Bitmap for building scrolling star

#record = 50   ' Initialized in main menu
CLS
MODE 0,0,0,0,0
BORDER 0
FOR c = 0 TO 60
WAIT
NEXT c
```

The arrays keep the positions of all the pseudo-3D things on screen. The arrays *fx* and *fy* keep the horizontal and vertical position. The array *t* indicates the type of "thing". The array *dx* keeps the horizontal distance from the player, although it starts from zero (the farthest distance) and increases toward 127 (the closest distance to player). The array *dy* keeps the state of the "thing," like a counter to move it to another position, and also a counter for the explosion timing when its value is greater than or equal to 128.

5.2 Graphics for the game

The graphics for this game have a great variety.

Sprite sheet. The four aliens can be seen in three animation frames (upper two rows). The explosion, scaled asteroids, and enemy rockets are in the bottom rows.

There are four types of alien ships, and these are animated with three frames of animation to give the illusion of rotating ships. There is a single sprite for the explosion. And all other sprites are used to increase proximity of the sprite to the player's spaceship.

```
aliens_bitmaps:
    BITMAP "........"   ' 9 Alien ship (1 of 3)
    BITMAP "...XX..."
    BITMAP ".XXXXX."
    BITMAP "X.XX..XX"
    BITMAP "XXXXXXXX"
    BITMAP ".XXXXX."
    BITMAP "XX.XX.XX"
    BITMAP "........"

    BITMAP "........"   ' 10 Alien ship (2 of 3)
    BITMAP "...XX..."
    BITMAP ".XXXXX."
    BITMAP "XX..XX.X"
    BITMAP "XXXXXXXX"
    BITMAP ".XXXXX."
    BITMAP "XX.XX.XX"
    BITMAP "........"

    BITMAP "........"   ' 11 Alien ship (3 of 3)
    BITMAP "...XX..."
    BITMAP ".XXXXX."
    BITMAP "X..XX..X"
    BITMAP "XXXXXXXX"
```

```
BITMAP ".XXXXXX."
BITMAP "XX.XX.XX"
BITMAP "........"

BITMAP "..XXXX.."
BITMAP "...XX..."
BITMAP "X.XXXX.X"
BITMAP "XX..XXXX"
BITMAP "XXXX..XX"
BITMAP "X.XXXX.X"
BITMAP "...XX..."
BITMAP "..XXXX.."

BITMAP "..XXXX.."
BITMAP "...XX..."
BITMAP "X.XXXX.X"
BITMAP "XX.XX.XX"
BITMAP "XXX..XXX"
BITMAP "X.XXXX.X"
BITMAP "...XX..."
BITMAP "..XXXX.."

BITMAP "..XXXX.."
BITMAP "...XX..."
BITMAP "X.XXXX.X"
BITMAP "XXXX..XX"
BITMAP "XX..XXXX"
BITMAP "X.XXXX.X"
BITMAP "...XX..."
BITMAP "..XXXX.."

BITMAP "XX....XX"
BITMAP "XX....XX"
BITMAP "X.XXXX.X"
BITMAP "XXXXXXXX"
BITMAP "XX.XX.XX"
BITMAP "..XXXX.."
BITMAP ".XX..XX."
BITMAP "XX....XX"

BITMAP ".XX..XX."
BITMAP "XX....XX"
BITMAP "X.XXXX.X"
BITMAP "XXXXXXXX"
BITMAP "XX.XX.XX"
BITMAP "..XXXX.."
BITMAP ".XX..XX."
BITMAP ".XX..XX."
```

```
        BITMAP ".XX..XX."
        BITMAP ".XX..XX."
        BITMAP "X.XXXX.X"
        BITMAP "XXXXXXXX"
        BITMAP "XX.XX.XX"
        BITMAP "..XXXX.."
        BITMAP ".XX..XX."
        BITMAP "..X..X.."

        BITMAP "..X.X..."
        BITMAP ".X....X."
        BITMAP "..XXXX.X"
        BITMAP "X.X..X.."
        BITMAP "X.XXXX.X"
        BITMAP "..XXXX.X"
        BITMAP ".X......"
        BITMAP "..X.XX.."

        BITMAP "...X.X.."
        BITMAP ".X....X."
        BITMAP "X.XXXX.."
        BITMAP "..X..X.X"
        BITMAP "X.X..X.X"
        BITMAP "X.XXXX.."
        BITMAP "......X."
        BITMAP "..XX.X.."

        BITMAP "..X.XX.."
        BITMAP "........"
        BITMAP "X.XXXX.X"
        BITMAP "X.XXXX.X"
        BITMAP "..XXXX.."
        BITMAP "X.XXXX.X"
        BITMAP ".X....X."
        BITMAP "...XX..."
```

The alien ships stay animated in the background, and the meteors
and enemy rockets approach the player, so these are drawn in several
frames to give the illusion of going from far to near.

```
storm_bitmaps_1:
    BITMAP "....X..."  ' 0 Explosion
    BITMAP "...X...."
    BITMAP ".X....X."
```

```
BITMAP "....X..."
BITMAP "XX....X."
BITMAP ".......X"
BITMAP "...X...."
BITMAP "....X..."

BITMAP "........"  ' 1 Meteor (1 of 8)
BITMAP "........"
BITMAP "........"
BITMAP "...X...."
BITMAP "........"
BITMAP "........"
BITMAP "........"
BITMAP "........"

BITMAP "........"  ' 2 Meteor (2 of 8)
BITMAP "........"
BITMAP "........"
BITMAP "...XX..."
BITMAP "...XX..."
BITMAP "........"
BITMAP "........"
BITMAP "........"

BITMAP "........"  ' 3 Meteor (3 of 8)
BITMAP "........"
BITMAP "...X...."
BITMAP "..X.X..."
BITMAP "...XX..."
BITMAP "........"
BITMAP "........"
BITMAP "........"

BITMAP "........"  ' 4 Meteor (4 of 8)
BITMAP "........"
BITMAP "...XX..."
BITMAP "..X..X.."
BITMAP "...X.X.."
BITMAP "....XX.."
BITMAP "........"
BITMAP "........"

BITMAP "........"  ' 5 Meteor (5 of 8)
BITMAP "..XXX..."
BITMAP ".X...X.."
BITMAP "..X..X.."
BITMAP "...X.X.."
BITMAP "....XX.."
```

```
      BITMAP "........"
      BITMAP "........"

      BITMAP "........"  ' 6 Meteor (6 of 8)
      BITMAP "..XXXX.."
      BITMAP ".X....X."
      BITMAP ".X.. X.."
      BITMAP "..X...X."
      BITMAP "...X..X."
      BITMAP "....XX.."
      BITMAP "........"

      BITMAP "..XXXX.."  ' 7 Meteor (7 of 8)
      BITMAP ".X....X."
      BITMAP "X....X.."
      BITMAP ".X...X.."
      BITMAP "..X...X."
      BITMAP "...X..X."
      BITMAP "....XXX."
      BITMAP "........"

      BITMAP "..XXXX.."  ' 8 Meteor (8 of 8)
      BITMAP "XX....XX"
      BITMAP "X......X"
      BITMAP ".X....X."
      BITMAP "..X...X."
      BITMAP "..XX...X"
      BITMAP "....X..X"
      BITMAP ".....XXX"

      BITMAP "........"  ' 9 Alien ship (1 of 3)
      BITMAP "...XX..."
      BITMAP ".XXXXXX."
      BITMAP "X.XX..XX"
      BITMAP "XXXXXXXX"
      BITMAP ".XXXXXX."
      BITMAP "XX.XX.XX"
      BITMAP "........"

      BITMAP "........"  ' 10 Alien ship (2 of 3)
      BITMAP "...XX..."
      BITMAP ".XXXXXX."
      BITMAP "XX..XX.X"
      BITMAP "XXXXXXXX"
      BITMAP ".XXXXXX."
      BITMAP "XX.XX.XX"
      BITMAP "........"
```

```
BITMAP "........"   ' 11 Alien ship (3 of 3)
BITMAP "...XX..."
BITMAP ".XXXXXX."
BITMAP "X..XX..X"
BITMAP "XXXXXXXX"
BITMAP ".XXXXXX."
BITMAP "XX.XX.XX"
BITMAP "........"

BITMAP "........"   ' 12 Alien shot (1 of 8)
BITMAP "........"
BITMAP "........"
BITMAP "...X...."
BITMAP "........"
BITMAP "........"
BITMAP "........"

BITMAP "........"   ' 13
BITMAP "........"
BITMAP "........"
BITMAP "...XX..."
BITMAP "...X...."
BITMAP "........"
BITMAP "........"
BITMAP "........"

BITMAP "........"   ' 14
BITMAP "........"
BITMAP "..X.X..."
BITMAP "...X...."
BITMAP "..X.X..."
BITMAP "........"
BITMAP "........"
BITMAP "........"

BITMAP "........"   ' 15
BITMAP "........"
BITMAP "..X..X.."
BITMAP "...XX..."
BITMAP "...XX..."
BITMAP "..X..X.."
BITMAP "........"
BITMAP "........"
```

This part of the bitmaps (*storm_bitmaps_2* and *storm_bitmaps_3*) is replicated in order to give graphics variety from time on time.

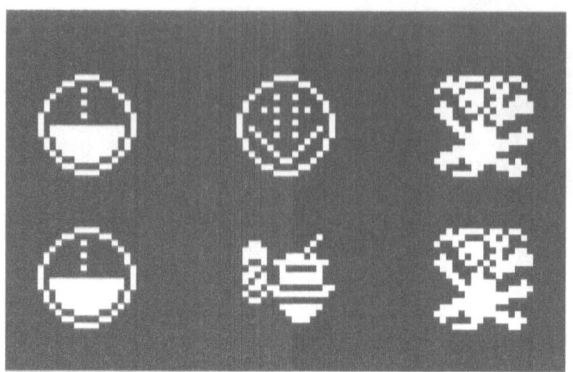

The two "round-indicator" images are bitmaps 20-23, The "kind-of-radar indicator" and coffee vase (bottom) are bitmaps 24-27. The "bug splat" images are bitmaps 28-31.

The bitmaps 20 to 23 are used to draw a round indicator with artificial horizon inside the cockpit.

Likewise the bitmaps 24 to 27 are for a kind-of-radar indicator, while in the alternate set of graphics these are a coffee vase. Notice the coffee vase is the only graphic changing between *storm_bitmaps_2* and *storm_bitmaps_3*.

Finally the bitmaps 28 to 31 show a bug crashing onto your windshield that is shown randomly.

```
storm_bitmaps_2:
    BITMAP "........"  ' 16        BITMAP "X.XXX.X."  ' 18
    BITMAP ".X.X.X.."                BITMAP ".XXXXX.."
    BITMAP "..XXX..."                BITMAP "XXXXXXX."
    BITMAP ".XX.XX.."                BITMAP "XXX.XXX."
    BITMAP "..XXX..."                BITMAP "XXXXXXX."
    BITMAP ".X.X.X.."                BITMAP ".XXXXX.."
    BITMAP "........"                BITMAP "X.XXX.X."
    BITMAP "........"                BITMAP "........"

    BITMAP "........"  ' 17        BITMAP "X.XXXX.X"  ' 19
    BITMAP ".X.XX.X."                BITMAP ".XXXXXX."
    BITMAP "..XXXX.."                BITMAP "XXXXXXXX"
    BITMAP ".XX.XXX."                BITMAP "XXX.XXXX"
    BITMAP ".XXXXXX."                BITMAP "XXXXXXXX"
    BITMAP "..XXXX.."                BITMAP "XXXXXXXX"
    BITMAP ".X.XX.X."                BITMAP ".XXXXXX."
    BITMAP "........"                BITMAP "X.XXXX.X"
```

```
                                      BITMAP "....X..."
BITMAP "......XX" ' 20               BITMAP ".X...X.."
BITMAP "....XX.."                    BITMAP "......X."
BITMAP "...X...X"                    BITMAP ".X.X..X."
BITMAP "..X....."                    BITMAP "........X"
BITMAP ".X.....X"                    BITMAP ".X.....X"
BITMAP ".X......"
BITMAP "X......X"                    BITMAP "X.X....." ' 26
BITMAP "X......."                    BITMAP "X..X..X."
                                      BITMAP ".X..X..."
BITMAP "XX......" ' 21               BITMAP ".X..X..."
BITMAP "..XX...."                    BITMAP "..X..X.."
BITMAP "....X..."                    BITMAP "...X...X"
BITMAP ".....X.."                    BITMAP "....XX.."
BITMAP "......X."                    BITMAP "......XX"
BITMAP "......X."
BITMAP ".......X"                    BITMAP ".....X.X" ' 27
BITMAP ".......X"                    BITMAP ".X..X..X"
                                      BITMAP "...X..X."
BITMAP "X.XXXXXX" ' 22               BITMAP "..X...X."
BITMAP "X.XXXXXX"                    BITMAP ".X...X.."
BITMAP ".X.XXXXX"                    BITMAP "X...X..."
BITMAP ".X.XXXXX"                    BITMAP "..XX...."
BITMAP "..X.XXXX"                    BITMAP "XX......"
BITMAP "...X..XX"
BITMAP "....XX.."                    BITMAP "..X.XXXX"
BITMAP "......XX"                    BITMAP ".XXXX..."
                                      BITMAP "X..X.XXX"
BITMAP "XXXXX.X" ' 23               BITMAP "....XXXX"
BITMAP "XXXXX.X"                    BITMAP ".X..X.XX"
BITMAP "XXXXX.X."                   BITMAP "XXX..XX."
BITMAP "XXXXX.X."                   BITMAP ".XX....X"
BITMAP "XXXX.X.."                   BITMAP "..XX..XX"
BITMAP "XX..X..."                   BITMAP "...XX.XX"
BITMAP "..XX...."                   BITMAP "....XXXX"
BITMAP "XX......"                   BITMAP ".....XXX"
                                      BITMAP "...XXXXX"
BITMAP "......XX" ' 24               BITMAP ".XXXXXXX"
BITMAP "....XX.."                   BITMAP "XXXX.XXX"
BITMAP "...X...."                   BITMAP ".X....XX"
BITMAP "..X...X."                   BITMAP "...XXXX."
BITMAP ".X......"
BITMAP ".X..X.X."                   BITMAP ".XX.XX.."
BITMAP "X......."                   BITMAP "XX.X..X."
BITMAP "X.....X."                   BITMAP ".XXX...."
                                      BITMAP "..X..XX."
BITMAP "XX......" ' 25               BITMAP ".XX.XXXX"
BITMAP "..XX...."                   BITMAP "X.XXXXXX"
```

```
        BITMAP ".XXXX..."              BITMAP "......XX"   ' 20
        BITMAP "..X....."              BITMAP "....XX.."
        BITMAP "XX....X."              BITMAP "...X...X"
        BITMAP "XX..XXXX"              BITMAP "..X....."
        BITMAP "XXXXXXX."              BITMAP ".X.....X"
        BITMAP "XXXX...."              BITMAP ".X......"
        BITMAP "XX......"              BITMAP "X......X"
        BITMAP "XXXX.X.."              BITMAP "X......."
        BITMAP "..XXXXX."
        BITMAP "....XX.."              BITMAP "XX......"   ' 21
                                       BITMAP "..XX...."
storm_bitmaps_3:                       BITMAP "....X..."
        BITMAP "........"   ' 16       BITMAP ".....X.."
        BITMAP ".X.X.X.."              BITMAP "......X."
        BITMAP "..XXX..."              BITMAP "......X."
        BITMAP ".XX.XX.."              BITMAP ".......X"
        BITMAP "..XXX..."              BITMAP ".......X"
        BITMAP ".X.X.X.."
        BITMAP "........"              BITMAP "X.XXXXXX"   ' 22
        BITMAP "........"              BITMAP "X.XXXXXX"
                                       BITMAP ".X.XXXXX"
        BITMAP "........"   ' 17       BITMAP ".X.XXXXX"
        BITMAP ".X.XX.X."              BITMAP "..X.XXXX"
        BITMAP "..XXXX.."              BITMAP "...X..XX"
        BITMAP ".XX.XXX."              BITMAP "....XX.."
        BITMAP ".XXXXXX."              BITMAP "......XX"
        BITMAP "..XXXX.."
        BITMAP ".X.XX.X."              BITMAP "XXXXXX.X"   ' 23
        BITMAP "........"              BITMAP "XXXXXX.X"
                                       BITMAP "XXXXX.X."
        BITMAP "X.XXX.X."   ' 18       BITMAP "XXXXX.X."
        BITMAP ".XXXXX.."              BITMAP "XXXX.X.."
        BITMAP "XXXXXXX."              BITMAP "XX..X..."
        BITMAP "XXX.XXX."              BITMAP "..XX...."
        BITMAP "XXXXXXX."              BITMAP "XX......"
        BITMAP ".XXXXX.."
        BITMAP "X.XXX.X."              BITMAP "........"   ' 24
        BITMAP "........"              BITMAP "........"
                                       BITMAP "..XX...."
        BITMAP "X.XXXX.X"   ' 19       BITMAP ".XXXX..."
        BITMAP ".XXXXXX."              BITMAP ".XXXX..."
        BITMAP "XXXXXXXX"              BITMAP ".X..X.XX"
        BITMAP "XXX.XXXX"              BITMAP "..XX...X"
        BITMAP "XXXXXXXX"              BITMAP ".XX.X..X"
        BITMAP "XXXXXXXX"
        BITMAP ".XXXXXX."              BITMAP "........"   ' 25
        BITMAP "X.XXXX.X"              BITMAP ".....X.."
                                       BITMAP "....X..."
```

```
BITMAP "...X...."              BITMAP ".....XXX"
BITMAP "XXX.X..."              BITMAP "...XXXXX"
BITMAP "XXXXXXX."              BITMAP ".XXXXXXX"
BITMAP ".....X.."              BITMAP "XXXX.XXX"
BITMAP "XXXXXX.."              BITMAP ".X....XX"
                              BITMAP "...XXXX."
BITMAP ".X.XX..X"  ' 26
BITMAP "..XX.XX."              BITMAP ".XX.XX.."
BITMAP ".X..X.XX"              BITMAP "XX.X..X."
BITMAP "..XX...."              BITMAP ".XXX...."
BITMAP ".......X"              BITMAP "..X..XX."
BITMAP "........"              BITMAP ".XX.XXXX"
BITMAP "........"              BITMAP "X.XXXXXX"
BITMAP "........"              BITMAP ".XXXX..."
                              BITMAP "..X....."
BITMAP "XXXXXX.."  ' 27       BITMAP "XX....X."
BITMAP "......XX"              BITMAP "XX..XXXX"
BITMAP "XXXXXXX."              BITMAP "XXXXXXX."
BITMAP "........"              BITMAP "XXXX...."
BITMAP "XXXXXX.."              BITMAP "XX......"
BITMAP "XXXXX..."              BITMAP "XXXX.X.."
BITMAP ".XXX...."              BITMAP "..XXXXX."
BITMAP "........"              BITMAP "....XX.."

BITMAP "..X.XXXX"          stars_bitmaps:
BITMAP ".XXXX..."              BITMAP "........"
BITMAP "X..X.XXX"              BITMAP "........"
BITMAP "....XXXX"              BITMAP "........"
BITMAP ".X..X.XX"              BITMAP "...X...."
BITMAP "XXX..XX."              BITMAP "........"
BITMAP ".XX....X"              BITMAP "........"
BITMAP "..XX..XX"              BITMAP "........"
BITMAP "...XX.XX"              BITMAP "........"
BITMAP "....XXXX"
```

5.3 Title screen

The title screen again is created using IntyColor. This is because it is easier to draw nice letters in a paint program (I like Paint.NET for these chores), and then pass the BMP graphic to IntyColor which takes care of assigning the tiles and converting the bitmaps to a format understandable by IntyBASIC.

The title screen for Meteor Storm. Not a full screen image; instead only the letters were drawn onto a smaller image.

```
         '
         ' Title screen
         '
storm_title:
    bullet_x = 0
    aliens = 0
    autofire = 0
    bug = 0
    sound_effect = 0

    CLS
    MODE 0,0,0,0,0
    BORDER 0
    FOR c = 0 TO 7
        SPRITE c,0
    NEXT c
    WAIT
    DEFINE 0,16,stormtitle_bitmaps_0
    WAIT
    DEFINE 16,16,stormtitle_bitmaps_1
    WAIT
    DEFINE 32,16,stormtitle_bitmaps_2
    WAIT
    DEFINE 48,7,stormtitle_bitmaps_3
    WAIT

    '
    ' Build it row by row
    '
    FOR c = 2 TO 6
        sound_effect = 7: sound_state = 0
        FOR d = 11 TO c STEP -1
            SCREEN stormtitle_cards,(c-2)*11,d*20+4,11,1
            IF d <> 11 THEN
```

```
                    e = d * 20 + 24
                    #backtab(e) = 0
                    #backtab(e + 1) = 0
                    #backtab(e + 2) = 0
                    #backtab(e + 3) = 0
                    #backtab(e + 4) = 0
                    #backtab(e + 5) = 0
                    #backtab(e + 6) = 0
                    #backtab(e + 7) = 0
                    #backtab(e + 8) = 0
                    #backtab(e + 9) = 0
                    #backtab(e + 10) = 0
                END IF
                WAIT
            NEXT d
        NEXT c

        '
        ' Crazy screen flash :P
        '
        sound_effect = 5: sound_state = 0
        FOR c = 0 TO 64
            d = c AND $0F
            MODE 0,d,d,d,d
            WAIT
        NEXT c

        PRINT AT 162 COLOR 3,"Record: ",<5>#record,"00"

        PRINT AT 200 COLOR 5,"Press Enter to start"

        debounce = 20
        DO
            WAIT
            IF debounce <> 0 THEN debounce = debounce - 1
            IF cont.key = 11 THEN
                EXIT DO
            END IF
        LOOP WHILE 1

        DO
            WAIT
            c = CONT
        LOOP WHILE c = 0

stuck:  GOTO stuck
    INCLUDE "titlem.bas"
```

155

Some variables are reset to zero like *bullet_x* (the player's lasers), *aliens* (indicator of aliens present), *autofire* (indicator of continuous firing), *bug* (a bug dropping from your windshield), and *sound_effect* (turning off any sound effect playing).

The code starts by defining the GRAM cards composing the title letters. Then it builds the title screen by moving one row at a time from the bottom of the screen up to the final position; this is accomplished by using the *SCREEN* sentence along offsets. The first offset is fixed *(c-2)*11* (the image size is 88 pixels wide); it points to the title's next row to move. The second offset is *(d*20)+4* and points to the row on screen (*d* gets decremented so it moves up on screen). The width is always eleven cards, and the height is always one card (one row). When it starts moving to offset 200 on screen, it needs to clean the next row downwards (as you can see the eleven *#backtab* lines to put a blank on screen).

Finally it starts a sound effect, and does an "attention-call" flashing by cycling the Color Stack background color through all the Intellivision colors (the variable *c* counts from 0 to 64, and *d* gets the modulo 16, so the colors go from 0 to 15 repeating another 3 times).

It shows the current record, and a message indicating to press Enter to start *(cont.key = 11)*.

Don't forget the graphics for the title screen in the source code file "titlem.bas":

```
REM IntyColor v1.1.5 Jul/25/2017
REM intycolor -b -n -e76 meteor_storm.bmp titlem.bas stormtitle
REM Created: Tue Mar 20 10:19:28 2018

' 55 bitmaps
stormtitle_bitmaps_0:
    DATA $1F1F,$3F1F,$3F3F,$7D7F
    DATA $C783,$FFCF,$FFFF,$FBFF
    DATA $EFE7,$EFEF,$CFCF,$CFCF
    DATA $FEFE,$80FE,$FC80,$8080
    DATA $FFFF,$1FFF,$DFDF,$1FDF
    DATA $E7E7,$07E7,$6767,$0767
    DATA $FEFE,$81FE,$FD81,$8080
    DATA $7F1F,$F8FF,$F0F0,$7FF8
    DATA $FBC3,$7CFD,$3C3C,$FC3C
```

```
     DATA $FFFF,$E1FF,$FFF1,$73FF
     DATA $E0C0,$F0F0,$F8F0,$C0F8
     DATA $787C,$7E02,$7A7E,$037B
     DATA $EBF3,$DFC8,$33BF,$C0E3
     DATA $8FCF,$CF00,$CFCF,$008F
     DATA $FCFC,$FC00,$CFCF,$00FC
     DATA $1F1F,$1F00,$1F1F,$001F
stormtitle_bitmaps_1:
     DATA $0707,$0700,$0707,$0007
     DATA $FEFE,$FE00,$FEFE,$00FE
     DATA $CF3F,$FFF0,$3F7F,$000F
     DATA $E0F8,$FC0C,$F8FC,$00F0
     DATA $7A78,$7F03,$797F,$0078
     DATA $78E0,$CC9C,$FCF0,$1C7C
     DATA $0F00,$1F1F,$3F3F,$3F3F
     DATA $FF00,$FFFF,$0000,$FE00
     DATA $7F00,$7F7F,$077F,$7777
     DATA $FE00,$FCFE,$C1FD,$DDDD
     DATA $0F00,$FF7F,$F8FF,$F0F0
     DATA $F800,$FEFC,$3FFF,$1F1F
     DATA $7F00,$7F7F,$3C7C,$3F3C
     DATA $FC00,$FEFE,$3E7E,$FE3E
     DATA $FC00,$FFFE,$7F7F,$7F7F
     DATA $1F00,$3F1F,$FFBF,$FFFF
stormtitle_bitmaps_2:
     DATA $E00C,$E0E0,$F0E0,$F0F0
     DATA $4000,$FF60,$FFFF,$FF00
     DATA $3E3E,$FC7C,$FAFC,$FE06
     DATA $0777,$0707,$0707,$0700
     DATA $C1DD,$C1C0,$C1C1,$C000
     DATA $F8F0,$7FFF,$8FBF,$FFF0
     DATA $3E1F,$FCFE,$C6FA,$FE1E
     DATA $3F3F,$3C3C,$3D3D,$3C01
     DATA $FCFE,$78F8,$CCBC,$FBE7
     DATA $7D7F,$3D3C,$3D3D,$BC01
     DATA $FDFF,$30F9,$CE96,$FCFE
     DATA $F8F0,$F8F8,$F8F8,$F800
     DATA $FFFF,$00FF,$0000,$0000
     DATA $FCFE,$00F8,$0000,$0000
     DATA $0707,$0007,$0000,$0000
     DATA $C0C0,$00C0,$0000,$0000
stormtitle_bitmaps_3:
     DATA $3F7F,$000F,$0000,$0000
     DATA $F8FC,$00E0,$0000,$0000
     DATA $3C3C,$003C,$0000,$0000
     DATA $3E7C,$070F,$0003,$0000
     DATA $3CBC,$80BC,$0080,$0000
     DATA $1078,$0000,$0000,$0000
```

```
    DATA $F8F8,$00F8,$0000,$0000

    REM 11x5 cards
stormtitle_cards:
    DATA $0806,$080E,$0816,$081E,$0826,$082E
    DATA $0836,$083E,$0846,$084E,$0856
    DATA $085E,$0866,$086E,$0876,$087E,$0886
    DATA $088E,$0896,$089E,$08A6,$08AE
    DATA $08B6,$08BE,$08C6,$08CE,$08D6,$08DE
    DATA $08E6,$08EE,$08F6,$08FE,$0906
    DATA $090E,$0916,$091E,$0926,$092E,$0936
    DATA $093E,$0946,$094E,$0956,$095E
    DATA $0966,$096E,$0976,$097E,$0986,$098E
    DATA $0996,$099E,$09A6,$09AE,$09B6
```

The option -e76 means to replace the color white (number 7) used in the bitmap for the color yellow we use at the title screen (number 6 in the Intellivision color palette).

5.4 Game start

The first step on starting the game is to reset the arrays containing the meteors, aliens, and bullets. Then it calls a subroutine to set up the bitmaps required by the game, and another to display the cockpit. This code replaces the line reading *stuck: GOTO stuck*.

```
    '
    ' Reset meteors
    '
    FOR c = 0 TO 5
        fx(c) = 0
        fy(c) = 0
        dx(c) = 0
        dy(c) = 0
        t(c) = 0
    NEXT c


    '
    ' Display cockpit and cannons
    '
    CLS
```

```
    GOSUB setup_bitmaps

    #score = 0
    level = 1

    GOSUB display_cockpit

    '
    ' Indicators
    '
    PRINT AT 205 COLOR 6,<2>level
    PRINT AT 208 COLOR 6,<5>#score,"00"
    FOR c = 224 TO 235
        #backtab(c) = 212 * 8 + 7
    NEXT c

    GOSUB setup_level

    window_x = 0
    window_y = 0
    power = 12

stuck:    goto stuck
```

You might wonder why it is calling *display_cockpit* when the code could be included just inside the main code. It is because this is a complicated subroutine, and it is called two times: one time here to display the cockpit, and another time after completing a level in order to clean the scratches on the pane.

It displays the current level number, and the current score (notice how the score displays two extra zeroes, so an internal increment of one appears to be one hundred). A bar is also drawn at the bottom of the screen.

Then it calls *setup_level* to start the game level, and sets the *window_x* and *window_y* displacement variables.

The last step is to set the current power of the spaceship at the maximum: 12.

```
setup_bitmaps:    PROCEDURE
    WAIT
    DEFINE 0,16,storm_bitmaps_1
```

```
        WAIT
        DEFINE 16,16,storm_bitmaps_2
        WAIT
        DEFINE 63,1,stars_bitmaps
        WAIT
        END

setup_level: PROCEDURE
        IF bug = 0 THEN bug = RANDOM(6) + 1
        bug = bug - 1
        IF level > 99 THEN level = 99
        IF level > 8 THEN c = 1 ELSE c = 64 - level / 4
        IF level > 8 THEN meteors = 24 ELSE meteors = 8 + level * 2
        next_meteor = RANDOM(32) + c
        start_level = 120
        animation = (level - 1) / 3 % 4
        DEFINE ALTERNATE 9,3,VARPTR aliens_bitmaps(animation * 12)
        shield = 0
        END
```

The bitmaps setup in the *setup_bitmaps* procedure is pretty basic, and only defines two of the main sets, and the bitmap of the stars.

The procedure *setup_level* creates a bug every 1 to 6 levels. It limits the game level number to 99, and meteors appear faster at each level, although the time gets capped at level 9 (variable *next_meteor*).

Also the number of meteors increases per level, again at a limit at level 9. The aliens change every 3 levels, and start attacking after 120 video frames (indicated by the *start_level* variable).

The *shield* variable keeps track of whether the sprite for the bug embedded into the windshield should be clipped to not get over the cockpit panel.

Although the Intellivision has very few GRAM cards available, in Color Stack mode we have access to the full range of GROM cards, and we use it to draw our cockpit on the screen.

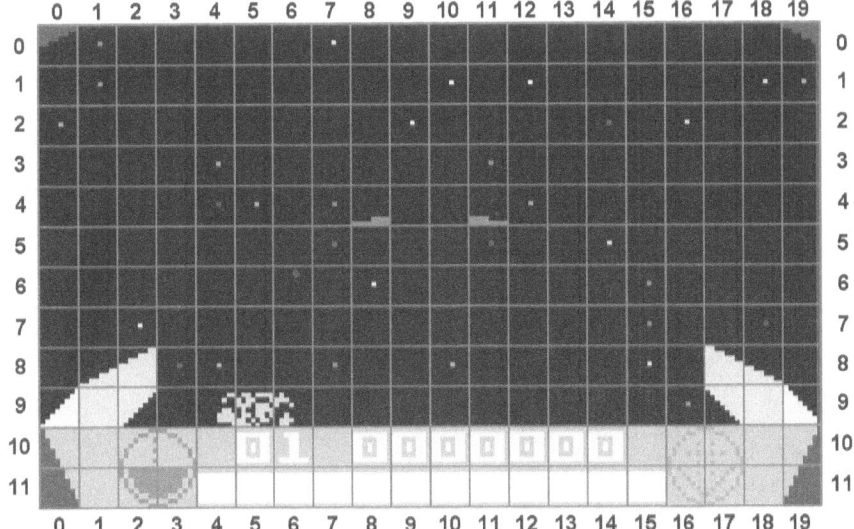

Spaceship cockpit screen. All geometric figures (diagonal filled cards) are taken from the predefined GROM graphics, referenced in appendix C, and this allows to have so many different sprites on screen at the same time. Notice the use of color to give an illusion of shadow in the laser cannons.

```
display_cockpit:   PROCEDURE
    IF (level - 1) AND 8 THEN snowanim = 7 ELSE snowanim = 1
    MODE 0,0,COCKPIT_COLOR2,0,0
    BORDER snowanim
    #backtab(0) = 111 * 8 + snowanim
    FOR c = 1 to 18
        #backtab(c) = 0
    NEXT c
    #backtab(19) = 110 * 8 + snowanim
    FOR c = 20 TO 87
        #backtab(c) = 0
    NEXT c
    #backtab(88) = 148 * 8 + 2
    #backtab(89) = 0
    #backtab(90) = 0
    #backtab(91) = 149 * 8 + 2
    FOR c = 92 TO 160
        #backtab(c) = 0
    NEXT c
    #backtab(161) = 108 * 8 + 3
    #backtab(162) = 112 * 8 + 3
    FOR c = 163 to 176
        #backtab(c) = 0
```

```
NEXT c
#backtab(177) = 113 * 8 + 3
#backtab(178) = 109 * 8 + 3
#backtab(179) = 0
#backtab(180) = 116 * 8 + 6
#backtab(181) = 95 * 8 + 3
#backtab(182) = 119 * 8 + 3
FOR c = 183 TO 196
    #backtab(c) = 0
NEXT c
#backtab(197) = 118 * 8 + 3
#backtab(198) = 95 * 8 + 3
#backtab(199) = 117 * 8 + 6

#backtab(200) = $2000 + 133 * 8 + snowanim
#backtab(219) = 132 * 8 + snowanim
#backtab(220) = 129 * 8 + snowanim
#backtab(239) = 128 * 8 + snowanim

#backtab(202) = 20 * 8 + $0802
#backtab(203) = 21 * 8 + $0802
#backtab(222) = 22 * 8 + $0802
#backtab(223) = 23 * 8 + $0802

IF (level - 1) AND 8 THEN
    #backtab(216) = 24 * 8 + $0807
    #backtab(217) = 25 * 8 + $0807
    #backtab(236) = 26 * 8 + $0807
    #backtab(237) = 27 * 8 + $0807
ELSE
    #backtab(216) = 24 * 8 + $0805
    #backtab(217) = 25 * 8 + $0805
    #backtab(236) = 26 * 8 + $0805
    #backtab(237) = 27 * 8 + $0805
END IF

'
' Create a stars backdrop
'
FOR c = 0 TO 30
    DO
        d = RANDOM(200)
    LOOP WHILE #backtab(d)
    #backtab(d) = $0801 + 63 * 8 + RANDOM(6)
NEXT c
WAIT
IF (level - 1) AND 8 THEN
    DEFINE 16,16,storm_bitmaps_3
```

```
ELSE
      DEFINE 16,16,storm_bitmaps_2
END IF
WAIT
END
```

5.5 Main game

The main game loop starts here, and we will implement this in parts. This code replaces the "stuck: goto stuck" line.

The first step is to scroll the stars per the displacement of the spaceship, but ten times slower than the displacement speed, so this gives an illusion of depth to the player.

For all the scrolling the player can do of enemies on the screen, the stars only move a maximum of 7 pixels in any direction, so the only pixel turned on in the bitmap doesn't exceed the GRAM card.

```
      '
      ' Main loop of game
      '
main_storm_loop:
      '
      ' Scroll stars
      '
      #star(0) = 0
      #star(1) = 0
      #star(2) = 0
      #star(3) = 0
      x = (window_x + 40)
      x = x / 10
      y = (window_y + 18)
      y = y / 5
      IF y AND 1 THEN
            #star(y / 2) = dots(x) * 256
      ELSE
            #star(y / 2) = dots(x)
      END IF
      DEFINE 63,1,VARPTR #star(0)

      WAIT
```

The *window_x* and *window_y* variables can get negative values. The center is 0,0. It gets the current position by adding *40* and *18* respectively and keeping it in the variables *x* and *y*. This is a good trick to adjust variables with 8-bit signed values in IntyBASIC, do the arithmetic and save the result into an 8-bit variable[10]

Remember we didn't enable the *SIGNED* sentence for the variables *window_x* and *window_y*[11].

Then the positive values are divided (per the real size of the window) and used to get the pixel to turn on for the star bitmap (card 63) and redefine it on the GRAM. As the bitmaps are saved as four words of 16-bit, there is the need for using *IF y AND 1* in order to choose the high-byte of the word, or the lower-byte of the word for the pixel. Notice how the *#star* array was reset to zero (empty) before drawing the pixel.

The player control is basically used to start a bullet when a side button is pressed (or continuously if auto fire has been enabled per key 4).

And if the disc is pressed in a direction, move the window in the X and Y directions by increments or decrements of two.

You can also see pressing key 0 makes it return to the title screen.

```
'
' Player control
'
c = CONT
IF c = $48 THEN
    IF #score > #record THEN #record = #score
    GOTO storm_title    ' Key 0
END IF
IF c = $82 THEN autofire = 4 ' Key 4
```

---

[10] This is because the processor always operates with 16-bit arithmetic, so reading a -1 value from 8-bit variables gives us 255 (hexadecimal $ff). Adding 2 would give us 257 if we continue working with 16-bit values, but if we save it as an 8-bit variable and read it again, it becomes 1, because it chops the higher part of the value.

[11] Although the SIGNED keyword existed at the time of writing Meteor Storm, I decided to not use it, maybe thinking of this book.

```
IF c = $22 THEN autofire = 0 ' key 6
c = c AND $E0
IF (c = $80) + (c = $40) + (c = $20) THEN
ELSE
    IF autofire + (c = $a0) + (c = $c0) + (c = $60) THEN
        IF bullet_x = 0 THEN
            bullet_x = 4
            bullet_y = 70
        END IF
    END IF
    IF cont.up THEN
        IF window_y <> 18 THEN window_y = window_y + 2
    END IF
    IF cont.down THEN
        IF window_y <> 256 - 18 THEN window_y = window_y - 2
    END IF
    IF cont.left THEN
        IF window_x <> 40 THEN window_x = window_x + 2
    END IF
    IF cont.right THEN
        IF window_x <> 256 - 40 THEN window_x = window_x - 2
    END IF
END IF
GOTO main_storm_loop
```

Let us not forget the dots data required to be able to paint each of the eight pixels available in a byte.

```
dots:
    DATA $80,$40,$20,$10,$08,$04,$02,$01,$01
```

5.6 Laser attack

Let us add the laser sprites for the player. This code goes just before the *WAIT* sentence:

```
IF bullet_x THEN    ' Bullet active
    SPRITE 6,$0308 + bullet_x,$0108 + bullet_y,$2000+180*8 + 5
    SPRITE 7,$03a0 - bullet_x,$0108 + bullet_y,$2000+181*8 + 5
ELSE
    SPRITE 6,0
    SPRITE 7,0
```

165

```
END IF
IF touched >= 5 THEN     ' Crash
     MODE 0,2,COCKPIT_COLOR2,0,0
ELSEIF touched AND 1 THEN
     MODE 0,2,COCKPIT_COLOR2,0,0
ELSE
     MODE 0,0,COCKPIT_COLOR2,0,0
END IF
```

It uses the sprites (MOB) 6 and 7 to show the twin lasers, one coming from the left ($0308 + bullet_x) and another coming from the right ($03a0 - bullet_x). There is no need to keep a separate variable for the right laser, as it is a twin. Also the laser shape is taken from the GROM.

This code goes just before the comment "player control":

```
'
' Move bullets
'
IF bullet_x THEN
     bullet_x = bullet_x + 4
     bullet_y = bullet_y - 2
     IF bullet_x = 76 THEN
          bullet_x = 0
          FOR c = 0 TO 5
               IF fx(c) THEN
                    d = dx(c) / 16
                    x = fx(c) + window_x + $0B
                    y = fy(c) + window_y + $0B
                    IF ABS(x - 88) < d THEN
                         IF ABS(y - 48) < d THEN
                              IF dy(c) < 128 THEN
                                   dy(c) = 255
                                   #score = #score + 1 + t(c)
                                   sound_effect = 4 + t(c)
                                   sound_state = 0
                                   GOSUB update_storm_score
                              END IF
                         END IF
                    END IF
               END IF
          NEXT c
     END IF
END IF
```

It displaces the left laser 4 pixels to the right and 2 pixels upward at each video frame. When the laser reaches the center of the screen (signaled by *bullet_x = 76*) it checks for collision against the array of enemies.

An enemy must be alive (*fx(c)* not equal to zero), and the distance is taken in account to calculate the size of the enemy (*d = dx(c) / 16*). The X and Y coordinates are adjusted per the window (for example, *fx(c) + window_x*) and a centering offset.

Remember the *ABS* function turns a negative number into a positive one, so if the enemy is to the left or the right we get a distance to the center for doing a comparison with the variable *d*.

If the enemy is hit, the explosion is started with *dy(c) = 255*, and the score is increased by the type of enemy. Also a unique sound effect is started, and the score display is updated.

This goes just after the sentence *GOTO main_storm_loop*:

```
update_storm_score:    PROCEDURE
    PRINT AT 208 COLOR 6,<5>#score
    END
```

It displays the actual score as 5 digits filled with zero at the left.

5.7 Aliens approaching

The first step is to add meteors at the start of the level. This code is added just before the "Move bullets" comment line, and we will break the code in parts for explanation:

```
    '
    ' Start level / add meteor
    '
    IF start_level THEN
        IF start_level = 120 THEN
            IF power < 12 THEN
                #backtab(224 + power) = 212 * 8 + 7
                power = power + 1
                sound_effect = 1:sound_state = 0
            END IF
            autofire = 0
```

```
          END IF
          start_level = start_level - 1
          IF ((level - 1) AND 7) = 0 THEN
              IF start_level = 115 THEN
                  sound_effect = 8: sound_state = 0
              END IF
              IF start_level = 30 THEN
                  sound_effect = 0
                  GOSUB display_cockpit
              ELSEIF start_level > 30 THEN
                d = -(FRAME / 2) AND 7
                FOR c = 0 TO 199
                #backtab(c)=light(c)+color_bright(color_frame(c)+d)
                NEXT c
              END IF
          END IF
          IF bug = 0 THEN
              IF start_level = 30 THEN
              DEFINE ALTERNATE 28,4,VARPTR storm_bitmaps_2(12 * 4)
                  sound_effect = 10: sound_state = 0
                  fx(1) = RANDOM(104) + 24
                  fy(1) = 8 + RANDOM(50)
                  t(1) = 3
              ELSEIF start_level = 1 THEN
                  IF fx(1) THEN
                      start_level = start_level + 1
                      fy(1) = fy(1) + 1
                      IF fy(1) > 79 THEN
                          fx(1) = 0
                          sound_effect = 0
                          shield = 0
                      ELSEIF fy(1) > 64 THEN
                          shield = 80 - fy(1)
                      END IF
                  END IF
              END IF
          END IF
      END IF
```

When the level is started, the variable *start_level* isn't zero (it starts at 120), so it is decremented by one in each video frame. If the *power* variable is less than twelve, the power bar is recharged one step, along with a sound effect.

If the level is a multiple of 8, then it starts an animation of going to light speed, including a sound effect when *start_level* is equal to 115. Then when *start_level* is counting down, it does the animation using the card table from the data table *light* and adds the color from the data table *color_bright*, using *color_frame* as base reference, adding the variable *d* for the animation.

If the random bug glued to the windshield is active (*bug* is equal to zero), and *start_level* goes to 30, it defines the bug graphics and uses the arrays to draw it at a random position of the windshield (*t(1)=3* defines it as a bug sprite). It stays there around 30 video frames, and then it goes down by means of *fy(1)=fy(1)+1* (and even stops the level from starting using *start_level=start_level+1*) until the bug disappears from the windshield.

```
ELSEIF (something + meteors) = 0 THEN
    level = level + 1
    IF ((level - 1) AND 7) = 0 THEN
        GOSUB rotating_planet
    END IF
    GOSUB setup_level
    PRINT AT 205 COLOR 6,<2>level
```

If there aren't things on the screen, and all meteors (and enemies) have appeared (*something + meteors = 0*), then it increases the level number, and if eight levels have been completed, it calls the *rotating_planet* animation.

```
ELSE
    IF next_meteor THEN
        IF meteors THEN
            next_meteor = next_meteor - 1
        END IF
    ELSE
        IF level > 20 THEN c = 16 ELSE c = 64 - level * 2
        next_meteor = RANDOM(32) + c - autofire
        FOR c = 0 TO 5
            IF fx(c) = 0 THEN
                fx(c) = RANDOM(80) + 40
                fy(c) = RANDOM(32) + 16
                IF (meteors AND 7) = 0 THEN
                    t(c) = 2
                    dx(c) = 112
                    pp(c) = RANDOM(16)
                    IF level>20 THEN e=12 ELSE e=96-level*4
                    dy(c) = RANDOM(32) + e - autofire
                ELSE
                    t(c) = 0
                    dx(c) = 0
                    dy(c) = RANDOM(2) + 1
```

```
                  END IF
                  meteors = meteors - 1
                  EXIT FOR
              END IF
          NEXT c
      END IF
  END IF
```

Finally after all the bells and whistles, it starts counting down the time for the next meteor to appear. Once the variable *next_meteor* reaches zero, it searches the array for a free space *(fx(c) = 0)*, and creates one enemy at a random position over the screen. For every eight meteors it creates an alien spaceship. For each increasing level, the alien spaceship fires even faster.

As a final note, all this code is invisible if there is no display of the meteors and aliens!

This code goes after the line reading *DEFINE 63,1,VARPTR #star(0)*:

```
    '
    ' Show meteors
    '
    something = 0
    FOR c = 0 TO 5
        IF fx(c) THEN ' Active
            ON t(c) GOTO display_meteor, display_shot,
display_alien, display_bug

display_bug:
        x = fx(c) + $08
        y = fy(c) + $08
        #mask = bug_color(level AND 7)
        IF level AND 1 THEN
            SPRITE c - 1, x + $0308, y + $0580, #mask + 28 * 8
            SPRITE c, x + $0300, y + $0580, #mask + 30 * 8
        ELSE
            SPRITE c - 1, x + $0300, y + $0180, #mask + 28 * 8
            SPRITE c, x + $0308, y + $0180, #mask + 30 * 8
        END IF
        GOTO display_continue

display_alien:
        x = fx(c) + window_x + $08
```

```
            y = fy(c) + window_y + $08
            IF dy(c) >= 128 THEN
                SPRITE c,x + (storm_xexp(d) AND $FF00)
                SPRITE c,,y + (storm_yexp(d) + #mask AND $FF00)
                SPRITE c,,,storm_sexp2(d)
            ELSE
                d = (FRAME AND 252) / 4 % 3
                SPRITE c,x + $0300
                SPRITE c,,y + $0100
                SPRITE c,,,alien_animation(d + animation * 3)
            END IF
            something = 1
            GOTO display_continue

display_shot:
            d = dx(c) / 16
            IF ((FRAME / 8) XOR C) AND 1 THEN
                #mask = $0c00
            ELSE
                #mask = 0
            END IF
            x = fx(c) + window_x + storm_xexp(d)
            y = fy(c) + window_y + storm_yexp(d)
            IF dy(c) >= 128 THEN
                SPRITE c,x + (storm_xexp(d) AND $FF00)
                SPRITE c,,y + (storm_yexp(d) + #mask AND $FF00)
                SPRITE c,,, storm_sexp2(d)
            ELSE
                SPRITE c,x + (storm_xexp(d) AND $FF00)
                SPRITE c,,y + (storm_yexp(d) + #mask AND $FF00)
                SPRITE c,,,storm_sexp3(d + animation * 16)
            END IF
            something = 1
            GOTO display_continue
display_meteor:
            d = dx(c) / 16
            IF ((FRAME / 8) XOR C) AND 1 THEN
                #mask = $0c00
            ELSE
                #mask = 0
            END IF
            x = fx(c) + window_x + storm_xexp(d)
            y = fy(c) + window_y + storm_yexp(d)
            IF dy(c) >= 128 THEN
                SPRITE c,x + (storm_xexp(d) AND $FF00)
                SPRITE c,,y + (storm_yexp(d) + #mask AND $FF00)
                SPRITE c,,,storm_sexp2(d)
            ELSE
```

```
                SPRITE c,x + (storm_xexp(d) AND $FF00)
                SPRITE c,,y + (storm_yexp(d) + #mask AND $FF00)
                SPRITE c,,,storm_sexp(d)
        END IF
        something = 1
        ELSE
                SPRITE c,0
        END IF
display_continue:
    NEXT c
```

If *fx(c)* is non-zero then there is an active enemy. The type of the enemy is determined by *t(c)* where 0 is a meteor, 1 is a shot, 2 is an alien, and 3 is the windshield bug (not affected by the pseudo-3D effect).

The x and y coordinates are taken from *fx(c)* and *fy(c)* and adjusted per the *window_x* and *windows_y* variables (except for the bug in the windshield), so the enemies displace if the player moves the spaceship. Furthermore the data tables *storm_xexp* and *storm_yexp* are used to integrate the zoom doing the effect of bullets getting near the player.

For meteors and shots, every 8 frames the sprite is mirrored both in X and Y directions to make it to look like it is rotating, this comparison is done by *IF ((FRAME / 8) XOR C) AND 1*. This gives the illusion of having even more animation frames.

The following data tables are required after the sentence *GOTO main_storm_loop*, plus a temporary stub for *rotating_planet*.

```
rotating_planet:   PROCEDURE
    END

storm_xexp:   ' Adjustments for X-size and offset
    DATA $0308,$0308,$0308,$0308,$0308,$0308,$0308,$0308
    DATA $0704,$0704,$0704,$0704,$0704,$0704,$0704,$0704

storm_yexp:   ' Adjustments for Y-size and offset
    DATA $0108,$0108,$0108,$0108,$0108,$0108,$0108,$0108
    DATA $0204,$0204,$0204,$0204,$0204,$0204,$0204,$0204

storm_sexp:   ' Sprites and color for meteor
    DATA $080E,$0816,$081E,$0826,$082E,$0836,$083E,$0846
    DATA $082E,$082E,$0836,$0836,$083E,$083E,$0846,$0846
```

```
storm_sexp2:  ' Sprites and color for explosion
    DATA $0802,$0802,$0802,$0802,$0802,$0802,$0802,$0802
    DATA $0802,$0802,$0802,$0802,$0802,$0802,$0802,$0802

storm_sexp3:  ' Sprites and color for alien shot
    DATA $1860,$1868,$1870,$1878,$1880,$1888,$1890,$1898
    DATA $1880,$1880,$1888,$1888,$1890,$1890,$1898,$1898

    DATA $1866,$186e,$1876,$187e,$1886,$188e,$1896,$189e
    DATA $1886,$1886,$188e,$188e,$1896,$1896,$189e,$189e

    DATA $1865,$186d,$1875,$187d,$1885,$188d,$1895,$189d
    DATA $1885,$1885,$188d,$188d,$1895,$1895,$189d,$189d

    DATA $1861,$1869,$1871,$1879,$1881,$1889,$1891,$1899
    DATA $1881,$1881,$1889,$1889,$1891,$1891,$1899,$1899

bug_color:
    DATA $0805,  $1806,  $1802,  $1807
    DATA $0803,  $1805,  $0804,  $0806

alien_animation:
    DATA $1848,  $1850,  $1858     ' Alien ship
    DATA $184e,  $1856,  $185e     ' Alien 4 sides
    DATA $184d,  $1855,  $185d     ' Alien monster
    DATA $1849,  $1851,  $1859     ' Alien wheel
```

The bug on the windshield needs to be clipped, so add this after the
WAIT sentence:

```
    '
    ' Hack: clip bug sprite
    '
    IF shield THEN POKE $3800+28*8+shield,0:POKE $3800+30*8+shield,0
```

Don't forget to add the following code at the very end of the source
code, because it contains the tables for the light speed effect.

```
    ASM ORG $F000

color_bright:
    DATA 0,1,4,5,2,6,3,7,0,1,4,5,2,6,3,7
```

```
color_frame:
    DATA 5,4,3,2,1,0,7,6,5,5,5,5,6,7,0,1,2,3,4,5
    DATA 4,3,2,1,0,7,6,5,4,4,4,4,5,6,7,0,1,2,3,4
    DATA 3,2,1,0,7,6,5,4,3,3,3,3,4,5,6,7,0,1,2,3
    DATA 2,1,0,7,6,5,4,3,2,2,2,2,3,4,5,6,7,0,1,2
    DATA 1,0,7,6,5,4,3,2,1,1,1,1,2,3,4,5,6,7,0,1
    DATA 1,0,7,6,5,4,3,2,1,1,1,1,2,3,4,5,6,7,0,1
    DATA 2,1,0,7,6,5,4,3,2,2,2,2,3,4,5,6,7,0,1,2
    DATA 3,2,1,0,7,6,5,4,3,3,3,3,4,5,6,7,0,1,2,3
    DATA 4,3,2,1,0,7,6,5,4,4,4,4,5,6,7,0,1,2,3,4
    DATA 5,4,3,2,1,0,7,6,5,5,5,5,6,7,0,1,2,3,4,5

light:
    DATA 111*8,183*8,181*8,000*8,000*8,000*8,060*8,000*8,189*8,000*8
    DATA 189*8,000*8,000*8,015*8,000*8,000*8,000*8,180*8,182*8,110*8
    DATA 177*8,175*8,000*8,183*8,181*8,000*8,000*8,060*8,000*8,188*8
    DATA 191*8,000*8,015*8,000*8,000*8,180*8,182*8,000*8,174*8,176*8
    DATA 167*8,000*8,179*8,177*8,175*8,183*8,181*8,000*8,060*8,190*8
    DATA 190*8,015*8,000*8,180*8,182*8,174*8,176*8,178*8,000*8,166*8
    DATA 000*8,173*8,171*8,169*8,167*8,179*8,177*8,183*8,181*8,191*8
    DATA 188*8,180*8,182*8,176*8,178*8,166*8,168*8,170*8,172*8,000*8
    DATA 207*8,207*8,207*8,207*8,207*8,173*8,171*8,169*8,167*8,000*8
    DATA 000*8,166*8,168*8,170*8,172*8,207*8,207*8,207*8,207*8,207*8
    DATA 000*8,000*8,000*8,000*8,000*8,166*8,168*8,170*8,172*8,000*8
    DATA 000*8,173*8,171*8,169*8,167*8,000*8,000*8,000*8,000*8,000*8
    DATA 000*8,166*8,168*8,170*8,172*8,174*8,176*8,180*8,182*8,189*8
    DATA 190*8,183*8,181*8,177*8,175*8,173*8,171*8,169*8,167*8,000*8
    DATA 172*8,000*8,174*8,176*8,178*8,180*8,182*8,000*8,015*8,191*8
    DATA 191*8,060*8,000*8,183*8,181*8,179*8,177*8,175*8,000*8,173*8
    DATA 176*8,108*8,112*8,180*8,182*8,000*8,000*8,015*8,000*8,190*8
    DATA 189*8,000*8,060*8,000*8,000*8,183*8,181*8,113*8,109*8,177*8
    DATA 116*8,095*8,119*8,000*8,000*8,000*8,015*8,000*8,000*8,188*8
    DATA 000*8,188*8,000*8,060*8,000*8,000*8,000*8,118*8,095*8,117*8
```

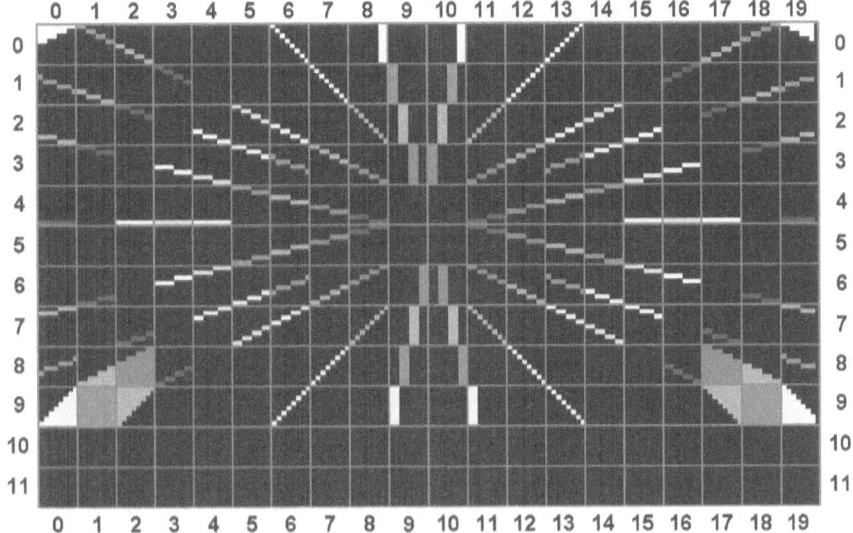

Lightspeed card grid. Again all these line shapes are taken from the predefined GROM character set (see appendix C), and each one is assigned a number which will get translated into a color for the movement effect.

The table *color_bright* is a circular table of 16 elements. This way adding a value from 0 to 7 makes it circulate the same colors (so the effect is continuous and not disrupted).

The table *color_frame* is the organization of the colors in a pseudo-circle. And finally the table *light* refers to GROM characters to draw the light lines on the screen. Each decimal number refers to the GROM character, and we multiply it by eight to get the right code for the screen.

Finally, we need the code to make meteors and enemy rockets approach the player, so add the following code before the "Start level" comment:

```
'
' Meteors approach spaceship
'
f = 0
FOR c = 0 TO 5
    IF fx(c) THEN
        IF dy(c) >= 128 THEN
            dy(c) = dy(c) - 1
```

```
                    IF dy(c) = 248 THEN fx(c) = 0
          ELSEIF t(c) = 2 THEN      ' Spaceship
               f = 1
               x = (pp(c) AND 3) - 1
               IF x = 2 THEN x = 0
               y = (pp(c) / 4) - 1
               IF y = 2 THEN y = 0
               x = x + fx(c)
               IF x < 40 THEN x = 40
               IF x > 118 THEN x = 118
               y = y + fy(c)
               IF y < 18 THEN y = 18
               IF y > 48 THEN y = 48
               fx(c) = x
               fy(c) = y
               IF dy(c) = 0 THEN
                    pp(c) = RANDOM(16)
                    IF level > 20 THEN
                         e = 12
                    ELSE
                         e = 96 - level * 4
                    END IF
                    dy(c) = RANDOM(32) + e - autofire
                    FOR d = 0 TO 5
                         IF fx(d) = 0 THEN
                              fx(d) = fx(c)
                              fy(d) = fy(c)
                              dx(d) = 0
                              dy(d) = 2
                              t(d) = 1
                              EXIT FOR
                         END IF
                    NEXT d
               ELSE
                    dy(c) = dy(c) - 1
               END IF
          ELSE
               dx(c) = dx(c) + dy(c)
               IF dx(c) < dy(c) THEN
                    touched = 10
                    fx(c) = 0
               END IF
          END IF
     END IF
  END IF
NEXT c
aliens = f
```

For each enemy, it checks first if it is active ($fx(c)$ is non-zero), and then handles the explosion (if $dy(c) \geq 128$), spaceship (when $t(c)=2$), or meteor/rocket (all other cases).

The meteors and rockets increase their proximity to the player simply by adding $dy(c)$ to $dx(c)$. When $dx(c)$ exceeds 8 bits it becomes less than $dy(c)$ and the player's ship is "touched" (we'll handle this in the following section), and the meteor or rocket disappears.

For aliens, the $pp(c)$ value contains the direction of movement so it doesn't remain static. The lower two bits contain the X direction, and the next two bits contain the Y direction. The table is relatively simple:

- 0 = -1 pixel
- 1 = 0 pixel displacement.
- 2 = 1 pixel.
- 3 = 0 pixel displacement.

These displacements are added to $fx(c)$ and $fy(c)$, and kept inside the "space" coordinates ($40 \leq x \leq 118$, and $18 \leq y \leq 48$).

The $dy(c)$ value is decremented continuously, and once it reaches zero, then the game tries to launch a rocket, looking for a free slot in the arrays, and setting accordingly $fx(d)$, $fy(d)$, $dx(d)$, $dy(d)$ and $t(d)$ (mostly copying the position of the shooter).

Finally the *aliens* variable is updated to indicate that alien spaceships are alive.

5.8 We are going down!

We didn't yet handle the case of the rocket or meteor hitting the player's spaceship. Already the *touched* variable is set up to indicate that.

Let us handle it. Add this code just after the line of the sentence reading *IF shield THEN POKE*:

```
IF touched THEN          ' Crash countdown
    touched = touched - 1
    IF touched = 0 THEN
```

```
IF power = 0 THEN  ' Out of power
    sound_effect = 2: sound_state = 0
    bullet_x = 0
    aliens = 0

    '
    ' Destruction
    '
    FOR c = 0 TO 127
        IF (c AND 15) < 8 THEN
            MODE 0,7,COCKPIT_COLOR2,0,0
        ELSEIF (c AND 15)<14 AND (c AND 1)<>0 THEN
            MODE 0,7,COCKPIT_COLOR2,0,0
        ELSE
            MODE 0,0,COCKPIT_COLOR2,0,0
        END IF
        WAIT
    NEXT c
    FOR c = 0 TO 7
        SPRITE c,0
    NEXT c

    DO
        GOSUB game_over_display
        WAIT
        c = CONT
    LOOP WHILE c
    DO
        GOSUB game_over_display
        WAIT
        c = CONT
    LOOP WHILE c = 0
    IF #score > #record THEN #record = #score
    GOTO storm_title
END IF
sound_effect = 3: sound_state = 0

'
' Make a scratch in cockpit
'
power = power - 1
#backtab(224 + power) = 212 * 8 + 2
loc = (RAND AND $0F)+((RAND AND $70)/16 % 7) * 20 + 2
c = (RAND AND $C0) / 64 * 6
#backtab(loc) = scratches(c + 1) * 8 + 7
c = c + 2
loc = loc + scratches(c)
#backtab(loc) = scratches(c + 1) * 8 + 7
```

```
                c = c + 2
                loc = loc + scratches(c)
                #backtab(loc) = scratches(c + 1) * 8 + 7
            END IF
        END IF
```

When the spaceship is touched, the variable *touched* gets a non-zero value. This value is decreased until it reaches zero, then the game removes a power unit from the spaceship.

If there is no power, then all of the screen flashes and a sound effect is invoked. Finally the **GAME OVER** message is displayed, and the game returns to the title screen.

But if there is still power, it is decremented by one (the removed card from the bar is painted red on screen with **GROM** character 212), a scratch is made onto the windshield at a random location, with a random shape (defined in the data array *scratches*).

The *scratches* data table, along with the *game_over_display* procedure, should be added after the line reading *GOTO main_storm_loop:*

```
scratches:
    DATA 0,185,1,186,20,184
    DATA 0,184,-1,187,20,185
    DATA 0,187,20,185,1,186
    DATA 0,186,20,184,-1,187

game_over_display: PROCEDURE
    c = FRAME AND 4
    IF c THEN c = 2 ELSE c = 7
    PRINT AT 85 COLOR c,"GAME  OVER"
    END
```

5.9 Sound effects

The game sound effects also use the IntyBASIC pseudo-multitasking capability, invoking a sound generator procedure on each video frame. We should add this line at the start of the game:

```
ON FRAME GOSUB play_effects
```

And this before the line reading *ASM ORG $F000*:

```
play_effects: PROCEDURE
    IF sound_effect = 8 THEN
        SOUND 0,640 - sound_state * 4,13-sound_state/32
        SOUND 1,320 - sound_state * 2,13-sound_state/32
        SOUND 2,160 - sound_state,13-sound_state/32
        SOUND 4,,$38
        sound_state = sound_state + 1
        IF sound_state = 160 THEN sound_effect = 0
        RETURN
    END IF
    IF bullet_x THEN
        SOUND 0,500 + bullet_x * 4,13
    ELSE
        SOUND 0,,0
    END IF
    IF aliens THEN
        SOUND 1,(FRAME AND $3E)+64,13
    ELSE
        SOUND 1,,0
    END IF
    ON sound_effect GOSUB
sse_none,sse_reload,sse_over,sse_scratch,sse_explosion,sse_explosion
2,sse_explosion3,sse_row,sse_none,sse_drop,sse_bug
    END

sse_none:    PROCEDURE
    SOUND 2,,0
    SOUND 4,,$38
    END

sse_reload:  PROCEDURE
    SOUND 2,214,13 - sound_state * 2
    SOUND 4,,$38
    sound_state = sound_state + 1
    IF sound_state = 3 THEN sound_effect = 0
    END

sse_over:    PROCEDURE
    SOUND 2,((sound_state AND $07) + 1) * 256,13
    SOUND 4,,$38
    sound_state = sound_state + 1
```

```
    IF sound_state = 100 THEN sound_effect = 0
    END

sse_scratch:  PROCEDURE
    SOUND 2,20+(RAND AND 7),15 - sound_state / 2
    SOUND 4,4+sound_state,$18
    sound_state = sound_state + 1
    IF sound_state = 8 THEN sound_effect = 0
    END

sse_explosion:    PROCEDURE
    SOUND 2,800,15 - sound_state / 4
    SOUND 4,31-sound_state/2,$18
    sound_state = sound_state + 1
    IF sound_state = 32 THEN sound_effect = 0
    END

sse_explosion2:    PROCEDURE
    SOUND 2,800 - sound_state * 8,15 - sound_state / 8
    SOUND 4,28-sound_state/4,$18
    sound_state = sound_state + 1
    IF sound_state = 64 THEN sound_effect = 0
    END

sse_explosion3:    PROCEDURE
    SOUND 2,600,15 - sound_state / 8
    SOUND 4,24-sound_state/2,$18
    sound_state = sound_state + 1
    IF sound_state = 48 THEN sound_effect = 0
    END

sse_row: PROCEDURE
    SOUND 2,sse_row_data(sound_state),13
    sound_state = sound_state + 1
    IF sound_state = 5 THEN sound_effect = 0
    END

sse_row_data:
    DATA 128,64,32,16,8

sse_drop:    PROCEDURE
    IF (sound_state AND 7) = 0 THEN SOUND 2,40 + RANDOM(20)
    IF (sound_state AND 7) >= 4 THEN
        SOUND 2,,0
    ELSE
        SOUND 2,,15-(sound_state AND 7)
    END IF
    SOUND 4,,$38
```

```
        sound_state = sound_state + 1

    END

sse_bug: PROCEDURE
    IF sound_state < 8 THEN
        SOUND 2,40+(RAND AND 7),15 - sound_state / 2
        SOUND 4,8+sound_state,$18
    ELSE
        SOUND 2,500 + fy(1) * 2, 13
        SOUND 4,,$38
    END IF
    sound_state = sound_state + 1
    END
```

The most special sound is the *sound_effect* number 8. It is generated when going to speed light, and it uses all three voices of the PSG (Programmable Sound Generator).

For all other cases, the twin lasers have an exclusive channel (*SOUND 0*), and when aliens appear, they use another exclusive channel to warn of their appearance (*SOUND 1*). This is a very good tip to "fill" the ears of the player.

The sound effects are:

- 1 = Laser shot. A single tone going down in volume.
- 2 = Game Over. Plays several low-pitch sounds
- 3 = Windshield scratch (hit).
- 4 = Explosion of meteor.
- 5 = Explosion of enemy rocket.
- 6 = Explosion of alien spaceship.
- 7 = Row of title screen being built.
- 9 = Supplies drop. A pseudo-random acute tone for four frames, and then four frames of silence. It sounds like a computer doing work[12].

---

[12] Okay, this only happens in movies.

- 10 = A bug hits the windshield. It starts with an acute noisy sound, following by a tone going low-pitch to signal displacement over the windshield.

5.10 The planet

We have forgotten the animation of the planet receiving supplies[13]

Replace the whole stub procedure *rotating_planet* with this:

```
INCLUDE "planet.bas"
INCLUDE "sphere1.bas"
INCLUDE "sphere2.bas"
INCLUDE "sphere3.bas"
INCLUDE "sphere4.bas"
INCLUDE "sphere5.bas"
```

And these are the corresponding files. For "planet.bas":

```
'
'  Shows a rotating planet
'
'  by Oscar Toledo G.
'
'  Creation date: Mar/21/2018.
'

rotating_planet:   PROCEDURE
    WAIT
    DEFINE 16,1,VARPTR package_bitmaps(7 * 4)
    FOR c = 0 TO 7
        SPRITE c,0
    NEXT c
    aliens = 0
    bullet_x = 0
    WAIT

    sound_effect = 9: sound_state = 0
```

---

[13] This has an interesting story, as I needed a 3-D wireframe rotating sphere. I couldn't find a free one on the Internet (Shutterstock wanted to sell me one for an outrageous $50 USD). So I wrote a 3-D Javascript program generating the animation in the required size and it looked beautiful. The program is available at: https://github.com/nanochess/sphere

```
x = 64
y = 20
f = 255
d = 0
FOR c = 0 TO 120
e = c % 5
IF d THEN
    IF e = 0 THEN DEFINE 0,16,sphere1_bitmaps_0
    IF e = 1 THEN DEFINE 0,16,sphere2_bitmaps_0
    IF e = 2 THEN DEFINE 0,16,sphere3_bitmaps_0
    IF e = 3 THEN DEFINE 0,16,sphere4_bitmaps_0
    IF e = 4 THEN DEFINE 0,16,sphere5_bitmaps_0
ELSE
    IF e = 0 THEN DEFINE 31,16,sphere1_bitmaps_0
    IF e = 1 THEN DEFINE 31,16,sphere2_bitmaps_0
    IF e = 2 THEN DEFINE 31,16,sphere3_bitmaps_0
    IF e = 3 THEN DEFINE 31,16,sphere4_bitmaps_0
    IF e = 4 THEN DEFINE 31,16,sphere5_bitmaps_0
END IF
GOSUB drop_supplies
WAIT
IF e = 0 THEN DEFINE 47,16,sphere1_bitmaps_1
IF e = 1 THEN DEFINE 47,16,sphere2_bitmaps_1
IF e = 2 THEN DEFINE 47,16,sphere3_bitmaps_1
IF e = 3 THEN DEFINE 47,16,sphere4_bitmaps_1
IF e = 4 THEN DEFINE 47,16,sphere5_bitmaps_1
GOSUB drop_supplies
WAIT
IF d = 0 THEN
    #backtab(48) = $0800 + 31 * 8 + 5
    #backtab(49) = $0800 + 32 * 8 + 5
    #backtab(50) = $0800 + 33 * 8 + 5
    #backtab(51) = $0800 + 34 * 8 + 5
    #backtab(67) = $0800 + 35 * 8 + 5
    #backtab(68) = $0800 + 36 * 8 + 5
    #backtab(69) = $0800 + 37 * 8 + 5
    #backtab(70) = $0800 + 38 * 8 + 5
    #backtab(71) = $0800 + 39 * 8 + 5
    #backtab(72) = $0800 + 40 * 8 + 5
    #backtab(87) = $0800 + 41 * 8 + 5
    #backtab(88) = $0800 + 42 * 8 + 5
    #backtab(89) = $0800 + 43 * 8 + 5
    #backtab(90) = $0800 + 44 * 8 + 5
    #backtab(91) = $0800 + 45 * 8 + 5
    #backtab(92) = $0800 + 46 * 8 + 5
ELSE
    #backtab(48) = $0800 + 0 * 8 + 5
```

```
      #backtab(49) = $0800 + 1 * 8 + 5
      #backtab(50) = $0800 + 2 * 8 + 5
      #backtab(51) = $0800 + 3 * 8 + 5
      #backtab(67) = $0800 + 4 * 8 + 5
      #backtab(68) = $0800 + 5 * 8 + 5
      #backtab(69) = $0800 + 6 * 8 + 5
      #backtab(70) = $0800 + 7 * 8 + 5
      #backtab(71) = $0800 + 8 * 8 + 5
      #backtab(72) = $0800 + 9 * 8 + 5
      #backtab(87) = $0800 + 10 * 8 + 5
      #backtab(88) = $0800 + 11 * 8 + 5
      #backtab(89) = $0800 + 12 * 8 + 5
      #backtab(90) = $0800 + 13 * 8 + 5
      #backtab(91) = $0800 + 14 * 8 + 5
      #backtab(92) = $0800 + 15 * 8 + 5
END IF
#backtab(107) = $0800 + 47 * 8 + 5
#backtab(108) = $0800 + 48 * 8 + 5
#backtab(109) = $0800 + 49 * 8 + 5
#backtab(110) = $0800 + 50 * 8 + 5
#backtab(111) = $0800 + 51 * 8 + 5
#backtab(112) = $0800 + 52 * 8 + 5
#backtab(127) = $0800 + 53 * 8 + 5
#backtab(128) = $0800 + 54 * 8 + 5
#backtab(129) = $0800 + 55 * 8 + 5
#backtab(130) = $0800 + 56 * 8 + 5
#backtab(131) = $0800 + 57 * 8 + 5
#backtab(132) = $0800 + 58 * 8 + 5
#backtab(148) = $0800 + 59 * 8 + 5
#backtab(149) = $0800 + 60 * 8 + 5
#backtab(150) = $0800 + 61 * 8 + 5
#backtab(151) = $0800 + 62 * 8 + 5


d = NOT d
GOSUB drop_supplies
DEFINE 16,1,VARPTR package_bitmaps(supplies_spr(f / 16))
WAIT

IF c < 80 THEN
      PRINT AT 166 COLOR 3
      IF c AND 4 THEN
            PRINT "Supplies"
            PRINT AT 186,"dropped"
      ELSE
            PRINT "        "
            PRINT AT 186,"       "
      END IF
ELSE
```

```
            IF c = 80 THEN
                #score = #score + 20
                sound_effect = 7
                sound_state = 0
                GOSUB update_storm_score
            END IF
            PRINT AT 165 COLOR 3
            IF c AND 4 THEN
                PRINT "Ready for"
                PRINT AT 184,"light-speed"
            ELSE
                PRINT "            "
                PRINT AT 184,"              "
            END IF
        END IF
    END IF

    NEXT c

    sound_effect = 0: sound_state = 0
    FOR c = 48 TO 151
        #backtab(c) = 0
    NEXT c

    GOSUB setup_bitmaps

    RETURN
    END

drop_supplies:    PROCEDURE
    IF f = 0 THEN
        SPRITE 0,0
        RETURN
    END IF
    IF f >= 128 THEN
        SPRITE 0,$0704+x,$0204+y,$0882
    ELSE
        SPRITE 0,$0308+x,$0108+y,$0882
    END IF
    f = f - 1
    IF FRAME AND 1 THEN
        IF f < 128 THEN
            x = x - 1
        ELSE
            x = x + 1
        END IF
    END IF
    IF (FRAME AND 7) = 0 THEN
        y = y + 1
```

```
        END IF
        END

supplies_spr:
        DATA 0*4,1*4,2*4,3*4,4*4,5*4,6*4,7*4
        DATA 4*4,4*4,5*4,5*4,6*4,6*4,7*4,7*4

package_bitmaps:
        BITMAP "........"
        BITMAP "........"
        BITMAP "........"
        BITMAP "...X...."
        BITMAP "........"
        BITMAP "........"
        BITMAP "........"
        BITMAP "........"

        BITMAP "........"
        BITMAP "........"
        BITMAP "........"
        BITMAP "...XX..."
        BITMAP "...XX..."
        BITMAP "........"
        BITMAP "........"
        BITMAP "........"

        BITMAP "........"
        BITMAP "........"
        BITMAP "..XXX..."
        BITMAP "..X.X..."
        BITMAP "..XXX..."
        BITMAP "........"
        BITMAP "........"
        BITMAP "........"

        BITMAP "........"
        BITMAP "........"
        BITMAP "..XXXX.."
        BITMAP "..X..X.."
        BITMAP "..X..X.."
        BITMAP "..XXXX.."
        BITMAP "........"
        BITMAP "........"

        BITMAP "........"
        BITMAP ".XXXXX.."
        BITMAP ".X...X.."
        BITMAP ".X...X.."
```

```
BITMAP ".X...X.."
BITMAP ".XXXXX.."
BITMAP "........"
BITMAP "........"

BITMAP "........"
BITMAP ".XXXXXX."
BITMAP ".X....X."
BITMAP ".X....X."
BITMAP ".X....X."
BITMAP ".X....X."
BITMAP ".XXXXXX."
BITMAP "........"

BITMAP "XXXXXXX."
BITMAP "X.....X."
BITMAP "X.....X."
BITMAP "X.....X."
BITMAP "X.....X."
BITMAP "X.....X."
BITMAP "XXXXXXX."
BITMAP "........"

BITMAP "XXXXXXXX"
BITMAP "X......X"
BITMAP "X......X"
BITMAP "X......X"
BITMAP "X......X"
BITMAP "X......X"
BITMAP "X......X"
BITMAP "XXXXXXXX"
```

The rotating planet is animated by redefining the **GRAM** cards in two steps, so the player doesn't see flickering graphics. The video frame steps for flicker-free animation of the planet are:

1. Load first half of the sphere in the non-displayed **GRAM** cards 0-15 or 31-46. Remember these are defined at the start of the next video frame.

2. Graphics are now defined. Load the second half of the sphere in the displayed **GRAM** cards 47-62. Again these are defined at the start of the next video frame.

3. Graphics are now defined. Now we are running against the raster (before video reaches the middle of screen where the GRAM cards 47-62 are displayed or the sphere would look disjointed), and it updates the cards for the first half of the sphere.

The package dropped onto the planet is a single GRAM being redefined to account for the effect of going farther away.

These are the five animated wireframe spheres used to represent the rotating planet.

These are the graphics for "sphere1.bas":

```
REM IntyColor v1.1.5 Jul/25/2017
REM intycolor -b -n -e75 sphere1.bmp sphere1.bas sphere1
REM Created: Wed Mar 21 17:18:34 2018

' 32 bitmaps
sphere1_bitmaps_0:
    DATA $0000,$0701,$3F0F,$FF7F
    DATA $3F00,$FFFF,$FFFF,$8AFB
    DATA $FC00,$FFFF,$FFFF,$878A
    DATA $0000,$E080,$BCF8,$EFDE
    DATA $0301,$0706,$0B0F,$171F
    DATA $DBFB,$FF93,$23FB,$7F63
    DATA $898B,$FD1F,$1F0D,$04FC
    DATA $7FC7,$21E1,$F0FF,$9F90
    DATA $9B97,$FF8D,$67C2,$E1FD
    DATA $C080,$F0E0,$F8F0,$F858
    DATA $3F37,$7F3F,$6A6A,$6A6A
    DATA $43E3,$E3FF,$C3C3,$41C3
    DATA $FF07,$06E4,$0606,$0302
    DATA $C8F8,$4C48,$444C,$FF5F
    DATA $3030,$1010,$7F19,$08F8
    DATA $ACFC,$6EEC,$F6FE,$7656
sphere1_bitmaps_1:
    DATA $6A6A,$7F6F,$3D7D,$3635
    DATA $7F41,$C1FF,$2061,$B0A0
    DATA $F2FF,$8383,$8181,$FFC1
    DATA $26E4,$3626,$3732,$D2FF
```

```
        DATA $0808,$0C0C,$FF0F,$0F0C
        DATA $7676,$5E76,$5EFE,$FCFC
        DATA $1A1A,$0F0B,$0607,$0103
        DATA $FE93,$EFF8,$F6FF,$B972
        DATA $60F0,$FE67,$33B0,$FC3E
        DATA $9F92,$DAFA,$FADF,$4E4A
        DATA $D8FC,$3F19,$3AFF,$7F3F
        DATA $B8BC,$F0F8,$E0E0,$80C0
        DATA $7EDF,$0F3F,$0107,$0000
        DATA $6E8C,$FF3F,$FFFF,$003F
        DATA $3F6E,$BFFF,$FFFF,$00FC
        DATA $FEFF,$F0FC,$80E0,$0000

        REM 6x6 cards
sphere1_cards:
        DATA $0000,$0805,$080D,$0815,$081D,$0000
        DATA $0825,$082D,$0835,$083D,$0845,$084D
        DATA $0855,$085D,$0865,$086D,$0875,$087D
        DATA $0885,$088D,$0895,$089D,$08A5,$08AD
        DATA $08B5,$08BD,$08C5,$08CD,$08D5,$08DD
        DATA $0000,$08E5,$08ED,$08F5,$08FD,$0000
```

The graphics for "sphere2.bas":

```
        REM IntyColor v1.1.5 Jul/25/2017
        REM intycolor -b -n -e75 sphere2.bmp sphere2.bas sphere2
        REM Created: Wed Mar 21 17:18:40 2018

        ' 32 bitmaps
sphere2_bitmaps_0:
        DATA $0000,$0701,$3F0F,$FF7F
        DATA $3F00,$FFFF,$FFD7,$91FB
        DATA $FC00,$FFFF,$FFFF,$8891
        DATA $0000,$E080,$7CF8,$EF9E
        DATA $0301,$0707,$1E0F,$3C1C
        DATA $F3F9,$FFF3,$C2FE,$FFC7
        DATA $9091,$F89F,$9F90,$98F8
        DATA $FE8F,$43C2,$E1FF,$3F60
        DATA $71E3,$FF39,$9FF4,$CBFE
        DATA $4080,$F0E0,$F8F0,$3C38
        DATA $3F3F,$7F79,$7179,$7171
        DATA $86E6,$E6FF,$8686,$8686
        DATA $FF9B,$88D8,$C8C8,$47CC
        DATA $30F8,$1030,$1818,$FF1F
        DATA $4D49,$2465,$7F25,$32FE
        DATA $1C3C,$9E9C,$FEFE,$CE8E
sphere2_bitmaps_1:
```

```
    DATA $7071,$7F7F,$7878,$3C38
    DATA $BF82,$C3FE,$C1C3,$6141
    DATA $FCFF,$6464,$2626,$BF22
    DATA $08C8,$0C0C,$0F0C,$C4FF
    DATA $1232,$1212,$FF17,$1712
    DATA $CECE,$CECE,$9EFE,$DCFC
    DATA $1E3C,$0F1F,$070F,$0103
    DATA $3E63,$1BF0,$8CFF,$A7CC
    DATA $93F3,$FFDF,$2FE9,$FC3E
    DATA $1F04,$06FE,$FE9F,$C686
    DATA $F3FF,$3F27,$64FF,$4F4D
    DATA $389C,$F038,$E0E0,$80C0
    DATA $7FFF,$0F3F,$0107,$0000
    DATA $C60E,$FFFF,$FFFF,$003F
    DATA $5F46,$EFFF,$FFFF,$00F8
    DATA $FEFF,$F0FC,$80E0,$0000

    REM 6x6 cards
sphere2_cards:
    DATA $0000,$0805,$080D,$0815,$081D,$0000
    DATA $0825,$082D,$0835,$083D,$0845,$084D
    DATA $0855,$085D,$0865,$086D,$0875,$087D
    DATA $0885,$088D,$0895,$089D,$08A5,$08AD
    DATA $08B5,$08BD,$08C5,$08CD,$08D5,$08DD
    DATA $0000,$08E5,$08ED,$08F5,$08FD,$0000
```

The graphics for "sphere3.bas":

```
    REM IntyColor v1.1.5 Jul/25/2017
    REM intycolor -b -n -e75 sphere3.bmp sphere3.bas sphere3
    REM Created: Wed Mar 21 17:18:46 2018

    ' 32 bitmaps
sphere3_bitmaps_0:
    DATA $0000,$0701,$3F0F,$FF7F
    DATA $1F00,$FFFF,$FFF7,$62FE
    DATA $FC00,$FFFF,$FFFF,$7063
    DATA $0000,$E080,$FCF0,$EFFE
    DATA $0301,$0F07,$1C0F,$391C
    DATA $B2F2,$FF26,$E4FC,$FFCF
    DATA $6163,$F97F,$7F60,$20F8
    DATA $FC3F,$97F4,$FBFF,$DFC9
    DATA $33E5,$FF31,$0FD8,$C6FC
    DATA $C080,$F0E0,$F8F0,$3C78
    DATA $3F3B,$7F7B,$7373,$7373
    DATA $48E8,$E8FF,$4848,$4C48
    DATA $FF23,$30F0,$3030,$1310
```

```
      DATA $C4FD,$6464,$2226,$FF3F
      DATA $8286,$C383,$7FC3,$41F9
      DATA $1C3C,$1E1C,$FEFE,$8E9E
sphere3_bitmaps_1:
      DATA $7173,$7F57,$7979,$3C38
      DATA $7F4C,$E4FE,$A624,$92B2
      DATA $F8FF,$1818,$0C08,$3F0D
      DATA $33F2,$1313,$1F11,$D9FF
      DATA $6161,$6161,$FF6F,$6761
      DATA $8E8E,$9E9E,$9EFE,$FCFC
      DATA $1C3C,$0F1F,$070F,$0103
      DATA $7FD3,$2FF9,$9CFF,$C78E
      DATA $06FC,$FF87,$43C2,$F37F
      DATA $1F19,$09F9,$F91F,$8909
      DATA $E3FF,$FF43,$CFFF,$9FCF
      DATA $3838,$F078,$E0E0,$80C0
      DATA $79EF,$1F3E,$0107,$0000
      DATA $8911,$FFFF,$FFFF,$003F
      DATA $DF89,$EBFF,$FFFF,$00FC
      DATA $FEFF,$F0FC,$80E0,$0000

      REM 6x6 cards
sphere3_cards:
      DATA $0000,$0805,$080D,$0815,$081D,$0000
      DATA $0825,$082D,$0835,$083D,$0845,$084D
      DATA $0855,$085D,$0865,$086D,$0875,$087D
      DATA $0885,$088D,$0895,$089D,$08A5,$08AD
      DATA $08B5,$08BD,$08C5,$08CD,$08D5,$08DD
      DATA $0000,$08E5,$08ED,$08F5,$08FD,$0000
```

The graphics for "sphere4.bas":

```
      REM IntyColor v1.1.5 Jul/25/2017
      REM intycolor -b -n -e75 sphere4.bmp sphere4.bas sphere4
      REM Created: Wed Mar 21 17:18:52 2018

      ' 32 bitmaps
sphere4_bitmaps_0:
      DATA $0000,$0701,$3F0F,$FF7F
      DATA $3F00,$FFFF,$FFFF,$76FC
      DATA $FC00,$FFFF,$FCFF,$3176
      DATA $0000,$E080,$FCF0,$FB7E
      DATA $0301,$0F07,$1F0F,$3D1D
      DATA $FCFE,$FF5C,$98F8,$3F1B
      DATA $5272,$FB7F,$5F5B,$49F9
      DATA $7C3F,$0DCC,$E6FF,$0F06
      DATA $4E9D,$FF6F,$1FF7,$C9FF
```

```
      DATA $C080,$E040,$D0F0,$7858
      DATA $3F3F,$7F7A,$6E6E,$6E6E
      DATA $30F0,$F0FF,$3030,$1010
      DATA $FF4B,$4CEC,$646C,$2764
      DATA $83FF,$8181,$C181,$FF5F
      DATA $050D,$8604,$FF83,$82FA
      DATA $AC6C,$9EB4,$F6FE,$56D6
sphere4_bitmaps_1:
      DATA $6A6E,$7F6F,$777E,$3735
      DATA $3F10,$98FE,$0808,$0C0C
      DATA $F6FF,$3222,$1232,$3F13
      DATA $40C0,$6060,$2760,$E0FF
      DATA $C382,$C3C3,$FFC7,$C7C2
      DATA $5656,$5656,$FCFE,$ECFC
      DATA $1A3F,$0F1F,$070F,$0103
      DATA $BF87,$47E6,$B1FF,$E9D9
      DATA $09F9,$FF0F,$8784,$E3FE
      DATA $3F20,$B0F8,$F8BF,$D191
      DATA $C6FE,$FFC4,$C9FF,$DFDB
      DATA $F8E8,$F0D0,$60E0,$80C0
      DATA $7BFF,$1F3D,$0107,$0000
      DATA $51E1,$FFFF,$FFFF,$003F
      DATA $DF51,$FFFF,$FFFF,$00FC
      DATA $FEFF,$F0FC,$80E0,$0000

      REM 6x6 cards
sphere4_cards:
      DATA $0000,$0805,$080D,$0815,$081D,$0000
      DATA $0825,$082D,$0835,$083D,$0845,$084D
      DATA $0855,$085D,$0865,$086D,$0875,$087D
      DATA $0885,$088D,$0895,$089D,$08A5,$08AD
      DATA $08B5,$08BD,$08C5,$08CD,$08D5,$08DD
      DATA $0000,$08E5,$08ED,$08F5,$08FD,$0000
```

And finally the graphics for "sphere5.bas":

```
      REM IntyColor v1.1.5 Jul/25/2017
      REM intycolor -b -n -e75 sphere5.bmp sphere5.bas sphere5
      REM Created: Wed Mar 21 17:18:57 2018

      ' 32 bitmaps
sphere5_bitmaps_0:
      DATA $0000,$0701,$3F1F,$FF7F
      DATA $3F00,$FFFF,$FFEB,$CCFC
      DATA $FC00,$FFFF,$F9FF,$46CC
      DATA $0000,$E080,$FCF8,$FB7E
      DATA $0301,$0707,$1B0F,$161B
```

```
     DATA $CCF4,$FFCC,$1CFC,$3F3F
     DATA $84CC,$FE9F,$9F86,$82FE
     DATA $7F67,$13F3,$E97F,$0F08
     DATA $8C9D,$FFC6,$A7E3,$D0FC
     DATA $C080,$E040,$90F0,$C898
     DATA $3E37,$7F36,$6C64,$6C6C
     DATA $29F8,$ECFF,$2C2C,$242C
     DATA $FF83,$83C3,$8181,$8381
     DATA $04FC,$0206,$0202,$FF1F
     DATA $48D8,$6848,$7F25,$24FC
     DATA $4CCC,$6664,$E6FE,$3626
sphere5_bitmaps_1:
     DATA $6464,$7F67,$2666,$3332
     DATA $3F24,$B6FE,$1216,$1B12
     DATA $F1FF,$4040,$6040,$3F20
     DATA $81C3,$8181,$C7C1,$C1FF
     DATA $3424,$3434,$FF37,$1F94
     DATA $3636,$2636,$6CFE,$EC7C
     DATA $1913,$0F09,$0607,$0103
     DATA $3F0B,$87E5,$63FF,$B931
     DATA $10F0,$FE97,$CFC8,$E6FE
     DATA $7F41,$61F9,$F97F,$3323
     DATA $FCFC,$3F38,$33FF,$2F33
     DATA $D868,$F0D0,$E0E0,$80C0
     DATA $7EDF,$1F3F,$0107,$0000
     DATA $3362,$FF9F,$FFFF,$003F
     DATA $3F33,$D7FF,$FFFF,$00FC
     DATA $FEFF,$F0FC,$80E0,$0000

     REM 6x6 cards
sphere5_cards:
     DATA $0000,$0805,$080D,$0815,$081D,$0000
     DATA $0825,$082D,$0835,$083D,$0845,$084D
     DATA $0855,$085D,$0865,$086D,$0875,$087D
     DATA $0885,$088D,$0895,$089D,$08A5,$08AD
     DATA $08B5,$08BD,$08C5,$08CD,$08D5,$08DD
     DATA $0000,$08E5,$08ED,$08F5,$08FD,$0000
```

Chapter 6

Dungeon Warrior

You are now into the dark dungeons. You wouldn't be here, but as a peasant you have dreamed of being a hero or a powerful warrior, and armed with your sword you decided to try your luck in these dungeons. Rumors are that the dungeons are filled with gold and jewels, but also with death, and strange undead enemies. Very few people have come out of these dungeons, most dead, and others severely hurt. But the idea of gold is enough to compel you to enter into the darkness...

This is the backstory for Dungeon Warrior, and it is an example of how the stories printed in game boxes were so amazing.

Dungeon Warrior is a Role-Playing-Game (RPG for short). It generates random mazes in each game, and fills them with random enemies, gold, and chests. The game is played in a first-person perspective using pseudo-3D graphics.

The role playing games were made famous by the Dungeons & Dragons board game, and many of its features made its way into personal computer games at the end of the 70's. One example is Akalabeth by Richard Garriot.[14]

6.1 Maze generation

The game depends heavily on a random maze generator. Although there are several algorithms for maze generation, we need an algorithm that doesn't require *too much* memory for data.

The logic for maze generation follows a simple algorithm:

1. Each square of the map indicates if there is a connection using a bitmap ($01 = Up, $02 = Right, $04 = Down, $08 = Left).

2. Start at the entry point of the maze.

3. For the current square, choose a random direction still not connected and that hasn't been reached before, and follow it saving the current position in the stack (also marking the map to signal a connection). If the direction isn't possible, choose another direction until filling the four possible directions, then backtrack using the stack.

If your map is 10x10 cells, then your stack for backtracking should be of the same size (i.e. 100 positions). In a standard Intellivision console using IntyBASIC, there are 228 memory cells of 8-bit.

---

[14] Akalabeth has the rare privilege of being the first RPG game widely sold. Was it made by a team of people? No. A big company? No. It was programmed by a high-school teenager on the Apple II computers available at the school during the summer of 1979. Surely we can imagine a bunch of boisterous teenagers testing the game in the school and playing endlessly while giving suggestions to the author. It happens he worked in Clear Lake City, Texas at a ComputerLand and demo'ed the game to his boss, who consented to sell the game in the store for $20. The game was packed as a floppy disk inside a Ziploc bag with photocopied instructions. California Pacific Computer Company received a copy of the game and contacted the teenager to publish the game. He flew to California with his parents and signed a contract to receive $5 USD for each copy sold. He sold 30,000 copies, and this is how Richard Garriott started one of the most prolific series of RPG games: Ultima. In fact Akalabeth is also known as Ultima 0 (zero). Apparently the name derives from Tolkien's Akallabêth, part of The Silmarillion. Even the final enemy is called Balrog. Apart from the names, no other reference to Tolkien exists.

We need a method to save space, and this method abuses the fact that only 4 bits are used from each map cell. So the stack is saved throughout the map, using the upper 4 bits to preserve the backtrack direction instead of the previous cell position, as it would require a full 8 bits!

So let's see our definitions for the maze generator:

```
'
' Dungeon Warrior
' by Oscar Toledo G.
' Creation date: May/08/2019.
'

    CONST EFFECT_WALKING = 1
    CONST EFFECT_CHEST = 2
    CONST EFFECT_LADDER = 3
    CONST EFFECT_MISS = 4
    CONST EFFECT_HIT = 5

    CONST MW = 12 ' Map width
    CONST MH = 12 ' Map height

    CONST M_MASK = $0F
    CONST M_UP = 1
    CONST M_RIGHT = 2
    CONST M_DOWN = 4
    CONST M_LEFT = 8
    CONST M_ITEM_MASK = $F0
    CONST M_ITEM_MONSTER1 = $10
    CONST M_ITEM_MONSTER2 = $20
    CONST M_ITEM_MONSTER3 = $30
    CONST M_ITEM_GOLD = $80
    CONST M_ITEM_CHEST = $90
    CONST M_ITEM_LADDER = $A0

    DIM map(MW * MH)

    PLAY SIMPLE

title_screen:
    CLS
    MODE 0,0,1,0,0
    WAIT

    #backtab(0) = $2000
    PRINT AT 22 COLOR 7,"Dungeon Warrior"
```

```
    #backtab(60) = $2000

    PRINT AT 81 COLOR 6,"Alone but impulsed"
    PRINT AT 100,"by your thirst for"
    PRINT AT 120,"adventures, you're"
    PRINT AT 140,"about to enter the"
    PRINT AT 160,"catacombs!"
    PRINT AT 201 COLOR 3,"Press keypad when"
    PRINT AT 221,"your soul is ready"

    GOSUB read_keypad

    level = 1
    current_armor = 1
    current_weapon = 1
    #hp = 10
    #max_hp = 10
    #gold = 0
    blind = 0
```

The definitions *MW* and *MH* give the size of the map in cells along width and height. *M_MASK* is the mask for connection of each cell, while the available directions are *M_UP*, *M_RIGHT*, *M_DOWN*, and *M_LEFT*.

Later we will use the *M_ITEM_ ** masks to add enemies and objects.

As always we command IntyBASIC to create an array for the map cells using *DIM map(MW * MH)*.

A simple title screen is enough for the purposes of the game as it has lots of text to explain what happens, plus initialization of certain important variables like the current dungeon level (*level*), the Health Points (*#hp*), and so on.

Now to the proper maze generation code:

```
    '
    ' Build the random map
    '

generate_maze:
    PLAY OFF

    CLS
    #backtab(0) = $2000
```

```
    IF level = 1 THEN MODE 0,4,0,4,0
    IF level = 2 THEN MODE 0,9,0,9,0
    IF level = 3 THEN MODE 0,8,0,8,0
    IF level = 4 THEN MODE 0,1,0,1,0
    IF level = 5 THEN MODE 0,13,0,13,0
    WAIT

    PRINT AT 239 COLOR 2,"*"

    ' Clear the map
    FOR c = 0 TO MW * MH - 1
        map(c) = 0
    NEXT c

    #seed = level * 31415 + RAND

    x = MW / 2
    y = 0
    GOSUB next_rand
    d = c
    WHILE 1
        p = y * MW + x
        IF c = 0 AND (map(p) AND M_UP) = 0 AND y > 0 AND (map(p -
MW) AND M_MASK) = 0 THEN
            map(p) = map(p) + M_UP
            map(stack_pos) = map(stack_pos) + $10
            stack_pos = stack_pos + 1
            y = y - 1
            p = p - MW
            map(p) = map(p) + M_DOWN
            GOSUB next_rand
            d = c
        ELSEIF c = 1 AND (map(p) AND M_RIGHT) = 0 AND x < MW - 1
AND (map(p + 1) AND M_MASK) = 0 THEN
            map(p) = map(p) + M_RIGHT
            map(stack_pos) = map(stack_pos) + $20
            stack_pos = stack_pos + 1
            x = x + 1
            p = p + 1
            map(p) = map(p) + M_LEFT
            GOSUB next_rand
            d = c
        ELSEIF c = 2 AND (map(p) AND M_DOWN) = 0 AND y < MH - 1 AND
(map(p + MW) AND M_MASK) = 0 THEN
            map(p) = map(p) + M_DOWN
            map(stack_pos) = map(stack_pos) + $30
            stack_pos = stack_pos + 1
            y = y + 1
```

```
                p = p + MW
                map(p) = map(p) + M_UP
                GOSUB next_rand
                d = c
            ELSEIF c = 3 AND (map(p) AND M_LEFT) = 0 AND x > 0 AND
(map(p - 1) AND M_MASK) = 0 THEN
                map(p) = map(p) + M_LEFT
                map(stack_pos) = map(stack_pos) + $40
                stack_pos = stack_pos + 1
                x = x - 1
                p = p - 1
                map(p) = map(p) + M_RIGHT
                GOSUB next_rand
                d = c
            ELSE
                c = (c + 1) % 4
                IF c = d THEN
                    IF stack_pos = 0 THEN EXIT WHILE
                    stack_pos = stack_pos - 1
                    c = map(stack_pos) AND $F0
                    map(stack_pos) = map(stack_pos) AND $0F
                    IF c = $10 THEN y = y + 1
                    IF c = $20 THEN x = x - 1
                    IF c = $30 THEN y = y - 1
                    IF c = $40 THEN x = x + 1
                    GOSUB next_rand
                    d = c
                END IF
            END IF
    WEND

stuck: GOTO stuck

next_rand:    PROCEDURE
    #seed = (#seed * 139 + 5) % 191
    c = #seed % 4
    END
```

Notice there are four lines with *IF* statements that are broken in two lines in this book. These should be only one line in the source code.

In the bottom-right corner of the screen is shown an asterisk as a way to indicate that the game is doing "things" (we can see it as a Loading message).

The map is reset to zero at the start of the code, and a random seed is created in the variable *#seed*. Then the entry point for the maze is set (top center), and a random number is chosen for the first cell connection in the map.

The main loop proceeds to check if the direction is possible (two conditions are required: not connected yet, and goes to a cell not yet visited).

When visiting another cell, it marks the newly-opened direction, and in the target cell it also opens the contrary direction. For example, if going UP, it marks the current cell with *M_UP*, and the new visited cell will be marked *M_DOWN*. It also saves the backtrack direction onto the stack – for example, when going up the value is $10.

Notice the *d=c* assignments; it allows the maze generator code to detect when all directions have been tried by means of the comparison *c = d*. The stack will become completely empty when each cell has been visited and all possible directions are searched, and then the maze generation will be finished exiting with *EXIT WHILE*.

6.2 Displaying the maze

A maze saved in the memory of the Intellivision isn't so useful, so let us code a screen display of each maze for testing.

Let us replace "stuck: GOTO stuck" with this code:

```
' >>>START OF TEMPORARY CODE<<<
'
' Show the maze
'
CLS
WAIT
DEFINE 0,16,walls_bitmaps
WAIT

FOR y = 0 TO MH - 1
    FOR x = 0 TO MW - 1
        PRINT AT y * 20 + x,$0805 + map(y * MW + x) * 8
    NEXT x
NEXT y
```

```
    PRINT AT 220 COLOR 7,<>level

    FOR c = 0 TO 60
        WAIT
    NEXT c

    level = level + 1
    GOTO generate_maze

    '
    ' Bitmaps for walls
    '
walls_bitmaps:
    BITMAP "XXXXXXXX"   ' 0
    BITMAP "X......X"
    BITMAP "X......X"
    BITMAP "X......X"
    BITMAP "X......X"
    BITMAP "X......X"
    BITMAP "X......X"
    BITMAP "XXXXXXXX"

    BITMAP "X......X"   ' 1
    BITMAP "X......X"
    BITMAP "X......X"
    BITMAP "X......X"
    BITMAP "X......X"
    BITMAP "X......X"
    BITMAP "X......X"
    BITMAP "XXXXXXXX"

    BITMAP "XXXXXXXX"   ' 2
    BITMAP "X......."
    BITMAP "X......."
    BITMAP "X......."
    BITMAP "X......."
    BITMAP "X......."
    BITMAP "X......."
    BITMAP "XXXXXXXX"

    BITMAP "X......X"   ' 3
    BITMAP "X......."
    BITMAP "X......."
    BITMAP "X......."
    BITMAP "X......."
    BITMAP "X......."
    BITMAP "X......."
```

```
BITMAP "XXXXXXXX"

BITMAP "XXXXXXXX"    ' 4
BITMAP "X......X"
BITMAP "X......X"
BITMAP "X......X"
BITMAP "X......X"
BITMAP "X......X"
BITMAP "X......X"
BITMAP "X......X"

BITMAP "X......X"    ' 5
BITMAP "X......X"
BITMAP "X......X"
BITMAP "X......X"
BITMAP "X......X"
BITMAP "X......X"
BITMAP "X......X"
BITMAP "X......X"

BITMAP "XXXXXXXX"    ' 6
BITMAP "X......."
BITMAP "X......."
BITMAP "X......."
BITMAP "X......."
BITMAP "X......."
BITMAP "X......."
BITMAP "X......X"

BITMAP "X......X"    ' 7
BITMAP "X......."
BITMAP "X......."
BITMAP "X......."
BITMAP "X......."
BITMAP "X......."
BITMAP "X......."
BITMAP "X......X"

BITMAP "XXXXXXXX"    ' 8
BITMAP ".......X"
BITMAP ".......X"
BITMAP ".......X"
BITMAP ".......X"
BITMAP ".......X"
BITMAP ".......X"
BITMAP "XXXXXXXX"

BITMAP "X......X"    ' 9
```

```
BITMAP ".......X"
BITMAP ".......X"
BITMAP ".......X"
BITMAP ".......X"
BITMAP ".......X"
BITMAP ".......X"
BITMAP "XXXXXXXX"

BITMAP "XXXXXXXX"    ' 10
BITMAP "........"
BITMAP "........"
BITMAP "........"
BITMAP "........"
BITMAP "........"
BITMAP "........"
BITMAP "XXXXXXXX"

BITMAP "X......X"    ' 11
BITMAP "........"
BITMAP "........"
BITMAP "........"
BITMAP "........"
BITMAP "........"
BITMAP "........"
BITMAP "XXXXXXXX"

BITMAP "XXXXXXXX"    ' 12
BITMAP ".......X"
BITMAP ".......X"
BITMAP ".......X"
BITMAP ".......X"
BITMAP ".......X"
BITMAP ".......X"
BITMAP "X......X"

BITMAP "X......X"    ' 13
BITMAP ".......X"
BITMAP ".......X"
BITMAP ".......X"
BITMAP ".......X"
BITMAP ".......X"
BITMAP ".......X"
BITMAP "X......X"

BITMAP "XXXXXXXX"    ' 14
BITMAP "........"
BITMAP "........"
BITMAP "........"
```

```
BITMAP "........"
BITMAP "........"
BITMAP "........"
BITMAP "X......X"

BITMAP "X......X"   ' 15
BITMAP "........"
BITMAP "........"
BITMAP "........"
BITMAP "........"
BITMAP "........"
BITMAP "........"
BITMAP "X......X"

'
' >>>END OF TEMPORARY CODE<<<
'
```

Each map cell contains a value from 0-15; basically it is a bit mask indicating the open directions from the cell. This can be translated easily using bitmaps with the open directions. For example, GRAM 0 is a closed square, GRAM 1 is a square with open top (*M_UP* open), GRAM 2 is a square with open right (*M_RIGHT*), GRAM 3 is a square with open top and right (*M_UP+M_RIGHT*), and so on.

To show the maze, two *FOR* loops are used, one for rows (*y*) and one for columns (*x*), then each cell is positioned on screen using the corresponding GRAM *$0805 + map(y * MW + x) * 8*. The multiplication by 8 converts the *map* array value into an offset for GRAM selection.

After running this code you'll see different random mazes being generated endlessly.

6.3 Adding monsters and treasures

Now we will get in charge of adding monsters and treasures to the maze. Remove the temporary code for this section, and insert this in the same place:

```
PRINT AT 239 COLOR 2,"+"
```

```
' Block starting square
p = 0
map(p) = map(p) + M_ITEM_LADDER

' Put exit ladder
p = MW * MH - 1
map(p) = map(p) + M_ITEM_LADDER

' Fill enemies
FOR d = 5 TO 5 + level * 2
    DO
        GOSUB next_rand
        p = #seed % (MW * MH)
    LOOP WHILE map(p) AND M_ITEM_MASK
    GOSUB next_rand
    ' Put tough enemies only near the exit
    IF p / MH < MH / 2 THEN
        IF c THEN c = c - 1
    ELSEIF p % MW < MW / 2 THEN
        IF c THEN c = c - 1
    END IF
    IF c <= 1 THEN map(p) = map(p) + M_ITEM_MONSTER1
    IF c = 2 THEN map(p) = map(p) + M_ITEM_MONSTER2
    IF c = 3 THEN map(p) = map(p) + M_ITEM_MONSTER3
NEXT d

' Fill gold
FOR d = 1 to 3
    DO
        GOSUB next_rand
        p = #seed % (MW * MH)
    LOOP WHILE map(p) AND M_ITEM_MASK
    map(p) = map(p) + M_ITEM_GOLD
NEXT d

' Fill chest
FOR d = 1 to 3
    DO
        GOSUB next_rand
        p = #seed % (MW * MH)
    LOOP WHILE map(p) AND M_ITEM_MASK
    map(p) = map(p) + M_ITEM_CHEST
NEXT d

' Unblock starting square
p = 0
map(p) = map(p) - M_ITEM_LADDER
```

```
    ' Show the maze

    CLS
    WAIT
    DEFINE 0,16,walls_bitmaps_0
    WAIT
    DEFINE 16,4,walls_bitmaps_1
    WAIT
    DEFINE 48,16,item_bitmaps
    WAIT

    p = 0
    curdir = 2
    PLAY music_background

explore_dungeon:
    ' Show current 3D view
    GOSUB show_room_3d

stuck:  GOTO stuck
```

The constant *ITEM_LADDERS* is added to the starting square (not really going to be used, but instead to mark a square where no monsters or items can appear).

The exit ladder is put into the bottom-right corner of the maze.

Now a number of enemies is filled into the maze; the *DO/LOOP* sentences enclose an empty random cell selection. The same is done with gold and chests.

Finally, the *ITEM_LADDER* value is removed from the starting square.

The graphics are loaded, the background music starts to play, and the pseudo-3D view is displayed.

Let us add also the background music at the end of the source code:

```
music_background:
    DATA 14
    MUSIC D4Y,D3W,-,M1
    MUSIC E4,S,-,M2
    MUSIC F4,D3,-,M3
    MUSIC S,S,-,M2
    MUSIC S,D3,-,M1
```

```
MUSIC S,S,-,M2
MUSIC G4,D3,-,M1
MUSIC A4,S,-,M2
MUSIC G4,G3,-,M3
MUSIC S,S,-,M2
MUSIC S,G3,-,M1
MUSIC S,S,-,M2
MUSIC F4,G3,-,M1
MUSIC E4,S,-,M2
MUSIC F4,D3,-,M3
MUSIC S,S,-,M2
MUSIC S,D3,-,M1
MUSIC S,S,-,M2
MUSIC E4,D3,-,M1
MUSIC D4,S,-,M2
MUSIC E4,C3,-,M3
MUSIC S,S,-,M2
MUSIC S,C3,-,M1
MUSIC S,S,-,M2
MUSIC D4,C3,-,M1
MUSIC E4,S,-,M2
MUSIC F4,D3,-,M3
MUSIC S,S,-,M2
MUSIC S,D3,-,M1
MUSIC S,S,-,M2
MUSIC G4,D3,-,M1
MUSIC A4,S,-,M2
MUSIC G4,G3,-,M3
MUSIC S,S,-,M2
MUSIC S,G3,-,M1
MUSIC S,S,-,M2
MUSIC C5,G3,-,M1
MUSIC D5,S,-,M2
MUSIC C5,F3,-,M3
MUSIC S,S,-,M2
MUSIC S,F3,-,M1
MUSIC S,S,-,M2
MUSIC A4,F3,-,M1
MUSIC G4,S,-,M2
MUSIC A4,A3,-,M3
MUSIC S,S,-,M2
MUSIC S,A3,-,M1
MUSIC S,S,-,M2
MUSIC A4,A3,-,M1
MUSIC C5,S,-,M2
MUSIC D5,D4,-,M2
MUSIC S,S,-,M3
MUSIC S,D4,-,M2
```

```
MUSIC S,S,-,M3
MUSIC E5,D4,-,M1
MUSIC F5,S,-,M2
MUSIC E5,E4,-,M3
MUSIC S,S,-,M2
MUSIC D5,E4,-,M3
MUSIC S,S,-,M2
MUSIC C5,E4,-,M3
MUSIC S,S,-,M2
MUSIC A4,C4,-,M3
MUSIC S,S,-,M2
MUSIC S,C4,-,M1
MUSIC S,S,-,M2
MUSIC G4,C4,-,M1
MUSIC F4,S,-,M2
MUSIC G4,B3,-,M3
MUSIC S,S,-,M2
MUSIC S,B3,-,M1
MUSIC S,S,-,M2
MUSIC F4,B3,-,M1
MUSIC E4,S,-,M2
MUSIC D4,D3,-,M3
MUSIC S,S,-,M2
MUSIC S,D3,-,M1
MUSIC S,S,-,M2
MUSIC E4,D3,-,M1
MUSIC F4,S,-,M2
MUSIC E4,C3,-,M3
MUSIC S,S,-,M2
MUSIC D4,C3,-,M3
MUSIC S,S,-,M2
MUSIC C4,C3,-,M3
MUSIC S,S,-,M2
MUSIC D4,D3,-,M3
MUSIC S,S,-,M2
MUSIC S,D3,-,M1
MUSIC S,S,-,M2
MUSIC S,D3,-,M1
MUSIC S,S,-,M2
MUSIC S,D3,-,M1
MUSIC S,S,-,M2
MUSIC S,D3,-,M1
MUSIC S,S,-,M2
MUSIC S,D3,-,M1
MUSIC S,S,-,M2
MUSIC S,D3,-,M1
MUSIC S,S,-,M3
MUSIC REPEAT
```

The game is not yet compilable by IntyBASIC. We are missing the graphics and pseudo-3D display code.

6.4 Pseudo-3D display of dungeons

The dungeons are displayed in four layers, and the walls require some special graphics not available in GROM.

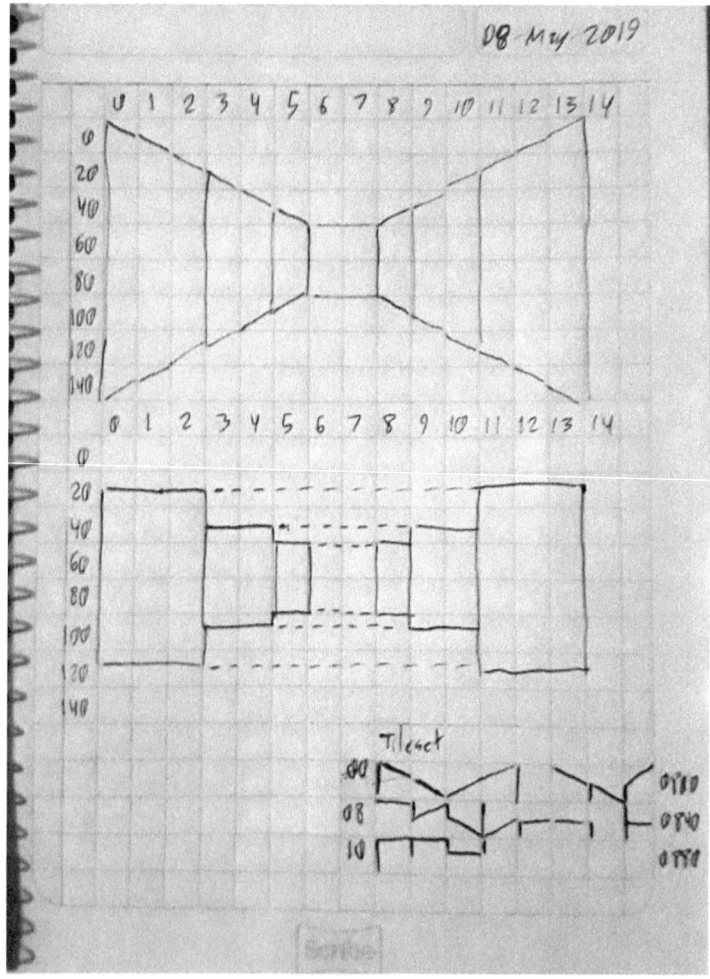

My notebook planning the required tiles for displaying the pseudo-3D dungeons. I went square by square making the GRAM table in the bottom right of the sheet.

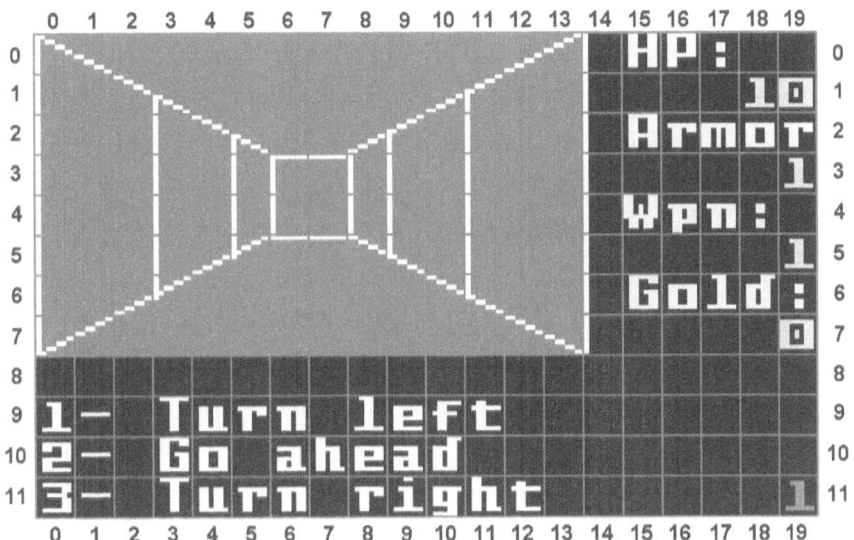

The game screen showing a corridor and the four layers.

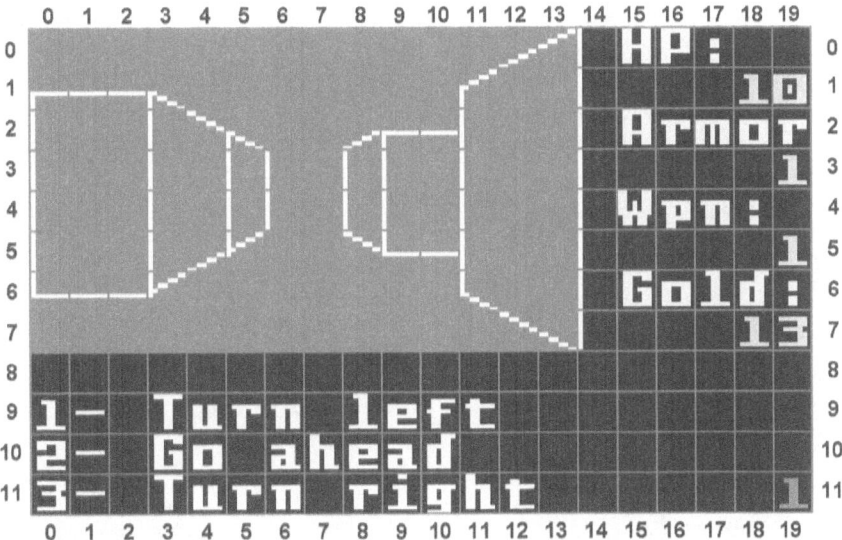

Another game screen to demonstrate the flat walls when a left or right path is available. Also you can see the flat wall in the fourth layer isn't shown here as the corridor keeps going.

If the player were to be displayed, his/her feet would be at row 7, column 7 of screen. From this position the display routine checks if the left side is open or closed, and same for the right side. So for each side there are two options to draw the walls: a diagonal wall, or a flat wall.

Notice how: the first layer has walls with a width of three columns, the next layer has walls with a width of two columns, the third layer has walls with a width of one column, and finally the fourth layer only can be a solid wall or nothing to signal there is more to be explored.

To simplify the drawing of the walls, notice how the white line making the right side of each wall bleeds into the next card (see column 14). These details are visible in the grid, but this is invisible to the player.

Also the Color Stack mode is used in order to have lowercase letters available for the status bars and indications. The color combination is *MODE 0,0,color,0,color;* this means the starting background color is black.

Each card located at column 0 in rows 0-7 must start with Bit 13 set (mask $2000) in order to change to the level color for walls. Also each card located at column 14 must have the mask $2000 in order to go back to the black background.

The graphics for this section of the game are added after the line saying "stuck: goto stuck":

```
        '                                    BITMAP "......XX"
    ' Bitmaps to create the
    ' pseudo-3D view of dungeons          BITMAP "........"   ' 2
        '                                    BITMAP "........"
walls_bitmaps_0:                           BITMAP "........"
    BITMAP "XX......"   ' 0                 BITMAP "........"
    BITMAP "X.XX...."                       BITMAP "......XX"
    BITMAP "X...XX.."                       BITMAP "....XX.."
    BITMAP "X.....XX"                       BITMAP "..XX...."
    BITMAP "X......."                       BITMAP "XX......"
    BITMAP "X......."
    BITMAP "X......."                       BITMAP "......XX"   ' 3
    BITMAP "X......."                       BITMAP "....XX.."
                                            BITMAP "..XX...."
    BITMAP "........"   ' 1                 BITMAP "XX......"
    BITMAP "........"                       BITMAP "........"
    BITMAP "........"                       BITMAP "........"
    BITMAP "........"                       BITMAP "........"
    BITMAP "XX......"                       BITMAP "........"
    BITMAP "..XX...."                       BITMAP "........"
    BITMAP "....XX.."
                                            BITMAP "X......."   ' 4
```

```
BITMAP "X......."             BITMAP "X......."
BITMAP "X......."             BITMAP "........"
BITMAP "X......."             BITMAP "........"
BITMAP "X......."             BITMAP "........"
BITMAP "X......."
BITMAP "X......."             BITMAP "X......."   ' 10
BITMAP "X......."             BITMAP "X......."
                             BITMAP "X......."
BITMAP "XX......"   ' 5       BITMAP "X......."
BITMAP "..XX...."             BITMAP "XX......"
BITMAP "....XX.."             BITMAP "..XX...."
BITMAP "......XX"             BITMAP "....XX.."
BITMAP "........"             BITMAP "......XX"
BITMAP "........"
BITMAP "........"             BITMAP "X......."   ' 11
BITMAP "........"             BITMAP "X......."
                             BITMAP "X......."
BITMAP "........"   ' 6       BITMAP "X......."
BITMAP "........"             BITMAP "X.....XX"
BITMAP "........"             BITMAP "X...XX.."
BITMAP "........"             BITMAP "X.XX...."
BITMAP "XX......"             BITMAP "XX......"
BITMAP "X.XX...."
BITMAP "X...XX.."             BITMAP "........"   ' 12
BITMAP "X.....XX"             BITMAP "........"
                             BITMAP "........"
BITMAP "......XX"   ' 7       BITMAP "........"
BITMAP "....XX.."             BITMAP "XXXXXXXX"
BITMAP "..XX...."             BITMAP "X......."
BITMAP "XX......"             BITMAP "X......."
BITMAP "X......."             BITMAP "X......."
BITMAP "X......."
BITMAP "X......."             BITMAP "........"   ' 13
BITMAP "X......."             BITMAP "........"
                             BITMAP "........"
BITMAP "XXXXXXXX"   ' 8       BITMAP "........"
BITMAP "........"             BITMAP "XXXXXXXX"
BITMAP "........"             BITMAP "........"
BITMAP "........"             BITMAP "........"
BITMAP "........"             BITMAP "........"
BITMAP "........"
BITMAP "........"             BITMAP "........"   ' 14
BITMAP "........"             BITMAP "........"
BITMAP "........"             BITMAP "........"
                             BITMAP "........"
BITMAP "X.....XX"   ' 9       BITMAP "X......."
BITMAP "X...XX.."             BITMAP "X......."
BITMAP "X.XX...."             BITMAP "X......."
BITMAP "XX......"
```

```
        BITMAP "X......."                    item_bitmaps:
                                                BITMAP "......XX"
        BITMAP "X......."   ' 15               BITMAP ".....XXX"
        BITMAP "X......."                      BITMAP ".X...X.X"
        BITMAP "X......."                      BITMAP ".X....XX"
        BITMAP "X......."                      BITMAP ".X...X.X"
        BITMAP "XXXXXXXX"                      BITMAP ".X......"
        BITMAP "X......."                      BITMAP ".X..X.XX"
        BITMAP "X......."                      BITMAP ".X..X..X"
        BITMAP "X......."                      BITMAP ".X.X..XX"
                                                BITMAP ".X.....X"
walls_bitmaps_1:                                BITMAP "XXX...X."
        BITMAP "XXXXXXXX"   ' 16               BITMAP ".X....XX"
        BITMAP "X......."                      BITMAP ".....X.X"
        BITMAP "X......."                      BITMAP ".....X.."
        BITMAP "X......."                      BITMAP "......X."
        BITMAP "X......."                      BITMAP "....XX.."
        BITMAP "X......."
        BITMAP "X......."                      BITMAP "XX......"
                                                BITMAP "XXX....."
        BITMAP "XXXXXXXX"   ' 17               BITMAP ".XX....."
        BITMAP "X......."                      BITMAP "X......."
        BITMAP "X......."                      BITMAP ".X......"
        BITMAP "X......."                      BITMAP "........"
        BITMAP "X......."                      BITMAP "XX.XX..."
        BITMAP "........"                      BITMAP "X...X..."
        BITMAP "........"                      BITMAP "XX.XXXX."
        BITMAP "........"                      BITMAP "X..XX.X."
                                                BITMAP ".X.X.XX."
        BITMAP "X......."   ' 18               BITMAP "XX..XX.."
        BITMAP "X......."                      BITMAP "X.X....."
        BITMAP "X......."                      BITMAP "..X....."
        BITMAP "X......."                      BITMAP ".X......"
        BITMAP "XXXXXXXX"                      BITMAP "..XX...."
        BITMAP "........"
        BITMAP "........"                      BITMAP "........"
        BITMAP "........"                      BITMAP "........"
                                                BITMAP "......XX"
        BITMAP "X......."   ' 19               BITMAP ".....X.."
        BITMAP "X......."                      BITMAP "....XXXX"
        BITMAP "X......."                      BITMAP ".....XXX"
        BITMAP "X......."                      BITMAP ".......X"
        BITMAP "X......."                      BITMAP "......XX"
        BITMAP "........"                      BITMAP ".....XXX"
        BITMAP "........"                      BITMAP "....XX.."
        BITMAP "........"                      BITMAP "....XX.X"
                                                BITMAP "...XX..X"
                                                BITMAP "...XXX.."
```

```
BITMAP "...XXXX."          BITMAP "XXXXX.X."
BITMAP "....XX.."          BITMAP "...XX.X."
BITMAP ".....XXX"          BITMAP "XXXXX.X."
                          BITMAP "X.XXX.X."
BITMAP "........"          BITMAP ".X.XXX.."
BITMAP "........"          BITMAP "XXXX...."
BITMAP "........"          BITMAP "........"
BITMAP "XXX....."
BITMAP "..X....."          BITMAP "..XXXX.."
BITMAP "XXX....."          BITMAP ".X.XX.X."
BITMAP "XX......"          BITMAP "..XXXX.."
BITMAP "XX......"          BITMAP "X..XX..."
BITMAP ".XX....."          BITMAP "X.XXXXXX"
BITMAP ".XXX...."          BITMAP "XX.XX.XX"
BITMAP "...XX..."          BITMAP "..X..X.."
BITMAP ".XXXX..."          BITMAP ".XX..XX."
BITMAP "..XXX..."
BITMAP "X.XXX..."          BITMAP ".XXXXXX."
BITMAP ".XXX...."          BITMAP "..X.XX.."
BITMAP "XXX....."          BITMAP "XX....XX"
                          BITMAP "XX.XXXXX"
BITMAP "........"          BITMAP "XX....XX"
BITMAP "........"          BITMAP "XXXXX.XX"
BITMAP "........"          BITMAP ".X....X."
BITMAP "........"          BITMAP "..X.XX.."
BITMAP "........"
BITMAP "...XXXXX"          BITMAP "........"
BITMAP "..X....."          BITMAP "........"
BITMAP ".XXXXXXX"          BITMAP ".XXXXXX."
BITMAP ".X......"          BITMAP "X.....XX"
BITMAP ".XXXXXXX"          BITMAP "XXXXXX.X"
BITMAP ".X...X.X"          BITMAP "XX..XX.X"
BITMAP ".XXXX.X."          BITMAP "XXXXXXX."
BITMAP ".XX.X..."          BITMAP "XXXXXX.."
BITMAP ".X.X.XXX"
BITMAP ".XXXXXXX"          BITMAP "..X..X.."
BITMAP "........"          BITMAP "..XXXX.."
                          BITMAP "..X..X.."
BITMAP "........"          BITMAP "..XXXX.."
BITMAP "........"          BITMAP "..X..X.."
BITMAP "........"          BITMAP ".XXXXXX."
BITMAP "........"          BITMAP "X.X..X.X"
BITMAP "........"          BITMAP ".XXXXXX."
BITMAP "XXXXXX.."
BITMAP "....XX.."
BITMAP "XXXX..X."
BITMAP "....XXX."
```

The walls' bitmaps from 0 to 19 are the minimum required to draw all the wall combinations that can appear at each depth layer.

The items' bitmaps are all elements that appear in the game. To have a reasonable detail, these are done in a grid of 16x16 pixels.

Before we can run this code we need to implement the pseudo-3D display. Add this code after the line saying "stuck: goto stuck":

```
advance_dir:  PROCEDURE
    IF curdir = 1 THEN p = p - MW
    IF curdir = 2 THEN p = p + 1
    IF curdir = 4 THEN p = p + MW
    IF curdir = 8 THEN p = p - 1
    END

get_item:       PROCEDURE
    d = 0
    c = map(p) AND M_ITEM_MASK
    IF c = M_ITEM_MONSTER1 THEN d = 1: e = 3
    IF c = M_ITEM_MONSTER2 THEN d = 1: e = 5
    IF c = M_ITEM_MONSTER3 THEN d = 1: e = 2
    IF c = M_ITEM_GOLD THEN d = 2: e = 6
    IF c = M_ITEM_CHEST THEN d = 3: e = 3
    IF c = M_ITEM_LADDER THEN d = 4: e = 3
    END

    ASM ORG $D000

    '
    ' Update stats
    '
update_stats: PROCEDURE
    PRINT AT 15 COLOR 6,"HP:"
    PRINT AT 35 COLOR 3,<.5>#hp
    PRINT AT 55 COLOR 6,"Armor"
    PRINT AT 75 COLOR 3,<.5>current_armor
    PRINT AT 95 COLOR 6,"Wpn:"
    PRINT AT 115 COLOR 3,<.5>current_weapon
    PRINT AT 135 COLOR 6,"Gold:"
    PRINT AT 155 COLOR 3,<.5>#gold
```

```
          END

          '
          ' Show a room in 3D view
          ' p = current position at map
          ' curdir = current viewing direction
          '          (1=up 2=right 4=down 8=left)
          '
show_room_3d: PROCEDURE
          save_pos = p

          left = curdir / 2
          IF left = 0 THEN left = 8

          right = curdir * 2
          IF right = 16 THEN right = 1


          '
          ' Clean wall drawing area
          '
          FOR c = 0 TO 140 STEP 20
              IF c = 0 THEN #backtab(c) = 0 ELSE #backtab(c) = $2000
              FOR d = 1 TO 13
                  #backtab(c + d) = 0
              NEXT d
              #backtab(c + 14) = $2000
          NEXT c

          GOSUB update_stats

          ' First depth layer
          IF (map(p) AND left) = 0 THEN      ' Wall at left
              PRINT AT 0,$0807,$080f
              PRINT AT 20,$2827,$0000,$082f
              PRINT AT 40,$2827
              PRINT AT 60,$2827
              PRINT AT 80,$2827
              PRINT AT 100,$2827
              PRINT AT 120,$2827,$0000,$0817
              PRINT AT 140,$285F,$081F
          ELSE ' Open path at left
              PRINT AT 20,$2867,$086F,$086F
              PRINT AT 40,$2827
              PRINT AT 60,$2827
              PRINT AT 80,$2827
              PRINT AT 100,$2827
              PRINT AT 120,$2897,$086F,$086F
```

```
        PRINT AT 140,$2000
END IF

IF (map(p) AND right) = 0 THEN    ' Wall at right
        PRINT AT 12,         $0817,$081f,$2827
        PRINT AT 31,$083f,$0000,$0000,$2827
        PRINT AT 51,$0827,$0000,$0000,$2827
        PRINT AT 71,$0827,$0000,$0000,$2827
        PRINT AT 91,$0827,$0000,$0000,$2827
        PRINT AT 111,$0827,$0000,$0000,$2827
        PRINT AT 131,$0857,$0000,$0000,$2827
        PRINT AT 152,        $082f,$080f,$2827
ELSE ' Open path at right
        PRINT AT 14,                  $2000
        PRINT AT 31,$0867,$086F,$086F,$2877
        PRINT AT 51,$0827,$0000,$0000,$2827
        PRINT AT 71,$0827,$0000,$0000,$2827
        PRINT AT 91,$0827,$0000,$0000,$2827
        PRINT AT 111,$0827,$0000,$0000,$2827
        PRINT AT 131,$0897,$086F,$086f,$289f
        PRINT AT 154,                 $2000
END IF

' Draw item/monster at current depth
GOSUB get_item

IF d = 0 THEN
        SPRITE 0,0
        SPRITE 1,0
ELSEIF d < 4 THEN
        SPRITE 0,$0708+5*8,$0288+4*8-2,$0800+48*8+e+(d - 1) * 4 * 8
        SPRITE 1,$0708+7*8,$0288+4*8-2,$0800+50*8+e+(d - 1) * 4 * 8
ELSE
        SPRITE 0,$0708+6*8,$0208+6*8-2,$0803+63*8
        SPRITE 1,0
END IF

IF (map(p) AND curdir) = 0 THEN    ' Corridor closed
        PRINT AT 23,$0867,$086F,$086F,$086F,$086F,$086F,$086F,$086F
        PRINT AT 43,$0827
        PRINT AT 63,$0827
        PRINT AT 83,$0827
        PRINT AT 103,$0827
        PRINT AT 123,$897,$086F,$086F,$086F,$086F,$086F,$086F,$086F
        p = save_pos
        SPRITE 2,0
        SPRITE 3,0
        SPRITE 4,0
```

```
      RETURN
END IF

' Second depth layer
GOSUB advance_dir

IF (map(p) AND left) = 0 THEN       ' Wall at left
      PRINT AT 23,$0837
      PRINT AT 43,$0827,$082F
      PRINT AT 63,$0827
      PRINT AT 83,$0827
      PRINT AT 103,$0827,$0817
      PRINT AT 123,$084F
ELSE ' Open path at left
      PRINT AT 23,$0877
      PRINT AT 43,$087F,$086F
      PRINT AT 63,$0827
      PRINT AT 83,$0827
      PRINT AT 103,$087F,$086F
      PRINT AT 123,$089F
END IF

IF (map(p) AND right) = 0 THEN      ' Wall at right
      PRINT AT 30,          $0817
      PRINT AT 49,$083F
      PRINT AT 69,$0827
      PRINT AT 89,$0827
      PRINT AT 109,$0857
      PRINT AT 130,          $082F
ELSE ' Open path at right
      PRINT AT 49,$0867,$086F
      PRINT AT 69,$0827
      PRINT AT 89,$0827
      PRINT AT 109,$0897,$086F
END IF

' Draw item/monster at current depth
GOSUB get_item

IF d = 0 THEN
      SPRITE 2,0
      SPRITE 3,0
ELSEIF d < 4 THEN
      SPRITE 2,$0308+6*8,$0188+4*8,$0800+48*8+e+(d - 1) * 4 * 8
      SPRITE 3,$0308+7*8,$0188+4*8,$0800+50*8+e+(d - 1) * 4 * 8
ELSE
      SPRITE 2,$0308+6*8+4,$0108+5*8,$0803+63*8
      SPRITE 3,0
```

```
    END IF

    IF (map(p) AND curdir) = 0 THEN   ' Closed corridor
        PRINT AT 45,$0867,$086F,$086F,$086F
        PRINT AT 65,$0827
        PRINT AT 85,$0827
        PRINT AT 105,$0897,$086F,$086F,$086F
        p = save_pos
        SPRITE 4,0
        RETURN
    END IF

    IF blind THEN ' If blind cannot see further
        SPRITE 4,0
        RETURN
    END IF

    ' Third depth layer
    GOSUB advance_dir

    IF (map(p) AND left) = 0 THEN     ' Wall at left
        PRINT AT 45,$0837
        PRINT AT 65,$0827
        PRINT AT 85,$0827
        PRINT AT 105,$084F
    ELSE ' Open path at left
        PRINT AT 45,$0877
        PRINT AT 65,$0887
        PRINT AT 85,$0827
        PRINT AT 105,$088F
    END IF

    IF (map(p) AND right) = 0 THEN    ' Wall at right
        PRINT AT 48,$0817
        PRINT AT 68,$0827
        PRINT AT 88,$0827
        PRINT AT 108,$082F
    ELSE ' Open path at right
        PRINT AT 68,$0887
        PRINT AT 88,$0827
        PRINT AT 108,$0847
    END IF

    ' Draw item/monster at current depth
    GOSUB get_item

    IF d = 0 THEN
        SPRITE 4,0
```

```
    ELSEIF d < 4 THEN
        SPRITE 4,$0308+6*8+4,$010a+4*8,$0800+60*8+e+(d - 1) * 8
    ELSE
        SPRITE 4,$0308+6*8+4,$0008+5*8-2,$0803+63*8
    END IF

    ' Fourth depth layer
    IF (map(p) AND curdir) = 0 THEN   ' Closed corridor
        PRINT AT 66,$0887,$0847
        PRINT AT 86,$0827
        PRINT AT 106,$0847,$0847
        p = save_pos
        RETURN
    END IF

    PRINT AT 66,$0827   ' Corridor keeps going
    PRINT AT 86,$0827

    p = save_pos
    END
```

The *advance_dir* procedure causes the current position to advance in the current viewing direction. It is used to advance through each depth layer for display.

The *get_item* procedure returns the type of object located at the current position in order to display it using sprites.

The *update_stats* procedure is used at each step to show the current stats at the right side of the screen, like the HP (Health Points).

The *show_room_3d* procedure is in charge of doing the full show of the pseudo-3D display. It receives from *p* the current position on the map, and *curdir* contains the current viewing direction as a bitmask using the same format of map cells (for example, 0x01 = Up).

To get the current left direction, the *curdir* mask is shifted to the right using a division by 2. If the resulting value is zero then it is changed to 8 as if it was a circular bit rotation, and assigned to the *left* variable. To get the current right direction, the *curdir* mask is shifted to the left using a multiplication by 2. If the resulting value is 16 then it is changed to 1 as if it was a circular bit rotation, and assigned to the *right* variable.

The first step in updating the display is to clear the area where the walls will be drawn. The *c* variable loops from 0 to 140 (the eight rows at top of the screen) and as explained before puts a $2000 card value at the first column, cleans to zero the following 13 columns, and finally puts a $2000 card value in the column 14.

The drawing of the first depth layer is straightforward. It checks the *map* array with the current position and does a logical AND operation to confirm if there is a wall or not at the left. It does same with the right side. Then it calls *get_item* in order to draw the sprite (if any) at the current depth. Notice it uses *SPRITE 0* and *1* in order to get the highest viewing priority, so a monster/treasure located near the player is shown over any other sprite. Finally it checks if the corridor is closed and draws a wall if that is the case, or calls *advance_dir* to get to the next map cell.

The drawing of the second and third depth layers is pretty much the same. The only difference is the sprite scaling: the first layer uses 16x16 double X and Y scaling (x2 in both directions for a total size of 32x32), the second layer uses 16x16 no scaling (x1 in both directions), and the third layer uses sprites drawn specially for 8x8 size.

When returning if a corridor is closed, it makes sure the remaining sprites are cleared, otherwise trash could remain on screen. It also restores the *p* variable because it contains the player position.

By the way, each **PRINT** statement uses hexadecimal values and this is interpreted by IntyBASIC as a direct value to be written into video memory. Remember this value is calculated as *$0800 + card_number * 8 + color*, where *color* is always 7 = white, and the *card_number* is one from the walls bitmaps, and *$0800* indicates to the STIC processor that the graphic is taken from the GRAM definable cards.

6.5 Player interface

The player interface reads the current map cell in order to choose the course of action. The player is only allowed to move if there is nothing in the way.

This code replaces the line saying "stuck: goto stuck".

```
' Battle or item
GOSUB clear_status
c = map(p) AND M_ITEM_MASK
map(p) = map(p) AND NOT M_ITEM_MASK
IF c = M_ITEM_MONSTER1 THEN
    c = 1
    GOSUB battle_monster
    IF #hp = 0 THEN GOTO game_over
    GOSUB show_room_3d
ELSEIF c = M_ITEM_MONSTER2 THEN
    c = 2
    GOSUB battle_monster
    IF #hp = 0 THEN GOTO game_over
    GOSUB show_room_3d
ELSEIF c = M_ITEM_MONSTER3 THEN
    c = 3
    GOSUB battle_monster
    IF #hp = 0 THEN GOTO game_over
    GOSUB show_room_3d
ELSEIF c = M_ITEM_GOLD THEN
    sound_effect = EFFECT_CHEST
    sound_state = 0
    c = RANDOM(200) + 10
    PRINT AT 180,"You've found"
    PRINT AT 200,<>c," pieces of gold"
    #gold = #gold + c
    GOSUB wait_for_read
    GOSUB show_room_3d
ELSEIF c = M_ITEM_CHEST THEN
    sound_effect = EFFECT_CHEST
    sound_state = 0
    c = RANDOM(5)
    IF c = 0 THEN
        PRINT AT 160,"You've found"
        c = RANDOM(3) + level - 1
        IF c > 4 THEN c = 4
        IF c = 0 THEN PRINT AT 180,"leather armor (+1)"
        IF c = 1 THEN PRINT AT 180,"ring mail (+2)"
        IF c = 2 THEN PRINT AT 180,"studded leather (+3)"
        IF c = 3 THEN PRINT AT 180,"scale mail (+4)"
        IF c = 4 THEN PRINT AT 180,"chain mail (+5)"
        PRINT AT 200,"Do you want to wear"
        PRINT AT 220,"it? 1-Yes, 0-No"
        DO
            GOSUB read_keypad
        LOOP WHILE d <> 0 AND d <> 1
```

```
                IF d = 1 THEN
                    current_armor = c + 1
                END IF
            ELSEIF c = 1 THEN
                PRINT AT 160,"You've found a"
                c = RANDOM(3) + level - 1
                IF c > 4 THEN c = 4
                IF c = 0 THEN PRINT AT 180,"dagger (+1)"
                IF c = 1 THEN PRINT AT 180,"short sword (+2)"
                IF c = 2 THEN PRINT AT 180,"mace (+3)"
                IF c = 3 THEN PRINT AT 180,"long sword(+4)"
                IF c = 4 THEN PRINT AT 180,"two handed sword(+5)"
                PRINT AT 200,"Do you want to use"
                PRINT AT 220,"it? 1-Yes, 0-No"
                DO
                    GOSUB read_keypad
                LOOP WHILE d <> 0 AND d <> 1
                IF d = 1 THEN
                    current_weapon = c + 1
                END IF
            ELSEIF c = 2 THEN
                PRINT AT 180,"You've found a"
                PRINT AT 200,"health potion!"
                #hp = #hp + #max_hp / 2
                IF #hp > #max_hp THEN #hp = #max_hp
            ELSEIF c = 3 THEN
                PRINT AT 160,"It contains evil"
                PRINT AT 180,"magic!!!"
                c = RANDOM(3)
                IF c = 0 THEN
                    PRINT AT 200,"Your armor"
                    PRINT AT 220,"disintegrated!!!"
                    current_armor = current_armor / 2
                ELSEIF c = 1 THEN
                    PRINT AT 200,"Fog everywhere!!!"
                    blind = 10 + RANDOM(10)
                ELSEIF c = 2 THEN
                    PRINT AT 200,"A succubus sucks your"
                    PRINT AT 220,"health!!!"
                    #hp = (#hp + 1) / 2
                END IF
            ELSEIF c = 4 THEN
                PRINT AT 180,"Nothing!!!"
            END IF
            GOSUB wait_for_read
            GOSUB show_room_3d
    ELSEIF c = M_ITEM_LADDER THEN
        sound_effect = EFFECT_LADDER
```

```
        sound_state = 0
        PRINT AT 180,"You've found a"
        PRINT AT 200,"ladder going down!"
        GOSUB wait_for_read
        #max_hp = #max_hp * 2
        #hp = (#hp + #max_hp) / 2
        level = level + 1
        IF level < 6 THEN GOTO generate_maze

        PLAY music_victory
        CLS
        GOSUB clear_sprites

        PRINT AT 2 COLOR 7,"YOU'RE A HERO!!!"

        PRINT AT 40 COLOR 6,"Upon descending you"
        PRINT AT 60,"find a tunnel that"
        PRINT AT 80,"goes out of the"
        PRINT AT 100,"catacombs! You're"
        PRINT AT 120,"now at a cliff, and"
        PRINT AT 140,"you can see a path"
        PRINT AT 160,"that promises new"
        PRINT AT 180,"adventures."

        PRINT AT 205 COLOR 3,<>#gold," gold"
        PRINT AT 227 COLOR 3,"Level ",<>level
        GOSUB read_keypad

        GOTO title_screen
    END IF

    GOSUB clear_status

    PRINT AT 180 COLOR 7,"1- Turn left"
    PRINT AT 200 COLOR 7,"2- Go ahead"
    PRINT AT 220 COLOR 7,"3- Turn right"

    GOSUB read_keypad

    IF d = 1 THEN
        curdir = curdir / 2
        IF curdir = 0 THEN curdir = 8
    END IF
    IF d = 2 THEN
        IF (map(p) AND curdir) <> 0 THEN
            sound_effect = EFFECT_WALKING
            sound_state = 0
            GOSUB advance_dir
```

```
            IF blind THEN blind = blind - 1
        END IF
    END IF
    IF d = 3 THEN
        curdir = curdir * 2
        IF curdir = 16 THEN curdir = 1
    END IF
    GOTO explore_dungeon
```

Let us take a break to explain what the code is doing. First, it assigns the variable c to contain the monster/object in the current map cell and ANDs it with *M_ITEM_MASK*. Then it removes it from the map cell, and proceeds to do comparisons with each possible item.

The monsters *M_ITEM_MONSTER1*, *M_ITEM_MONSTER2*, and *M_ITEM_MONSTER3* are processed immediately as battles by calling *battle_monster* and exiting to *game_over* if the HP is 0.

The item *M_ITEM_GOLD* adds a random quantity of gold to the player's stash. Notice the gold is only an extra feature here and cannot be used for anything.

The chest (*M_ITEM_CHEST*) can contain one of five things: armor, weapon, health, evil magic (further subdivided into no armor, blindness, and a succubus sucking your health), or nothing.

Finally, *M_ITEM_LADDER* allows the player to descend to another dungeon. When reaching level 6 a victory message appears, and after waiting for the keypad, it returns to the title screen.

When no items or monsters are found, it shows a small guide indicating the keypad buttons to turn left, turn right, or advance in the current direction.

Turning to the left or right uses the same trick shown in *show_room_3d*, circularly bit-shifting the current direction.

When advancing in the current direction, it decreases the variable *blind* if non-zero, in order to remove the effect of blindness (if found in chest).

```
game_over:
    CLS
    MODE 0,2,2,2,2
    WAIT
    PLAY music_game_over

    GOSUB clear_sprites

    PRINT AT 68 COLOR 7,"\100\104\105\101"
    PRINT AT 88      ,"\147\095\000\095\133"
    PRINT AT 108     ,"\160\158\095\128\135"
    PRINT AT 128     ,"\196\196\196\143"
    PRINT AT 148     ,"\098\102\103\164\164"

    PRINT AT 184 COLOR 0,"You're dead!"
    PRINT AT 205 COLOR 0,<>#gold," gold"
    PRINT AT 227 COLOR 0,"Level ",<>level
    GOSUB read_keypad

    GOTO title_screen
```

The Game Over screen uses only the GROM available cards, and these are displayed using *PRINT* and embedding the numeric GROM code along the backslash character. It can be a good tip when you are running low on ROM space.

The grid for the Game Over screen.

Some utility subroutines are necessary for the game to work:

```
read_keypad:  PROCEDURE
    FOR d = 0 TO 15
        WAIT
    NEXT d

    DO
        WAIT
    LOOP WHILE cont.key = 12

    d = cont.key
    END

clear_sprites:     PROCEDURE
    FOR c = 0 TO 7
        SPRITE c, 0
    NEXT c
    END

clear_status: PROCEDURE
    FOR c = 160 TO 238
        #backtab(c) = 0
    NEXT c
    #backtab(239) = $0082 + level * 8
    PRINT COLOR 7
    END

wait_for_read:     PROCEDURE
    FOR d = 0 TO 60
        WAIT
    NEXT d
    END
```

The procedure *read_keypad* debounces the keypad, and waits for a key to be pressed, assigning the number of the pressed key to the *d* variable.

The procedure *clear_sprites* simply removes all sprites from screen. The procedure *clear_status* cleans the bottom four rows of the screen, and puts the level number in the bottom-right corner. Finally, *wait_for_read* is a small delay of one second so the player can read the messages.

```
    '
    ' Battle monster
    ' c = Monster (1-3)
```

```
    '
battle_monster:          PROCEDURE
     monster_type = c + level
     monster_hp = monster_type * monster_type * 2

     DO
         damage = RANDOM(current_weapon * 10 + 1)

         GOSUB clear_status
         IF damage = 0 THEN
             PRINT AT 180,"You miss!!!"
             sound_effect = EFFECT_MISS
             sound_state = 0
         ELSE
             IF damage > monster_hp THEN damage = monster_hp
             PRINT AT 180,"You hit for ",<>damage
             PRINT AT 200,"damage"
             sound_effect = EFFECT_HIT
             sound_state = 0
         END IF

         GOSUB wait_for_read

         monster_hp = monster_hp - damage
         IF monster_hp = 0 THEN EXIT DO

         damage = RANDOM(monster_type + 1)
         IF current_armor > damage THEN
             damage = 0
         ELSE
             damage = damage - current_armor
         END IF

         GOSUB clear_status

         IF damage > #hp THEN damage = #hp

         IF damage = 0 THEN
             PRINT AT 180,"Monster miss"
             sound_effect = EFFECT_MISS
             sound_state = 0
         ELSE
             PRINT AT 180,"Monster hits you"
             PRINT AT 200,"for ",<>damage," damage!"
             sound_effect = EFFECT_HIT
             sound_state = 0
         END IF
         #hp = #hp - damage
```

```
        GOSUB update_stats

        GOSUB wait_for_read

        IF #hp = 0 THEN EXIT DO

    LOOP UNTIL #hp < 1 OR monster_hp < 1

    IF #hp = 0 THEN
        GOSUB clear_status
        PRINT AT 180,"You've been killed!"
    ELSE
        GOSUB clear_status
        PRINT AT 180,"Monster killed!!!"
        c = RANDOM(50)
        IF c THEN PRINT AT 200,<>c," gold found"
        #gold = #gold + c
    END IF
    GOSUB wait_for_read

    END
```

The *battle_monster* procedure assigns a Health Points value to the monster based on the type and depth inside the dungeon. The damage is calculated randomly as the current weapon multiplied by ten, plus one. The monster damage to the player is calculated randomly as the number of monster plus the depth level.

If the monster is defeated then a random quantity of gold is added to the player's *#gold* variable.

To almost complete the game, add these Game Over and Victory melodies at the end of the code:

```
music_game_over:
    DATA 10
    MUSIC A3W,A4W,-,M1
    MUSIC S,S,-,-
    MUSIC E4,E5,-,-
    MUSIC S,S,-,-
    MUSIC C4,C5,-,-
    MUSIC S,S,-,-
    MUSIC E4,E5,-,-
    MUSIC S,S,-,-
```

```
MUSIC A4,A5,-,M2
MUSIC S,S,-,-
MUSIC E4,E5,-,-
MUSIC S,S,-,-
MUSIC C4,C5,-,-
MUSIC S,S,-,-
MUSIC E4,E5,-,M1
MUSIC S,S,-,-
MUSIC G3,G4,-,-
MUSIC S,S,-,-
MUSIC D4,D5,-,-
MUSIC S,S,-,-
MUSIC B3,B4,-,M1
MUSIC S,S,-,M1
MUSIC D4,D5,-,M1
MUSIC S,S,-,-
MUSIC G4,G5,-,-
MUSIC S,S,-,-
MUSIC D4,D5,-,-
MUSIC S,S,-,-
MUSIC B3,B4,-,-
MUSIC S,S,-,-
MUSIC D4,D5,-,-
MUSIC S,S,-,-
MUSIC A4,A5,-,M1
MUSIC S,S,-,-
MUSIC F4,F5,-,-
MUSIC S,S,-,-
MUSIC D4,D5,-,-
MUSIC S,S,-,-
MUSIC C4,C5,-,-
MUSIC S,S,-,-
MUSIC B3,B4,-,-
MUSIC S,S,-,-
MUSIC A3,A4,-,-
MUSIC S,S,-,-
MUSIC G3#,G4#,-,-
MUSIC S,S,-,-
MUSIC E3,E4,-,-
MUSIC S,S,-,-
MUSIC G3#,G4#,-,-
MUSIC S,S,-,-
MUSIC A3,A4,-,-
MUSIC S,S,-,-
MUSIC B3,B4,-,-
MUSIC S,S,-,-
MUSIC C4,C5,-,-
MUSIC S,S,-,-
```

```
      MUSIC D4,D5,-,-
      MUSIC S,S,-,-
      MUSIC C4,C5,-,-
      MUSIC S,S,-,-
      MUSIC A3,A4,-,M3
      MUSIC S,S,-,-
      MUSIC STOP

music_victory:
      DATA 10
      MUSIC E4X,A3W,-,M1
      MUSIC S,S,-,-
      MUSIC G4,C3,-,M2
      MUSIC S,S,-,-
      MUSIC C5,D3,-,M1
      MUSIC S,S,-,-
      MUSIC A4,C3,-,M2
      MUSIC S,S,-,-
      MUSIC S,A2,-,M1
      MUSIC S,S,-,-
      MUSIC S,C3,-,M2
      MUSIC S,S,-,-
      MUSIC E4,D3,-,M1
      MUSIC S,S,-,-
      MUSIC S,E3,-,M2
      MUSIC S,S,-,-
      MUSIC S,E3,-,M1
      MUSIC S,S,-,-
      MUSIC D4,A2,-,M2
      MUSIC S,S,-,-
      MUSIC S,E3,-,M1
      MUSIC S,S,-,-
      MUSIC G4,A2,-,M2
      MUSIC S,S,-,-
      MUSIC E4,E3,-,M1
      MUSIC S,S,-,-
      MUSIC S,A2,-,M2
      MUSIC S,S,-,-
      MUSIC S,E3,-,M1
      MUSIC S,S,-,-
      MUSIC D4,A2,-,M2
      MUSIC S,S,-,-
      MUSIC S,E3,-,M1
      MUSIC S,S,-,-
      MUSIC E4,A2,-,M2
      MUSIC S,S,-,-
      MUSIC S,E3,-,M1
      MUSIC S,S,-,-
```

```
MUSIC D4,A2,-,M2
MUSIC S,S,-,-
MUSIC S,E3,-,M1
MUSIC S,S,-,-
MUSIC A3,A2,-,M2
MUSIC S,S,-,-
MUSIC A3,E3,D2W,M1
MUSIC S,S,E3,-
MUSIC S,A2,F2,M2
MUSIC S,S,G3,-
MUSIC S,E3,A2,M1
MUSIC S,S,-,-
MUSIC S,A2,-,M2
MUSIC S,S,-,-
MUSIC S,E3,-,M1
MUSIC S,S,-,-
MUSIC S,A2,-,M2
MUSIC S,S,-,-
MUSIC S,E3,-,M1
MUSIC S,S,-,-
MUSIC S,A2,-,M2
MUSIC S,S,-,-
MUSIC S,E3,-,M1
MUSIC S,S,-,-
MUSIC S,A2,-,M2
MUSIC S,S,-,-
MUSIC S,-,-,M1
MUSIC S,-,-,-
MUSIC S,-,-,M2
MUSIC S,-,-,-
MUSIC S,-,-,M1
MUSIC S,-,-,-
MUSIC STOP
```

6.6 Sound effects

The sound effects are the last thing remaining to implement in Dungeon Warrior. As with all the other games shown in this book, the sound effects are generated using the pseudo multitask capability of IntyBASIC, and the *play_effects* procedure is called in each video frame.

Add this as the first line of the program:

```
ON FRAME GOSUB play_effects
```

And add this just before the *music_background* label:

```
play_effects: PROCEDURE
    ON sound_effect GOSUB sound_none, sound_walking, sound_chest,
sound_ladder, sound_miss, sound_hit
    END

sound_none:  PROCEDURE
    SOUND 2,1,0
    END

sound_walking:    PROCEDURE
    SOUND 2,3072,12
    sound_state = sound_state + 1
    IF sound_state = 8 THEN sound_effect = 0
    END

sound_chest:  PROCEDURE
    IF sound_state AND 2 THEN
        SOUND 2,480 - sound_state * 16,12
    ELSE
        SOUND 2,64 + sound_state * 16,12
    END IF
    sound_state = sound_state + 1
    IF sound_state = 16 THEN sound_effect = 0
    END

sound_ladder: PROCEDURE
    IF sound_state AND 4 THEN
        SOUND 2,2048,12
    ELSE
        SOUND 2,,0
    END IF
    sound_state = sound_state + 1
    IF sound_state = 32 THEN sound_effect = 0
    END

sound_miss:  PROCEDURE
    IF sound_state AND 2 THEN
        SOUND 2,1024,12
    ELSE
        SOUND 2,512,12
    END IF
    sound_state = sound_state + 1
```

```
    IF sound_state = 16 THEN sound_effect = 0
    END

sound_hit:    PROCEDURE
    SOUND 2,64 - sound_state * 2,12
    sound_state = sound_state + 1
    IF sound_state = 16 THEN sound_effect = 0
    END
```

The sound effects used in this game are a walking sound effect, an opening chest sound effect, a descending ladder sound effect, a missed hit sound effect, and a successful hit sound effect.

,

Appendix A

Tombs surrounding a tile

This is a small C program that calculates the tombs surrounding a tile. As I wanted it to be easy to understand, it has a small representation of the Intellivision screen as array *screen*. You can see the X characters representing a tomb, while the dots represent the positions where the player can walk.

It circulates the 16x9 array generating the numbers of the tombs that surround each walkable tile.

```
/*
** Calculate squares referred from screen
**
** by Oscar Toledo G.
**
** Creation date: Dec/13/2016.
*/

#include <stdio.h>
#include <string.h>

char screen[12][20] = {
    "                    ",
    "                    ",
    "    ................    ",
    "    .XX.XX.XX.XX.XX.    ",
    "    ................    ",
    "    .XX.XX.XX.XX.XX.    ",
    "    ................    ",
    "    .XX.XX.XX.XX.XX.    ",
    "    ................    ",
```

```c
    "  .XX.XX.XX.XX.XX.   ",
    "  ..............   ",
    "                   ",
};

/*
** Main program
*/
int main(void)
{
  int x;
  int y;
  int array[4];
  int c;
  int a;
  int b;
  int d;

  for (y = 2; y < 11; y++) {     /* Row */
    for (x = 2; x < 18; x++) {   /* Column */
      array[0] = -1;
      array[1] = -1;
      array[2] = -1;
      array[3] = -1;
      if (screen[y][x] == '.') {
        for (a = -1; a <= 1; a++) {
          for (b = -1; b <= 1; b++) {
            if (screen[y + a][x + b] == 'X') {
              c = ((y + a) - 3) / 2 * 5 + ((x + b) / 3) - 1;
              d = 0;
              while (array[d] != -1 && array[d] != c) {
                d++;
                if (d == 4) {
                  fprintf(stderr, "boink\n");
                  break;
                }
              }
              array[d] = c;
            }
          }
        }
      }
      printf("\tDATA %d,%d,%d,%d\n",
        array[0], array[1], array[2], array[3]);
    }
  }
}
```

238

Appendix B

Boogie-woogie generator

I was watching a video teaching how to play boogie-woogie style songs on the piano keyboard, and although I thought I learned it, I forgot it very fast.

But not enough that I couldn't write a program that follows the principles taught in the video!

```c
/*
** Generate boogie-woogie music
**
** by Oscar Toledo G.
**
** Creation date: Oct/24/2018.
*/

#include <stdio.h>
#include <stdlib.h>
#include <time.h>

#define ALL_NOTES       // Use all three channels

#define OFFSET_ADJUST  0

char left_pattern[3][8] = {
    13,
    13,
    16,
    17,
    20,
    13,
    22,
```

```c
  20,
};

char right_pattern[6][8] = {
  25, 32, 25, 34, 25, 37, 25, 34,
  37, 25, 34, 31, 32, 25,  0,  0,
  25, 32, 34, 32, 25,  0,  0,  0,
  41,  0, 41,  0, 41,  0, 41,  0,
  41, 41, 41, 41, 41, 41, 41, 41,
  41,  0,  0,  0, 41,  0,  0,  0,
};

char right_pattern2[6][8] = {
   0, 29,  0, 30,  0, 32,  0, 30,
  32,  0, 30, 28, 29,  0,  0,  0,
   0, 29, 30, 29,  0,  0,  0,  0,
  49,  0, 49,  0, 49,  0, 49,  0,
  49, 49, 49, 49, 49, 49, 49, 49,
  49,  0,  0,  0, 49,  0,  0,  0,
};

/*
** Left pattern 1: (3rd octave)
** C - C - Eb - E - G - C - A - G
** Transpose to F
** Transpose to G
**
** Right hand:
** E5 G5 A5 C6 (C6 chord)
** One time per chord
** Then two times per chord (half)
** Then four times per chord (quarter)
** Then swing eighth notes
** Then triplets
**
** D5# G5 A5 C6 (F chord)
** F5 G5 B5 D6 (G chord)
**
** Right hand lick:
** C E+G C F + A C G + C5 C F + A C E + G
**
** Right hand lick variation 1:
** G+C5 C F+A D#+F# E+G C
**
** Right hand lick variation 2:
** C E+G F+A E+G C
**
** Options:
```

```
** One left
** One left, one right (repeat)
*+
** One left, one right
** One left, one right.
**
** Two times, elevate one note, two times.
** Go back, two times, elevate two notes, two times.
*/


/*
** The notes are arranged per the internal
** IntyBASIC tracker note numbers.
*/
char *notes[64] = {
  "-",

  "C2", "C2#", "D2", "D2#",
  "E2", "F2", "F2#", "G2",
  "G2#", "A2", "A2#", "B2",

  "C3", "C3#", "D3", "D3#",
  "E3", "F3", "F3#", "G3",
  "G3#", "A3", "A3#", "B3",

  "C4", "C4#", "D4", "D4#",
  "E4", "F4", "F4#", "G4",
  "G4#", "A4", "A4#", "B4",

  "C5", "C5#", "D5", "D5#",
  "E5", "F5", "F5#", "G5",
  "G5#", "A5", "A5#", "B5",

  "C6", "C6#", "D6", "D6#",
  "E6", "F6", "F6#", "G6",
  "G6#", "A6", "A6#", "B6",

  "C7",
  "?",
  "S",
};

int tables[6][64] = {
  {0, 0, 0, -1, 0, 0, 0, -1, 99},
  {0, 0, 0, 0, 0, 0, 0, 0, 99},
  {0, 0, 0, 0, 5, 5, 7, 7, 99},
  {0, 0, 5, 5, 7, 7, 5, 5, 99},
  {0, 0, 0, 0, 5, 5, 5, 5, 5, 5, 5, 5, 7, 7, 7, 7, 7, 7, 7, 7, 99},
```

```c
  {0, 0, 0, 0, 7, 7, 7, 7, 99},
};

/*
** Main program
*/
int main(void)
{
  int base;
  int vivace;
  int vivace_step;
  int c;
  int d;
  int e;
  int f;
  int g;
  int h;
  int prev_d;
  int pat1;
  int pat2;
  unsigned int seed;

  srand(seed = time(0));
  printf("\tFOR c = 0 TO 60\n");
  printf("\t\tWAIT\n");
  printf("\tNEXT c\n");
  printf("\tPLAY FULL\n");
  printf("\tPLAY music_1\n");
  printf("\tWHILE 1: WEND\n");
  printf("\n");
  printf("\t' Automagically generated by boogie.c srand(%d)\n",
          seed);
  printf("music_1:\n");
  printf("\tDATA 6\n");

  prev_d = 3;
  vivace = -1;
  vivace_step = 0;
  for (c = 0; c < 60; c++) {
    if (vivace == -1) {
      vivace = rand() % 6;
      vivace_step = 0;
    }
    do {
      d = rand() % 6;
    } while (prev_d >= 3 && d >= 3) ;
    prev_d = d;
    pat1 = tables[vivace][vivace_step * 2] + OFFSET_ADJUST;
```

```c
    pat2 = tables[vivace][vivace_step * 2 + 1];
    if (pat2 != -1)
      pat2 += OFFSET_ADJUST;
    for (e = 0; e < 8; e++) {
      printf("\tMUSIC ");
      f = left_pattern[0][e];
      if (f) {
        f += pat1;
      }
      printf("%s", notes[f]);
      if (pat2 == -1) {
        g = 0;
        h = 0;
        printf(",-");
      } else {
        g = right_pattern[d][e];
        if (g) {
          g += pat2;
        }
#ifdef ALL_NOTES
        h = right_pattern2[d][e];
        if (h) {
          h += pat2;
        }
#else
        h = 0;
#endif
        printf(",%s,%s", notes[g], notes[h]);
      }
      printf(",-\n\0\t' %d,%d,%d,%d\n", vivace, vivace_step, d, e);
      if (e & 1) {
        printf("\tMUSIC %s,%s,%s\n",
          f ? "S" : "-", g ? "S" : "-", h ? "S" : "-");
      }
    }
    vivace_step++;
    if (tables[vivace][vivace_step * 2] == 99)
      vivace = -1;
  }
  printf("\tMUSIC STOP\n");
}
```

Appendix C

GROM table

This is a reference card of the GROM table. To avoid manual errors (and a lot of work) it has been generated automatically by a special program written by myself so it looks like an old Texas Instruments video databook.

The graphics for codes 213 onwards aren't included because these contain executable code from the Intellivision ROM and fall under copyright constraints. You can think of these as random noise.

Each card includes the offset number into ROM (hexadecimal on the left side, and decimal on the right side), and you can use it directly in IntyBASIC by using the backlash along with the number in the *PRINT* statement. For example, for the exclamation point:

```
PRINT COLOR 5 "\1"
```

Or if you want to directly use the code to be put on the screen:

```
PRINT 1 * 8 + 5
```

It is the same but we do all the work, including offsetting the card number by 3 bits (multiplication by 8), and adding the color number.

You can also use these cards for generating the reverse shapes. For example, in Color Stack mode with setup MODE 0,0,7,0,7 you can use the mask $2000 to change backgrounds between black/white.

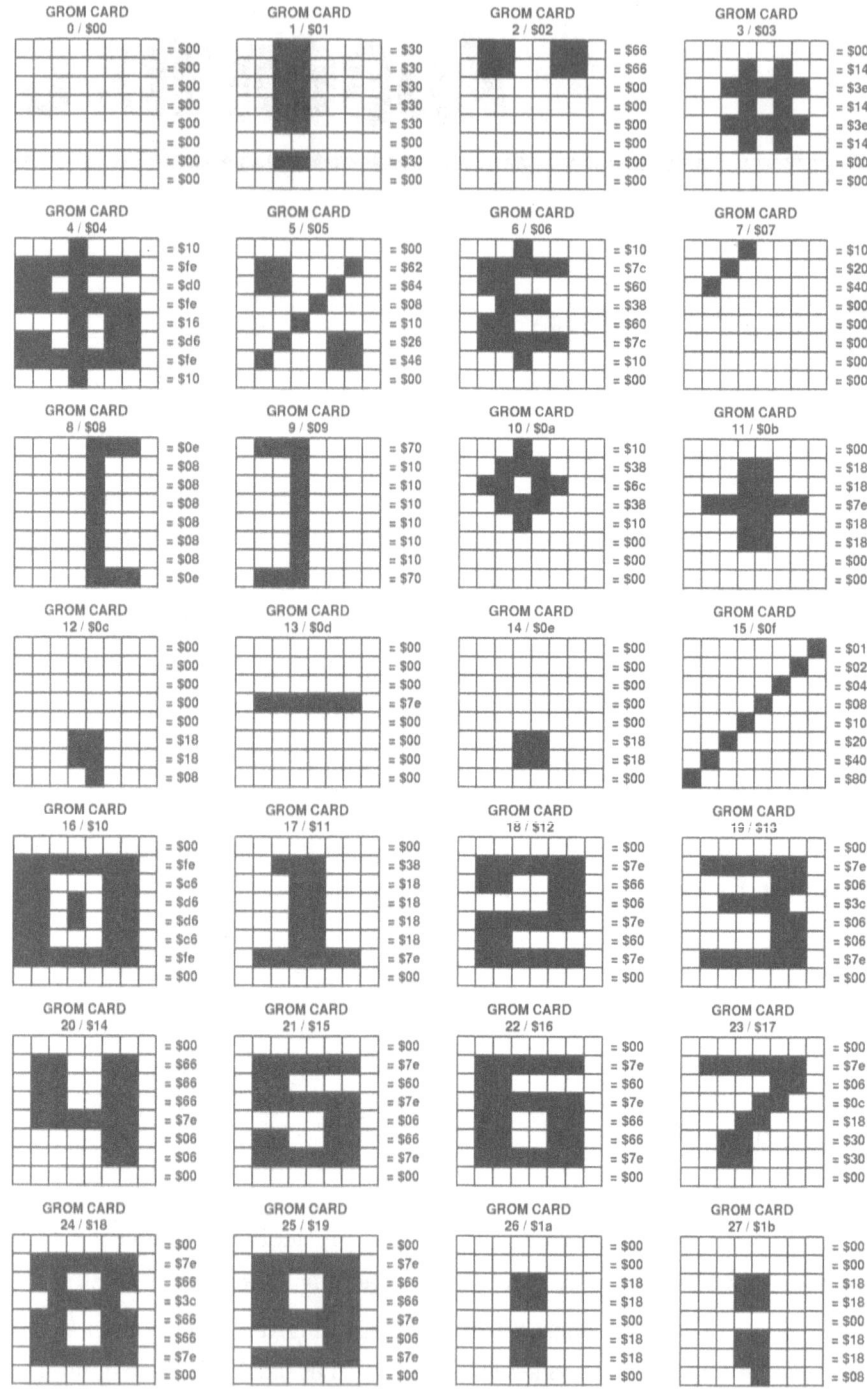

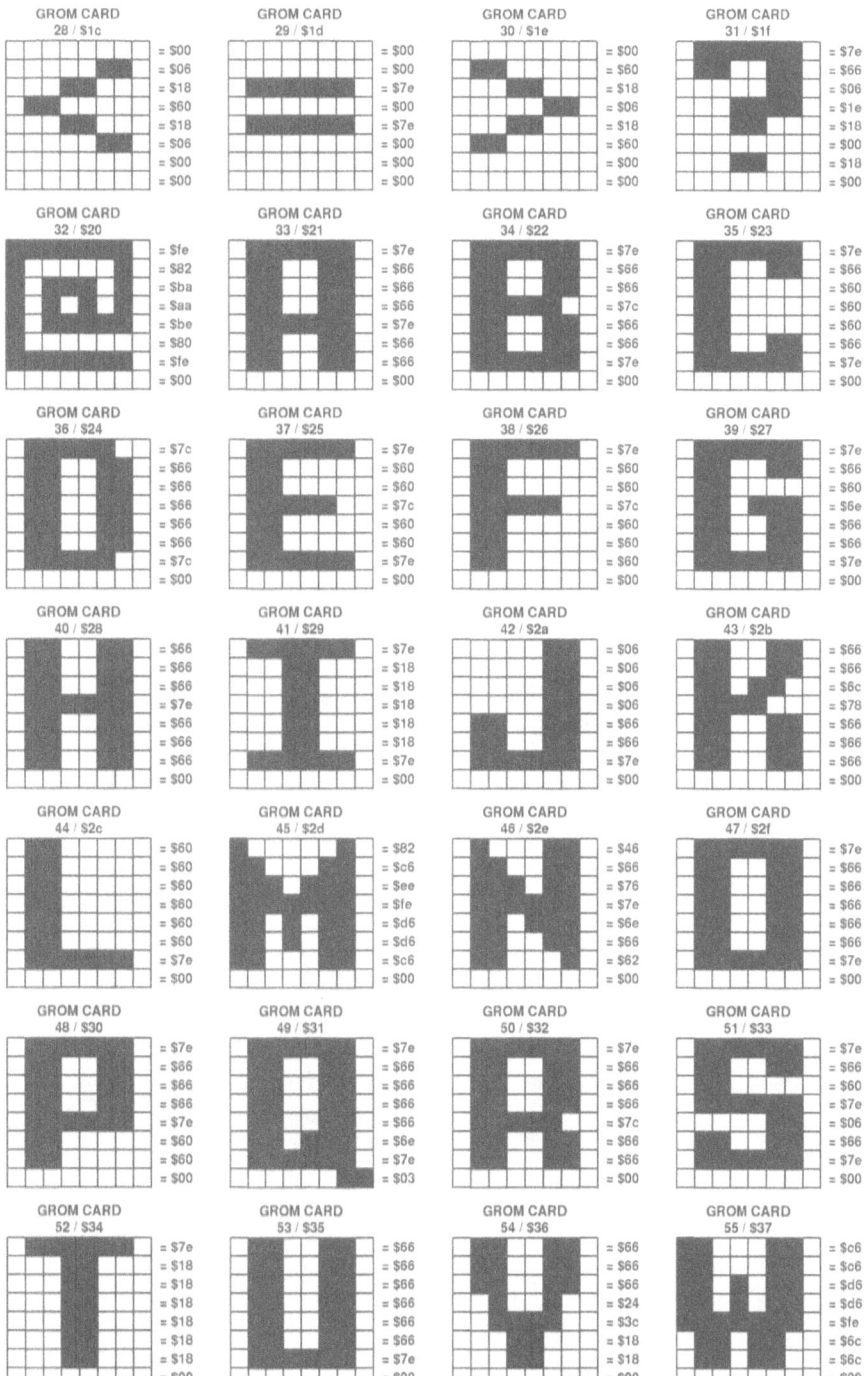

GROM CARD 28 / $1c
= $00
= $06
= $18
= $60
= $18
= $06
= $00
= $00

GROM CARD 29 / $1d
= $00
= $00
= $7e
= $00
= $7e
= $00
= $00
= $00

GROM CARD 30 / $1e
= $00
= $60
= $18
= $06
= $18
= $60
= $00
= $00

GROM CARD 31 / $1f
= $7e
= $66
= $06
= $1e
= $18
= $00
= $18
= $00

GROM CARD 32 / $20
= $fe
= $82
= $ba
= $aa
= $be
= $80
= $fe
= $00

GROM CARD 33 / $21
= $7e
= $66
= $66
= $66
= $7e
= $66
= $66
= $00

GROM CARD 34 / $22
= $7e
= $66
= $66
= $7c
= $66
= $66
= $7e
= $00

GROM CARD 35 / $23
= $7e
= $66
= $60
= $60
= $60
= $66
= $7e
= $00

GROM CARD 36 / $24
= $7c
= $66
= $66
= $66
= $66
= $66
= $7c
= $00

GROM CARD 37 / $25
= $7e
= $60
= $60
= $7c
= $60
= $60
= $7e
= $00

GROM CARD 38 / $26
= $7e
= $60
= $60
= $7c
= $60
= $60
= $60
= $00

GROM CARD 39 / $27
= $7e
= $66
= $60
= $6e
= $66
= $66
= $7e
= $00

GROM CARD 40 / $28
= $66
= $66
= $66
= $7e
= $66
= $66
= $66
= $00

GROM CARD 41 / $29
= $7e
= $18
= $18
= $18
= $18
= $18
= $7e
= $00

GROM CARD 42 / $2a
= $06
= $06
= $06
= $06
= $66
= $66
= $7e
= $00

GROM CARD 43 / $2b
= $66
= $66
= $6c
= $78
= $66
= $66
= $66
= $00

GROM CARD 44 / $2c
= $60
= $60
= $60
= $60
= $60
= $60
= $7e
= $00

GROM CARD 45 / $2d
= $82
= $c6
= $ee
= $fe
= $d6
= $d6
= $c6
= $00

GROM CARD 46 / $2e
= $46
= $66
= $76
= $7e
= $6e
= $66
= $62
= $00

GROM CARD 47 / $2f
= $7e
= $66
= $66
= $66
= $66
= $66
= $7e
= $00

GROM CARD 48 / $30
= $7e
= $66
= $66
= $66
= $7e
= $60
= $60
= $00

GROM CARD 49 / $31
= $7e
= $66
= $66
= $66
= $66
= $6e
= $7e
= $03

GROM CARD 50 / $32
= $7e
= $66
= $66
= $66
= $7c
= $66
= $66
= $00

GROM CARD 51 / $33
= $7e
= $66
= $60
= $7e
= $06
= $66
= $7e
= $00

GROM CARD 52 / $34
= $7e
= $18
= $18
= $18
= $18
= $18
= $18
= $00

GROM CARD 53 / $35
= $66
= $66
= $66
= $66
= $66
= $66
= $7e
= $00

GROM CARD 54 / $36
= $66
= $66
= $66
= $24
= $3c
= $18
= $18
= $00

GROM CARD 55 / $37
= $c6
= $c6
= $d6
= $d6
= $fe
= $6c
= $6c
= $00

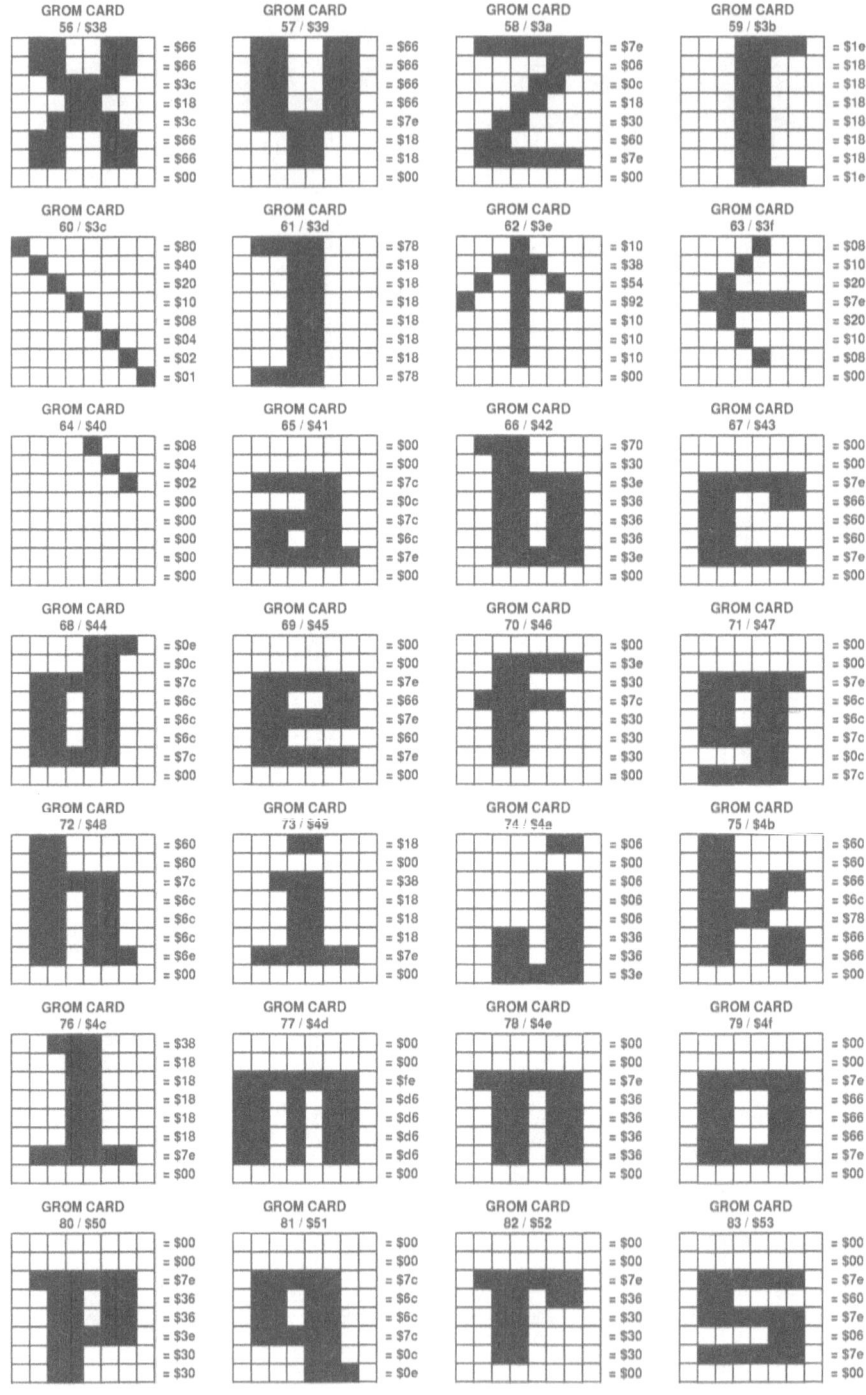

GROM CARD 56 / $38
= $66, = $66, = $3c, = $18, = $3c, = $66, = $66, = $00

GROM CARD 57 / $39
= $66, = $66, = $66, = $66, = $7e, = $18, = $18, = $00

GROM CARD 58 / $3a
= $7e, = $06, = $0c, = $18, = $30, = $60, = $7e, = $00

GROM CARD 59 / $3b
= $1e, = $18, = $18, = $18, = $18, = $18, = $18, = $1e

GROM CARD 60 / $3c
= $80, = $40, = $20, = $10, = $08, = $04, = $02, = $01

GROM CARD 61 / $3d
= $78, = $18, = $18, = $18, = $18, = $18, = $18, = $78

GROM CARD 62 / $3e
= $10, = $38, = $54, = $92, = $10, = $10, = $10, = $00

GROM CARD 63 / $3f
= $08, = $10, = $20, = $7e, = $20, = $10, = $08, = $00

GROM CARD 64 / $40
= $08, = $04, = $02, = $00, = $00, = $00, = $00, = $00

GROM CARD 65 / $41
= $00, = $00, = $7c, = $0c, = $7c, = $6c, = $7e, = $00

GROM CARD 66 / $42
= $70, = $30, = $3e, = $36, = $36, = $36, = $3e, = $00

GROM CARD 67 / $43
= $00, = $00, = $7e, = $66, = $60, = $60, = $7e, = $00

GROM CARD 68 / $44
= $0e, = $0c, = $7c, = $6c, = $6c, = $6c, = $7c, = $00

GROM CARD 69 / $45
= $00, = $00, = $7e, = $66, = $7e, = $60, = $7e, = $00

GROM CARD 70 / $46
= $00, = $3e, = $30, = $7c, = $30, = $30, = $30, = $00

GROM CARD 71 / $47
= $00, = $00, = $7e, = $6c, = $6c, = $7c, = $0c, = $7c

GROM CARD 72 / $48
= $60, = $60, = $7c, = $6c, = $6c, = $6c, = $6e, = $00

GROM CARD 73 / $49
= $18, = $00, = $38, = $18, = $18, = $18, = $7e, = $00

GROM CARD 74 / $4a
= $06, = $00, = $06, = $06, = $06, = $36, = $36, = $3e

GROM CARD 75 / $4b
= $60, = $60, = $66, = $6c, = $78, = $66, = $66, = $00

GROM CARD 76 / $4c
= $38, = $18, = $18, = $18, = $18, = $18, = $7e, = $00

GROM CARD 77 / $4d
= $00, = $00, = $fe, = $d6, = $d6, = $d6, = $d6, = $00

GROM CARD 78 / $4e
= $00, = $00, = $7e, = $36, = $36, = $36, = $36, = $00

GROM CARD 79 / $4f
= $00, = $00, = $7e, = $66, = $66, = $66, = $7e, = $00

GROM CARD 80 / $50
= $00, = $00, = $7e, = $36, = $36, = $3e, = $30, = $30

GROM CARD 81 / $51
= $00, = $00, = $7c, = $6c, = $6c, = $7c, = $0c, = $0e

GROM CARD 82 / $52
= $00, = $00, = $7e, = $36, = $30, = $30, = $30, = $00

GROM CARD 83 / $53
= $00, = $00, = $7e, = $60, = $7e, = $06, = $7e, = $00

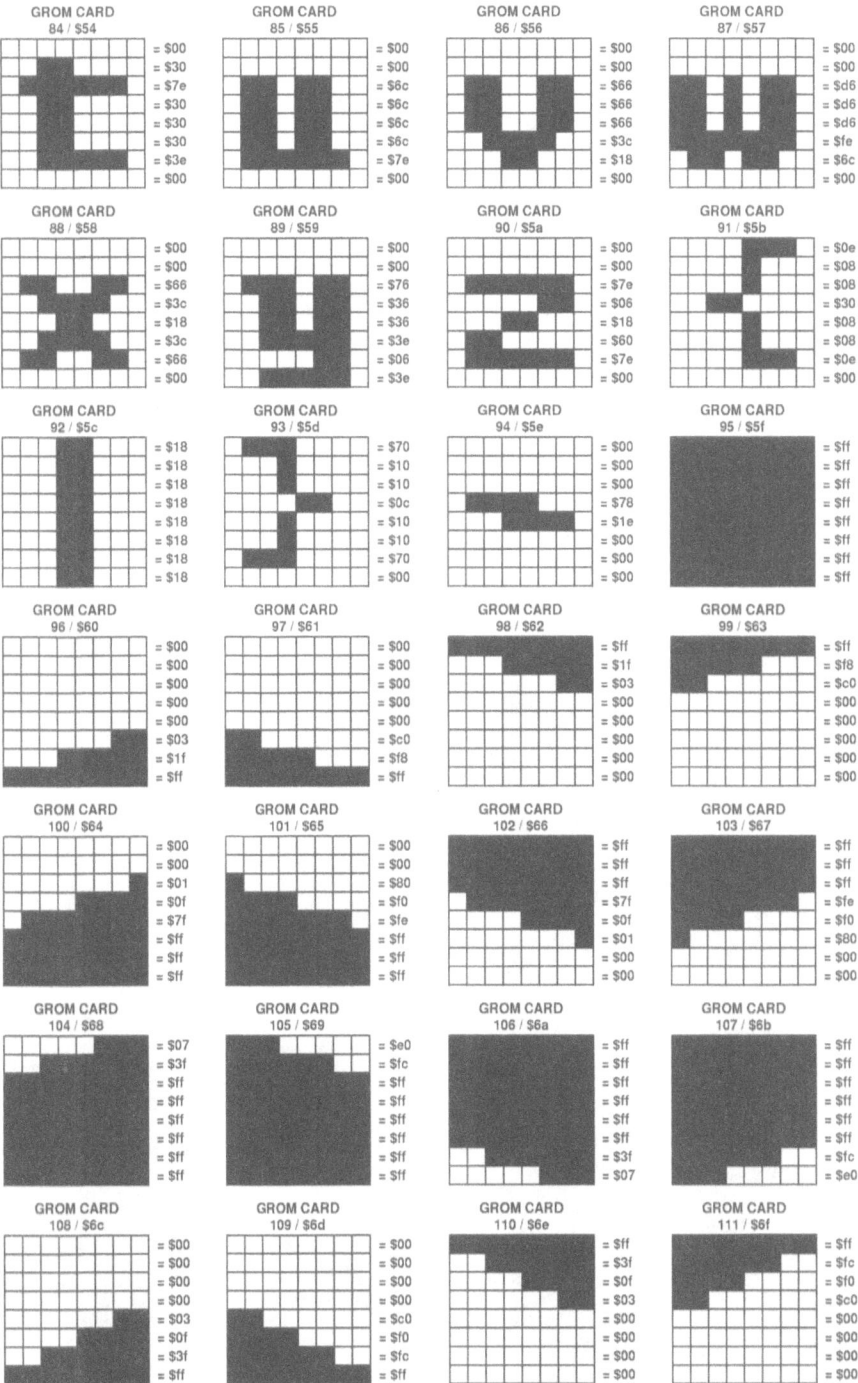

GROM CARD
84 / $54

= $00
= $30
= $7e
= $30
= $30
= $30
= $3e
= $00

GROM CARD
85 / $55

= $00
= $00
= $6c
= $6c
= $6c
= $6c
= $7e
= $00

GROM CARD
86 / $56

= $00
= $00
= $66
= $66
= $66
= $3c
= $18
= $00

GROM CARD
87 / $57

= $00
= $00
= $d6
= $d6
= $d6
= $fe
= $6c
= $00

GROM CARD
88 / $58

= $00
= $00
= $66
= $3c
= $18
= $3c
= $66
= $00

GROM CARD
89 / $59

= $00
= $00
= $76
= $36
= $36
= $3e
= $06
= $3e

GROM CARD
90 / $5a

= $00
= $00
= $7e
= $06
= $18
= $60
= $7e
= $00

GROM CARD
91 / $5b

= $0e
= $08
= $08
= $30
= $08
= $08
= $0e
= $00

GROM CARD
92 / $5c

= $18
= $18
= $18
= $18
= $18
= $18
= $18
= $18

GROM CARD
93 / $5d

= $70
= $10
= $10
= $0c
= $10
= $10
= $70
= $00

GROM CARD
94 / $5e

= $00
= $00
= $00
= $78
= $1e
= $00
= $00
= $00

GROM CARD
95 / $5f

= $ff
= $ff
= $ff
= $ff
= $ff
= $ff
= $ff
= $ff

GROM CARD
96 / $60

= $00
= $00
= $00
= $00
= $00
= $03
= $1f
= $ff

GROM CARD
97 / $61

= $00
= $00
= $00
= $00
= $00
= $c0
= $f8
= $ff

GROM CARD
98 / $62

= $ff
= $1f
= $03
= $00
= $00
= $00
= $00
= $00

GROM CARD
99 / $63

= $ff
= $f8
= $c0
= $00
= $00
= $00
= $00
= $00

GROM CARD
100 / $64

= $00
= $00
= $01
= $0f
= $7f
= $ff
= $ff
= $ff

GROM CARD
101 / $65

= $00
= $00
= $80
= $f0
= $fe
= $ff
= $ff
= $ff

GROM CARD
102 / $66

= $ff
= $ff
= $ff
= $7f
= $0f
= $01
= $00
= $00

GROM CARD
103 / $67

= $ff
= $ff
= $ff
= $fe
= $10
= $80
= $00
= $00

GROM CARD
104 / $68

= $07
= $3f
= $ff
= $ff
= $ff
= $ff
= $ff
= $ff

GROM CARD
105 / $69

= $e0
= $fc
= $ff
= $ff
= $ff
= $ff
= $ff
= $ff

GROM CARD
106 / $6a

= $ff
= $ff
= $ff
= $ff
= $ff
= $ff
= $3f
= $07

GROM CARD
107 / $6b

= $ff
= $ff
= $ff
= $ff
= $ff
= $ff
= $fc
= $e0

GROM CARD
108 / $6c

= $00
= $00
= $00
= $00
= $03
= $0f
= $3f
= $ff

GROM CARD
109 / $6d

= $00
= $00
= $00
= $00
= $c0
= $f0
= $fc
= $ff

GROM CARD
110 / $6e

= $ff
= $3f
= $0f
= $03
= $00
= $00
= $00
= $00

GROM CARD
111 / $6f

= $ff
= $fc
= $f0
= $c0
= $00
= $00
= $00
= $00

249

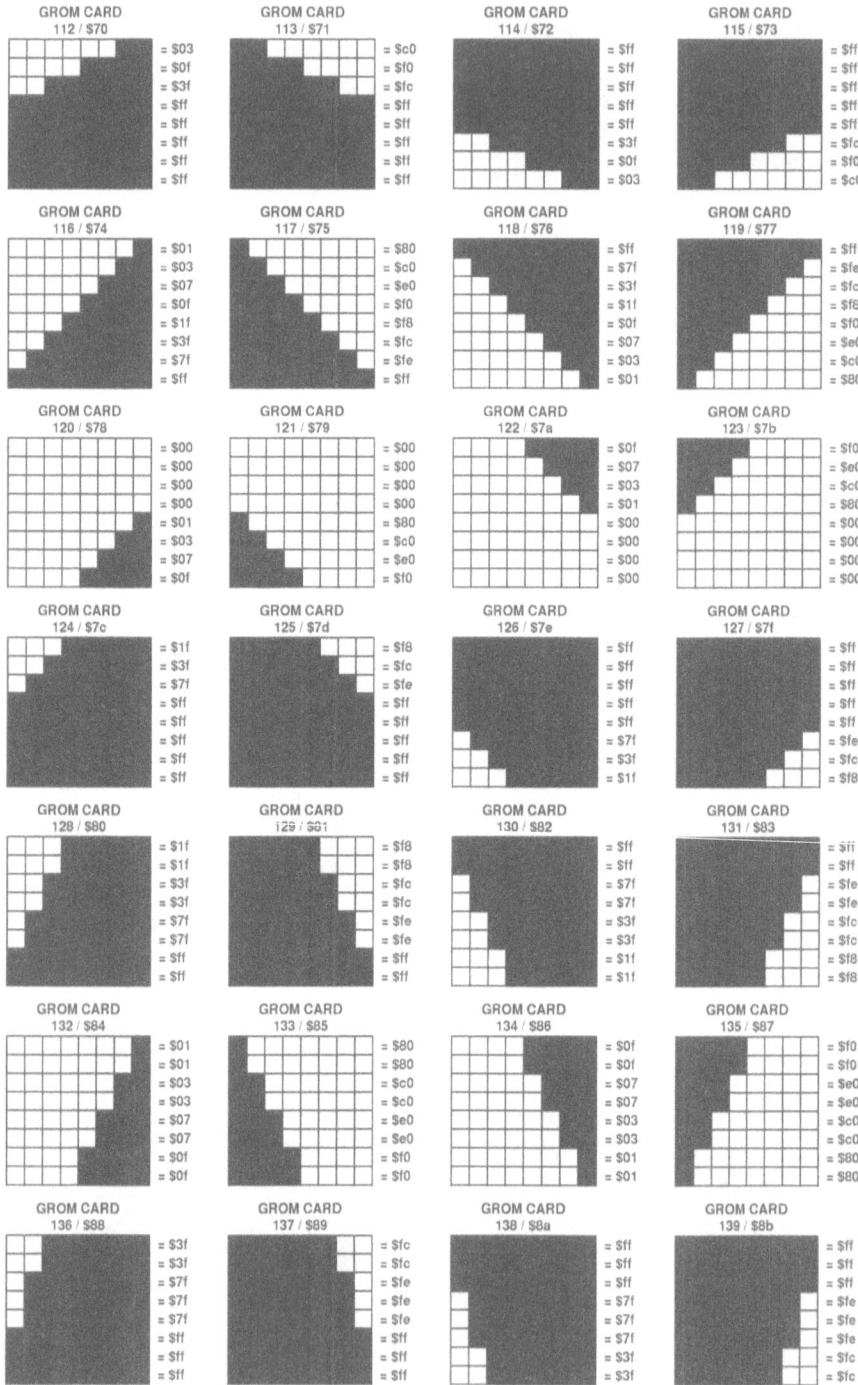

GROM CARD
112 / $70
= $03
= $0f
= $3f
= $ff
= $ff
= $ff
= $ff
= $ff

GROM CARD
113 / $71
= $c0
= $f0
= $fc
= $ff
= $ff
= $ff
= $ff
= $ff

GROM CARD
114 / $72
= $ff
= $ff
= $ff
= $ff
= $ff
= $3f
= $0f
= $03

GROM CARD
115 / $73
= $ff
= $ff
= $ff
= $ff
= $ff
= $fc
= $f0
= $c0

GROM CARD
116 / $74
= $01
= $03
= $07
= $0f
= $1f
= $3f
= $7f
= $ff

GROM CARD
117 / $75
= $80
= $c0
= $e0
= $f0
= $f8
= $fc
= $fe
= $ff

GROM CARD
118 / $76
= $ff
= $7f
= $3f
= $1f
= $0f
= $07
= $03
= $01

GROM CARD
119 / $77
= $ff
= $fe
= $fc
= $f8
= $f0
= $e0
= $c0
= $80

GROM CARD
120 / $78
= $00
= $00
= $00
= $00
= $01
= $03
= $07
= $0f

GROM CARD
121 / $79
= $00
= $00
= $00
= $00
= $80
= $c0
= $e0
= $f0

GROM CARD
122 / $7a
= $0f
= $07
= $03
= $01
= $00
= $00
= $00
= $00

GROM CARD
123 / $7b
= $f0
= $e0
= $c0
= $80
= $00
= $00
= $00
= $00

GROM CARD
124 / $7c
= $1f
= $3f
= $7f
= $ff
= $ff
= $ff
= $ff
= $ff

GROM CARD
125 / $7d
= $f8
= $fc
= $fe
= $ff
= $ff
= $ff
= $ff
= $ff

GROM CARD
126 / $7e
= $ff
= $ff
= $ff
= $ff
= $ff
= $7f
= $3f
= $1f

GROM CARD
127 / $7f
= $ff
= $ff
= $ff
= $ff
= $ff
= $fe
= $fc
= $f8

GROM CARD
128 / $80
= $1f
= $1f
= $3f
= $3f
= $7f
= $7f
= $ff
= $ff

GROM CARD
129 / $81
= $f8
= $f8
= $fc
= $fc
= $fe
= $fe
= $ff
= $ff

GROM CARD
130 / $82
= $ff
= $ff
= $7f
= $7f
= $3f
= $3f
= $1f
= $1f

GROM CARD
131 / $83
= $ff
= $ff
= $fe
= $fe
= $fc
= $fc
= $f8
= $f8

GROM CARD
132 / $84
= $01
= $01
= $03
= $03
= $07
= $07
= $0f
= $0f

GROM CARD
133 / $85
= $80
= $80
= $c0
= $c0
= $e0
= $e0
= $f0
= $f0

GROM CARD
134 / $86
= $0f
= $0f
= $07
= $07
= $03
= $03
= $01
= $01

GROM CARD
135 / $87
= $f0
= $f0
= $e0
= $e0
= $c0
= $c0
= $80
= $80

GROM CARD
136 / $88
= $3f
= $3f
= $7f
= $7f
= $7f
= $ff
= $ff
= $ff

GROM CARD
137 / $89
= $fc
= $fc
= $fe
= $fe
= $fe
= $ff
= $ff
= $ff

GROM CARD
138 / $8a
= $ff
= $ff
= $ff
= $7f
= $7f
= $7f
= $3f
= $3f

GROM CARD
139 / $8b
= $ff
= $ff
= $ff
= $fe
= $fe
= $fe
= $fc
= $fc

250

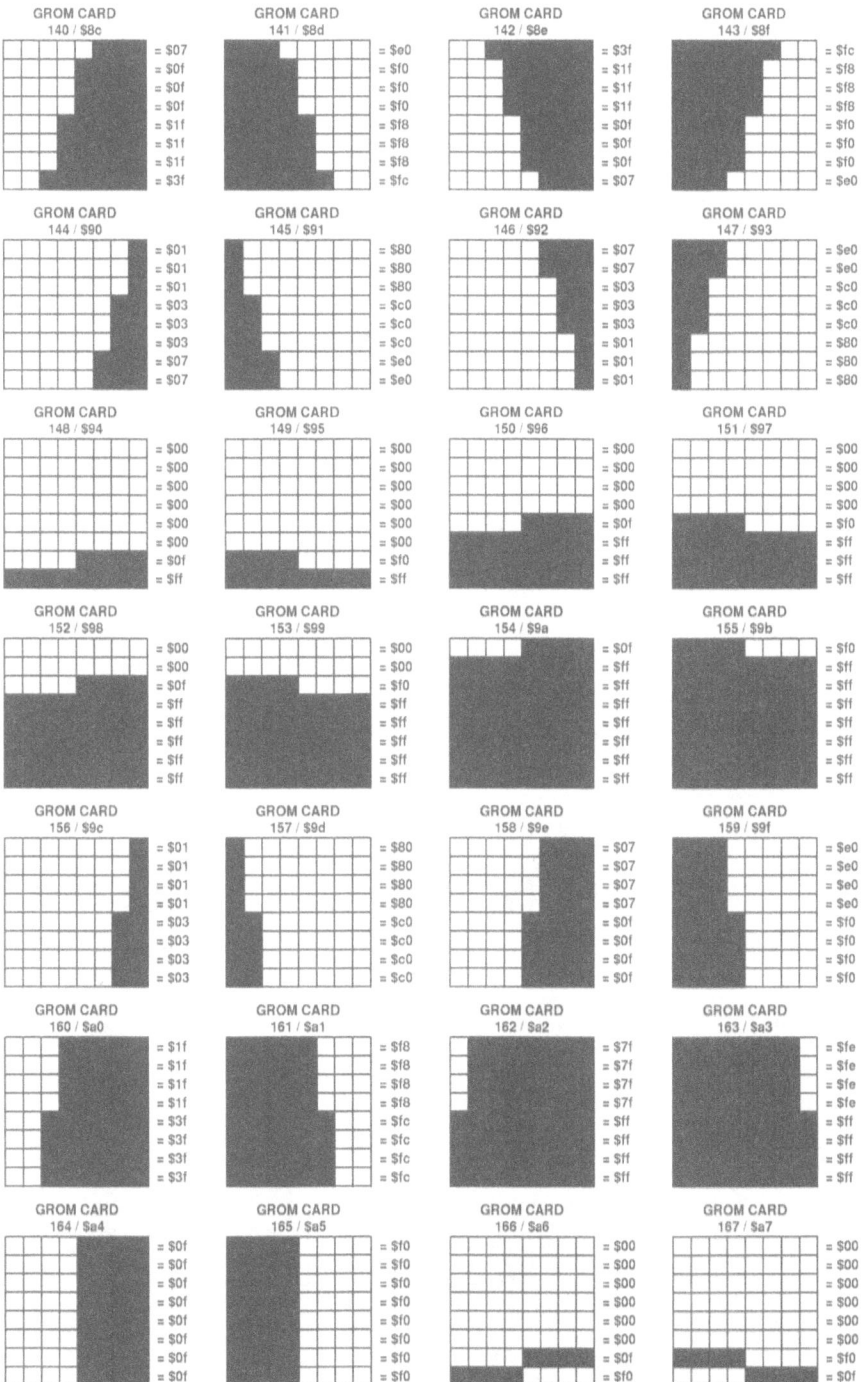

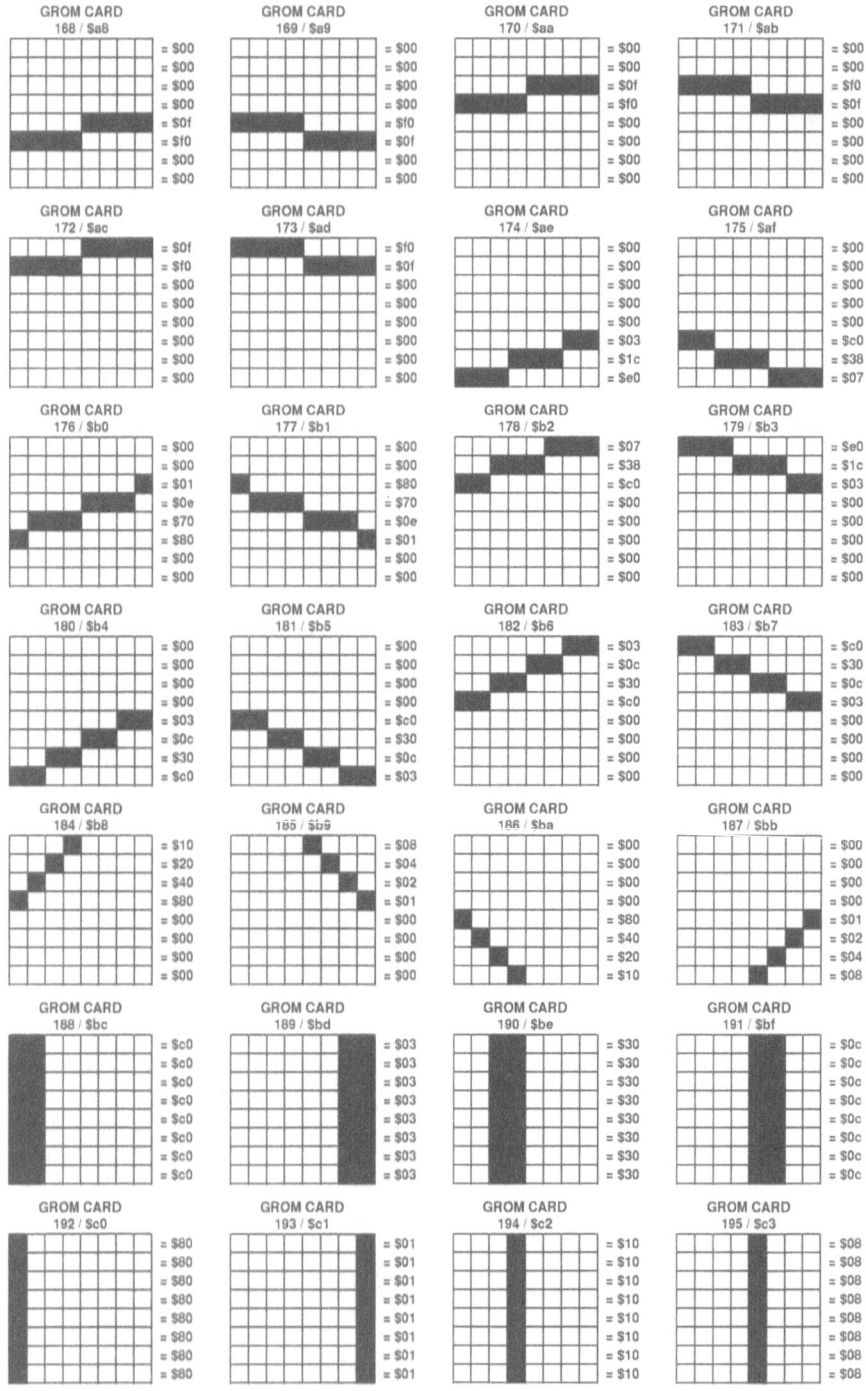

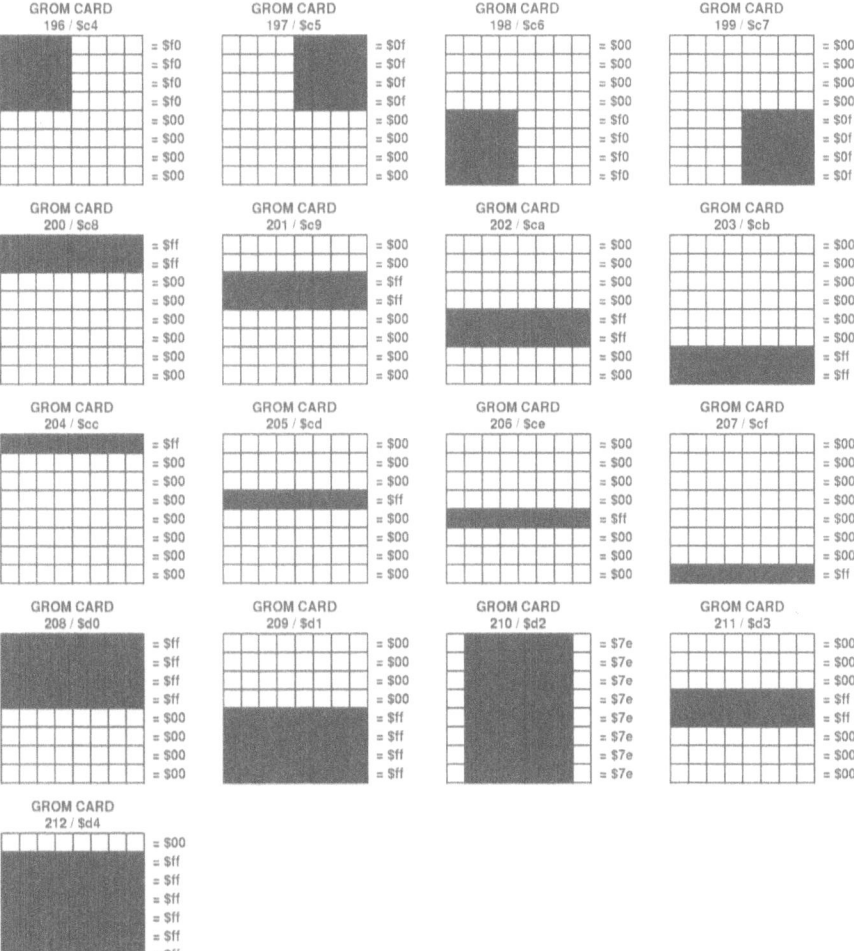

GROM CARD
196 / $c4

= $f0
= $f0
= $f0
= $f0
= $00
= $00
= $00
= $00

GROM CARD
197 / $c5

= $0f
= $0f
= $0f
= $0f
= $00
= $00
= $00
= $00

GROM CARD
198 / $c6

= $00
= $00
= $00
= $00
= $f0
= $f0
= $f0
= $f0

GROM CARD
199 / $c7

= $00
= $00
= $00
= $00
= $0f
= $0f
= $0f
= $0f

GROM CARD
200 / $c8

= $ff
= $ff
= $00
= $00
= $00
= $00
= $00
= $00

GROM CARD
201 / $c9

= $00
= $00
= $ff
= $ff
= $00
= $00
= $00
= $00

GROM CARD
202 / $ca

= $00
= $00
= $00
= $00
= $ff
= $ff
= $00
= $00

GROM CARD
203 / $cb

= $00
= $00
= $00
= $00
= $00
= $00
= $ff
= $ff

GROM CARD
204 / $cc

= $ff
= $00
= $00
= $00
= $00
= $00
= $00
= $00

GROM CARD
205 / $cd

= $00
= $00
= $ff
= $00
= $00
= $00
= $00
= $00

GROM CARD
206 / $ce

= $00
= $00
= $00
= $ff
= $00
= $00
= $00
= $00

GROM CARD
207 / $cf

= $00
= $00
= $00
= $00
= $00
= $00
= $ff

GROM CARD
208 / $d0

= $ff
= $ff
= $ff
= $ff
= $00
= $00
= $00
= $00

GROM CARD
209 / $d1

= $00
= $00
= $00
= $00
= $ff
= $ff
= $ff
= $ff

GROM CARD
210 / $d2

= $7e
= $7e
= $7e
= $7e
= $7e
= $7e
= $7e
= $7e

GROM CARD
211 / $d3

= $00
= $00
= $00
= $ff
= $ff
= $00
= $00
= $00

GROM CARD
212 / $d4

= $00
= $ff
= $ff
= $ff
= $ff
= $ff
= $ff
= $00

Appendix D

Digitized sound

Although in chapter 2 we saw the generation of sound effects and introduction of music sheets, we can also play digitized sound using the PSG chip, albeit with some limitations.

The generation of sound effects updates the PSG chip at least 50 or 60 times per second (the video frame rate). The playing of digitized sound samples requires playing a sample 8000 times per second! In order to do this we need to fully use the CP1610 processor to only play sound samples, so this means the sound samples cannot be played as the game happens, but only in static situations.

The source sound file is a WAV file with 8 kHz. frequency, 16-bit sound samples, and monoaural. It also should be amplified to occupy the full range of volume. All this can be achieved using the Audacity free edition sound software.

Every two samples from the WAV file will be translated into a word. So one second of digitized audio will use 4K words (8K bytes). This is pretty expensive in terms of space (very few effects can be included) but the results can be pretty impressive.

The conversion program is written in C language and goes like this:

```
/*
** Convert WAV to playable AY-3-8910/AY-3-8914
**
** by Oscar Toledo G. (nanochess)
```

```
**
** (c) Copyright 2018 Oscar Toledo G.
**
** Creation date: Sep/18/2018.
** Revision date: Nov/14/2020.
*/

#include <stdio.h>
#include <stdlib.h>

#define VERSION    2

#define EXTRA_VOLUME  1.414

/*
** Create a map of each positive volume value
** (negative values are assumed to be zero)
*/
unsigned char map[32768];

/*
** Here is created a table of volume values in 16-bit range
**
** Each one is equivalent to an AY-3 volume value.
*/
int v[16];

/*
** Main program
*/
int main(int argc, char *argv[])
{
    FILE *a;
    signed short sample[2];
    int size[1];
    int c;
    int d;
    int e;
    int vol;
    int val;
    int min;

    /*
    ** Using a single channel for playing audio.
    **
    ** The coarseness of the volume sample causes it
    ** to be low fidelity.
    */
```

```
#if VERSION == 1   /* Simple and pretty cool */
    val = 32768;
    vol = 32767;
    c = 15;
    while (c >= 1) {
        for (d = vol; d < val; d++)
            map[d] = c;
        c--;
        val = vol;
        vol = vol / 1.414;
    }
#endif

    /*
    ** Using two channels for playing audio.
    **
    ** It can get fine volume control using the two
    ** channels.
    */
#if VERSION == 2

    /*
    ** Get the real 16 volume levels of AY-3-8910
    */
    vol = 32767;
    c = 15;
    while (c >= 1) {
        v[c] = vol;
        vol = vol / 1.414;
        c--;
    }

    /*
    ** Now for each possible positive volume found
    ** on a WAV file, try to get the optimum
    ** combination of volumes for two channels.
    **
    ** It assumes (simplistically) that addition
    ** of volumes is linear.
    */
    for (c = 0; c < 32767; c++) {
        min = 100000;
        vol = 0;
        for (d = 15; d >= 0; d--) { /* Start from louder */
            for (e = 0; e < 16; e++) {   /* Start from quiet */
                /* See difference versus input */
                if (abs(v[d] + v[e] - c) < min) {
                    /* New best difference */
```

```c
                    min = abs(v[d] + v[e] - c);
                    /* Take note of combination */
                    vol = d | (e << 4);
                }
            }
        }
        map[c] = vol; /* Save the best combination */
    }
#endif

    if (argc != 2) {
        fprintf(stderr, "Usage: wave input.wav\n");
        fprintf(stderr, "Where the input file should be ");
        fprintf(stderr, "a 8khz 16-bit mono WAV file\n");
        exit(1);
    }
    a = fopen(argv[1], "rb");
    if (a == NULL) {
        fprintf(stderr, "Couldn't open: %s\n", argv[1]);
        exit(1);
    }
    fseek(a, 0x28, SEEK_SET);
    fread(&size[0], 1, sizeof(size), a);
    size[0] = size[0] / 4;
    printf("test_loop:\n");
    printf("\tDO\n");
    printf("\t\tWAIT\n");
    printf("\tLOOP WHILE cont.key <> 12\n");
    printf("\n");
    printf("\tDO\n");
    printf("\t\tWAIT\n");
    printf("\tLOOP WHILE cont.key = 12\n");
    printf("\n");
    printf("\tCALL play_wave(VARPTR wave(0), %d)\n", size[0]);
    printf("\n");
    printf("\tGOTO test_loop\n");
    printf("\n");
    printf("\tASM INCLUDE \"wave_helper.asm\"\n");
    printf("\n");
    printf("wave: ' %d length\n", size[0]);

    /*
    ** Proceed to convert wave file
    */
    c = 0;
    while (size[0]) {

        /*
```

```
        ** Read two samples each time
        */
        fread(&sample[0], 1, sizeof(sample), a);
        if (sample[0] < 0)
            sample[0] = 0;
        if (sample[1] < 0)
            sample[1] = 0;

        /*
        ** Increase volume
        */
        vol = sample[0] * EXTRA_VOLUME;
        if (vol > 32767) {
            fprintf(stderr, "Exceeded range!\n");
            exit(1);
        }
        val = sample[1] * EXTRA_VOLUME;
        if (val > 32767) {
            fprintf(stderr, "Exceeded range!\n");
            exit(1);
        }

        /*
        ** Map samples as two bytes, fit in a word
        */
        if (c == 0)
            printf("\tDATA ");
        else
            printf(",");
        printf("$%02x%02x", map[val], map[vol]);
        if (c == 7)
            printf("\n");
        c = (c + 1) & 7;
        size[0]--;
    }
    if (c)
        printf("\n");
    fclose(a);
}
```

As the samples are 16-bit, both negative and positive values are
allowed, but the negative values are zero'ed as the AY-3-8914 doesn't allow
negative volume outputs. The positive values (32768 possible options) are
calculated for the most approximate combination of two volume values of

the AY-3-8914. These two volume values are combined in a single byte for every sample.

The command is *wave input.wav >output.bas* and it will create the IntyBASIC source code output based on the input WAV file.

You will need the following *wave_helper.asm* code that is in charge of playing the digitized sound:

```
        ;
        ; Plays a waveform sample at 8 khz.
        ;
        ; by Oscar Toledo G. (nanochess)
        ;
        ; (c) Copyright 2018 Oscar Toledo G.
        ;
        ; Creation date: Sep/18/2018.
        ; Revision date: Nov/14/2020.
        ;


        ;
        ; The commented out code is fine tuning for jzintv.
        ; The timing isn't well known for me.
        ;
PLAY_WAVE_ISR:      PROC
    MVO R0,$20      ; Activates display
    JR R5
    ENDP


        ;
        ; Play wave at 8 khz. (7990 hz. +/-)
        ; Input:
        ;    r0 = address of waveform
        ;    r1 = size in words
        ;
        ; It disables interrupts but keeps screen enabled while playing
        ;
PLAY_WAVE:    PROC
    BEGIN

    MOVR R0,R4

    CLRR R0
    MVO R0,$01FD
    MVII #$3f,R0
    MVO R0,$01F8

    MVII #PLAY_WAVE_ISR,R0
```

```
        DIS
        MVO     R0,ISRVEC
        SWAP    R0
        MVO     R0,ISRVEC+1
        EIS
.1:
        MVI@ R4,R0      ; 8
        MOVR R0,R2      ; 6
        ANDI #$0F,R2    ; 8
        MOVR R0,R3      ; 6
        SLR R3,2        ; 8
        SLR R3,2        ; 8
        ANDI #$0F,R3    ; 8
        MVO R2,$01FB    ; 11
        MVO R3,$01FC    ; 11
;       MVO R3,$01FC    ; 11
        DECR R4         ; 6
        MVI@ R4,R0      ; 8
        TSTR R1         ; 6
        BNE .2          ; 9
.2:
        MVO R0,$20      ; 11
        SWAP R0         ; 6
        MOVR R0,R2      ; 6
        ANDI #$0F,R2    ; 8
        MOVR R0,R3      ; 6
        SLR R3,2        ; 8
        SLR R3,2        ; 8
        ANDI #$0F,R3    ; 8
        MVO R2,$01FB    ; 11
        MVO R3,$01FC    ; 11
;       MVO R3,$01FC    ; 11
        NOP             ; 6
;       NOP             ; 6
        DECR R1         ; 6
        BNE .1          ; 9
        CLRR R0
        MVO R0,$01FB
        MVO R0,$01FC
        MVO R0,$01FD
        MVII #$38,R0
        MVO R0,$01F8

        MVII #_int_vector,R0

        DIS
        MVO     R0,ISRVEC
```

```
        SWAP    R0
        MVO     R0,ISRVEC+1
        EIS
        RETURN

        ENDP
```

For playing back the sound, the mixer register is set to all ones ($3F) in order to keep the outputs high **and** controllable with the volume values.

The volume values are extracted for each sample, and put into the volume registers of the AY-3-8914, then a small wait is done in order to keep the playback frequency to around 8000 samples per second.

When the sound playback is complete, the mixer register is set back to $38, and all volumes are set back to zero.

This same code has been used in my new game Frankenstein's Monster to add a digitized voice phrase in the Game Over screen.

Appendix E

Tips from the Trench

This is a contribution by Michael J. Hayes. Incidentally he is also the proofreader of the book. As we were talking about the book, he came out with some good ideas about some IntyBASIC programming areas, and I told him "I didn't think about that style of focusing it, could you present your ideas as an appendix?" and so, this appendix was born.

E.1 In the beginning

I'm very happy to have this chance to share some of my design tips that I felt could be useful, if there had ever been another IntyBASIC programming book released. Now here we are.

When we were planning the Intellivision Virtual Expo that took place in November 2020, I had first considered taking a lot of time to go into excruciating "behind the scenes" detail about the implementation of my game FUBAR. But since we only had so much time, I ended up devoting my segment to showcasing the games I had developed so far, including X-Ray & DILLIGAS, which by the time you're reading this might have already been released. I didn't even have time to showcase the Portable Intellivision Development Environment (PIDE) that I had built, in case anybody else might have had a use for such an environment.

Now that I have some space to share a few implementation details with you, I'll focus on what is most relevant when working within

IntyBASIC. First, I'll start with a condensed version of my Intellivision development personal story.

I had wanted to get into game development ever since my family first bought an Intellivision in 1981, and we all gathered around the TV and took turns playing Astrosmash and Space Battle. Even when the Intellivision had faded from relevancy with the end of INTV, I could not bring myself to plant my flag somewhere else. At one point, I thought I would get into programming state-of-the-art computer games, but I got off to a false start in my last semester of Undergraduate School, and lost all my self-confidence in my programming ability.

During that time, I maintained a fan-based Intellivision website, first called The ECS BASIC Library, where I posted all the games I had developed in ECS BASIC in grade school. Very humble beginnings indeed, but I learned to make the most of whatever resources I had, and find optimization techniques when necessary. Thankfully, with the ability to use virtual ECS tapes in newer releases of jzIntv, I made the best of my games[15].

I broadened the scope of that website and renamed it The Intellivision Library, where I hosted a couple ECS BASIC programming contests, among other things like reviews of rare games. Before I left Graduate School and abandoned my website, I renamed it once again to The Intellivision Laboratory, to shift focus toward future indie game development. This was in response to the MAGUS II board that people could pre-order from the Blue Sky Rangers, who promised to recognize "Next-Generation Blue Sky Rangers" – which would be my big chance! Even if I wasn't developing games commercially, I still cared about the Intellivision, even to this day.

When the MAGUS II didn't happen, the Blue Sky Rangers refunded the money and sent a copy of Your Friend The EXEC to everybody who pre-ordered one. My first attempt at developing an Intellivision game was Hunt The Wumpus, with the only available tool at the time being the

---

[15] Readily available at http://www.midnightblueinternational.com/archive.php#ECS

Assembler bundled with the emulator INTVPC, which in turn was bundled with Intellivision Lives! for PC. When Joseph Zbiciak released jzIntv and the included Assembler as1600, I made another attempt at an Intellivision game and to regain my self-confidence. That resulted in SameGame, which I hadn't quite finished but had gotten playable just in time for PhillyClassic in April 2001. Surprisingly, SameGame was well-received by the other upcoming indie developers.

Later, I developed another game Robots, based on the game Daleks, which I had played on Windows 3.1. I added it to SameGame, which Joe Zbiciak had modified to fix the Stack Overflow issue that caused it to crash after the player tried to start a new game. I also conceived FUBAR, and had worked out the pseudocode and took a week off from work to devote to programming it. During that week, I got a phone call from Chris Neiman, who had attended PhillyClassic and also enjoyed SameGame. He was working with David Harley and was planning on releasing four games under the brand Intelligentvision, and he wanted to find out whether I was interested in releasing SameGame in physical form. Of course I was! But I would have loved to release FUBAR even more, so I told him I'll try to get this new game FUBAR done before the end of the week. If not, then I would send him the source code for what is now SameGame & Robots to release instead.

When I received my copy of the first Intelligentvision release, Stonix, I was all the more excited to know that my game would "land among the stars" with this one, along with 4-Tris, which Joe Zbiciak had already released independently. Although I finished the prototype for FUBAR, along the way I realized I made a couple mistakes which would require a complete rewrite of the code. There were also slowdown issues when multiple AI players were at play, which I could not avoid.

I ended up sitting on FUBAR for 15 years before I came back to it, and rewrote it to a finished product.

Three things came about during that time which made a released version of FUBAR possible. One was IntyBASIC. The second was JLP, which allowed for: additional memory (which is why I could only have 4 AI players in the prototype), saving data through EEPROM (because having to set all the player and game settings each time was annoying, saying nothing of reprogramming all the AI players), and also real-time multiplication & division, which handled the slowdown issue. Finally there was the aforementioned PIDE which I built so I could create Intellivision games in the cracks of the very little free time I had.

Within my PIDE, I also added Chocolate Mine to another game Blix, which I released through GoodDealGames / Homebrew Heaven. I also developed X-Ray & DILLIGAS, which I created from start to finish in this environment. To make the PIDE friendlier, I developed two front-ends, one for playing Intellivision games, and one for development. From here, the blue sky is the limit, and I'm looking forward to future development on the Amico.

E.2 CALL and USR

E.2.1 USR

I felt this could have used a little more explanation in the original book. These allow for calls to procedures written in Assembly Language. Obviously you will need to know how to write code in Assembly, particularly 1600 Assembly. It helps to have had experience writing games before IntyBASIC, when Assembly was the only choice you had. If you don't know Assembly, you can at least benefit from the samples of code which I provide.

First, what is *CALL*, and what is *USR*? If you've written a *PROCEDURE* in IntyBASIC before, you know about *GOSUB*, which executes the code within that Procedure, and then returns to code execution from where you left off. *CALL* works the same way, except it goes to a "PROC" written in Assembly. The difference with *USR* is that it returns the value in Register R0. If you've written in other languages before, this is like the difference between subroutines and functions: one passes back a value, and one doesn't.

Here's an example of a function. I call it *POWEROF2*, which takes a value between 0 and 15, and returns the value 2 to that power. Because it returns a value, it would be invoked using *USR*.

```
ASM POWEROF2: PROC
     ' Returns a power of 2.
     ' Input:
     ' R0 = Number in 4-bit range (0-15)
     ' Output:
     ' R0 = 2 to the power of the given input
     ASM BEGIN
          ASM ANDI #$f, R0 ; Enforce valid range.
          ASM MOVR R0, R1
          ASM MVII #1, R0
     ASM PowerOf2Loop:
          ASM CMPI #2, R1
          ASM BLT PowerOf2AlmostDone
          ASM SLL R0, 2
          ASM SUBI #2, R1
          ASM B PowerOf2Loop
     ASM PowerOf2AlmostDone:
          ASM TSTR R1
          ASM BZE PowerOf2Done
          ASM SLL R0, 1
     ASM PowerOf2Done:
          ASM RETURN
     ASM ENDP
```

You'll notice each line begins with *ASM*, so IntyBASIC knows it's a line of Assembly code and leaves it for as1600 to handle. The first line is the procedure name, followed by "PROC" after the colon. Then we have comments, prefaced with apostrophes since IntyBASIC scans these lines first. The procedure begins with "ASM BEGIN" and ends with "ASM RETURN" and "ASM ENDP". I indented all the intermediate lines once for labels and twice otherwise.

The first line of code after "ASM BEGIN" has a comment after it. Notice the comment in this line is prefaced with a semicolon and not an apostrophe. as1600 uses only semicolons, and IntyBASIC uses apostrophes and not semicolons.

First, we're using ANDI "logical-AND Immediate value" to zero-out any raised bits that would put the input outside of valid range. This is here for dummy-proofing, to avoid "garbage-in, garbage-out". R0 (and that's a zero) is the register that contains the value that is passed to it whenever the function is invoked with something like $\#y = USR\ POWEROF2(x)$ with x being the passed value, and $\#y$ being the value returned at the end. As you should know, y is prefaced with a hash symbol so IntyBASIC treats it as a 16-bit value. It should also be *UNSIGNED*, in the case $x = 15$, so it doesn't end up *-32,768*.

Because the same register, R0, is used for the output, we're going to copy the value to register R1 with the following line: "MOVR R0, R1" (MOVe Register value from R0 into R1). Then we're writing the value 1 to R0 with "MVII #1, R0" (MoVe In Immediate value 1 to R0). Note that immediate values must be prefaced with a hash symbol. We're using the value 1 because in the case our passed value is 0, we want to return the value 1 ($2^0 = 1$). The remainder of the procedure will bit-shift R0 to the left by the number of places specified in R1.

Now we have the label for the loop, called "PowerOf2Loop" followed by a colon. This is not unlike other labels you're used to, that your code could jump to with IntyBASIC *GOTO* instructions.

Within the loop, first we're checking to see whether R1 (which initially contains the passed value) is less than 2. The first line "CMPI #2, R1" CoMPares the Immediate value 2 against register R1. If R1's value is lower than that, then we exit the loop: "BLT PowerOf2AlmostDone" (Branch if Less Than). Following that, we bit-shift R0's value two positions to the left with "SLL R0, 2" (Shift Logical Left R0 by 2 positions) and subtract 2 from R1 since its value is 2 or higher at this point: "SUBI #2, R1" (SUBtract Immediate value 2 from R1). We then go back to the beginning of the loop with a simple Branch instruction: "B PowerOf2Loop".

You might be wondering why we only shift two positions at a time within a loop. It turns out the Intellivision CPU has one set of instructions for shifting one position, and another set of instructions for shifting two positions. There really is no argument for how many positions. Depending on whether you specify one or two positions, as1600 uses the opcode for the appropriate instruction. That's why there's no hash symbol before the 2 in this instruction.

Finally, at the "Almost Done" label, we check to see if R1's value is zero or not (its only other possible value is 1, since we know it's less than 2 at this point). To check for a zero value, we TeST the Register value with "TSTR R1" and Branch if equal to ZEro with "BZE PowerOf2Done". The line that follows is executed if R1 contained a nonzero value, which we know is 1. Shift-Logical R0's bits one more position to the Left with "SLL R0, 1". Then in either case, we reach the "Done" label and RETURN to the original code.

Now how would we invoke this? Earlier I mentioned $\#y = USR$ $POWEROF2(x)$, so we'll look at it in more detail. x is the power to which 2 is raised (otherwise known as the Logarithm) to give us $\#y$. Obviously x does not need to be more than an 8-bit value, because 15 is as high as it will go. Assuming x has the value 10, $\#y$ will end up being 1,024, which is 2^{10}.

The only other thing to know is that you can pass up to four values. In our example, we passed only one value, x. The second, third, and fourth values passed would be contained in R1, R2, and R3, in that order.

E.2.2 CALL

If you've seen one of my releases since 2019, each game opens up with "MIDNIGHT BLUE INTERNATIONAL" text that unfolds and then pans to the bottom of the screen, with a musical sting that is different with each game. When the text disappears, a large blue sphere in the background quickly shifts upward as the remainder of the title text appears, and then the logo reappears from the top of the screen, now flattened to make room for all the other text.

Near the top of the screen are eight icons whose image is also different each game. I put them in the title screen to mimic the eight color blocks from the original Mattel Electronics title screens, but I use the eight "pastel colors" due to the black background behind them. One line of text is drawn at the bottom of the screen each video frame during panning, which then shifts up eight pixels at a time along with the blue sphere. This repeats very rapidly until the top of the sphere nearly touches the eight icons.

What's important is that each of the eight icon's position is static while everything else moves. That means I can't use IntyBASIC's *SCROLL* routine. I could just use a simple *FOR* loop before writing text in the bottom row, like this:

```
FOR Iteration = 40 TO 219
    #backtab(Iteration) = #backtab(Iteration+20)
NEXT Iteration
```

... but this simple-looking loop takes longer than a single video frame to execute, making the panning effect look jerky. That means I must write the equivalent Assembly code, which executes much faster.

```
ASM TITLESCROLL: PROC
    ' Assembly function to quickly pan only part of the screen.
    ' No arguments, no return value.
    ASM BEGIN
        ASM MVII #$23c, R4
        ASM MVII #$228, R5
    ASM TitleScrollLoop:
        ASM MVI@ R4, R0
        ASM MVO@ R0, R5
```

```
      ASM CMPI #$2f0, R4
      ASM BLT TitleScrollLoop
      ASM RETURN
ASM ENDP
```

I'll just cover what's new in this example. We begin by using MVII to write immediate hexadecimal values this time, and we're using registers R4 and R5. First, you know the values are hexadecimal (base-16) because they're prefaced with a dollar sign in addition to the hash symbol for immediate values. Second, in case you're not aware, the address range $200 through $2ef, which is 16-bit, covers the image on the screen – $228 is the beginning of the third row (*#backtab(40)*), and $23c is the beginning of the fourth row (*#backtab(60)*). Third, why R4 and R5? It turns out these two registers auto-increment when you use them with pointer instructions, making them ideal for loops that involve blocks of contiguous addresses.

Now we get into TitleScrollLoop. MVI@ is the mnemonic to MoVe In a value that's "at" the address pointed to by the first register, and save it to the second register. We're using R0, which isn't otherwise being used, to get the #backtab data, and then MoVe Out the value "at" the other #backtab location. R4 and R5 are handily pointing to *#backtab(60)* and *#backtab(40)*, in that order, to begin with, and then they automatically increment to point to the next index each iteration.

Next we have a CoMParison to an Immediate value, which I explained before, followed by a Branch if Less Than that value to the beginning of the Loop. That means that until R4 is pointing off the screen, there's more #backtab data to copy. Otherwise we're done.

Because it was the screen that was affected, we don't need to return a value from R0. Therefore it gets invoked with *CALL*. I have another subroutine written in IntyBASIC that draws the next line of text in the bottom row, so in my main code, I have these three lines where the screen panning is taking place, copied a few times.

```
      WAIT
      CALL TITLESCROLL
      GOSUB BottomRowText
```

In our case, there are no arguments, but *CALL* can pass up to 4 arguments to procedures that need them, same as with USR. The only other thing I'll point out before we move on is that you might get errors from as1600 that you didn't get from the IntyBASIC compiler, for the obvious reason that IntyBASIC didn't examine your Assembly code, but as1600 does.

E.3 Optimizing IF statements

E.3.1 Conversion to and from TRUE and FALSE.

A good trick to know involves knowing IntyBASIC's Binary conversion to and from TRUE and FALSE[16]. It's the same as with most modern languages.

FALSE has a value of 0. In Binary, all bits are set to 0.

TRUE has a Binary value of -1. You might wonder, why -1. In case you're not familiar with Two's Complement Notation, in Binary -1 is represented by setting all bits to 1.

Now, what about conversion from Binary values? The value 0 evaluates to FALSE. All other values evaluate to TRUE, including negative numbers.

To put it another way, a TRUE expression raises all bits. Any bit raised makes an expression TRUE.

Let us see an example from X-Ray: Board Generation.

At this point, I'll show you a snippet of code from X-Ray, which ties together what I've demonstrated so far. First, I'll explain a few rules of the game and the internal representation of the boards. In case you haven't seen at least the preview, the game takes place on an 8x8 board. Anywhere between 4 and 7 diffusers are hidden somewhere on the board. It's up to the player to find them by firing discovery lasers (or "beams", as I guess I should have called them for x-rays) into the grid.

---

[16] Notice there aren't TRUE or FALSE constants defined in IntyBASIC. These names are used to illustrate the concept of sucessful/non-succesful comparisons.

There's no need for me to go further with the rules here, except to say that it's possible the diffusers can be arranged in a way that makes it impossible for any laser to reveal a diffuser's position. Therefore, I built an "integrity check" that scraps the arrangement and tries again if necessary.

As for the board's representation, the two boards (the game only requires half the screen, so I built two instances of the game to run concurrently, in case a second person wants to play at the same time) are represented by an 8-bit array, with each of the 16 indexes representing one row (8 rows per board), and each bit representing one cell within that row. When you start the game, the code to generate a new board is invoked for each of the two halves of the screen, one at a time. This is where the code is that I want to show you.

```
XRayCreateBoard: PROCEDURE
    ' Places diffusers onto a temp board.
    ' Then runs an integrity check to make sure
    ' all the diffusers can be found.
    ' If not, try again.
    ' Along the way, predetermines the value of each entry point.
    ' Inputs:
        ' Arg: number of diffusers (range 4-7)
    ' Outputs:
        ' #TempRow array: low 8 bits ready to be copied
        ' to the BoardRow array
        ' TempEntry array: ready to be copied
        ' to the BoardEntry array
XRayCreateBoardRetry:
    FOR Iteration = 0 TO 7
        #TempRow(Iteration) = $ff00 ' Raise the high order bits
            ' to be lowered when spaces are visited.
    NEXT Iteration
    FOR Iteration = 0 TO 31
        TempEntry(Iteration) = 0 ' Initialize the entry points.
    NEXT Iteration
    FOR Iteration = 1 TO Arg ' Ready to place diffusers
        DO
            Temp = RANDOM(64) ' 6 random bits
            Temp2 = USR POWEROF2 (Temp AND 7) ' Bitmask for col.
            Temp = Temp / 8 ' Row
        LOOP WHILE #TempRow(Temp) AND Temp2 ' Try again if
            ' there is already a diffuser there.
        #TempRow(Temp) = #TempRow(Temp) XOR Temp2 ' Place diffuser
    NEXT Iteration
```

The variables *Temp*, *Temp2*, and *Iteration* are incidental. *Arg* (argument) is already set to the number of diffusers for the player whose board is being initialized. The array *#TempRow* is 16-bit, hence the hash symbol, and has 8 indexes, one for each row. TempEntry is an 8-bit array with 32 indexes, each value of which contains information for the tile to be revealed at the Entry Point specified by the player. No need to worry about the Entry Points though, except to say that *BoardEntry* has 64 indexes, 32 for each player.

After a passed integrity check, the *#TempRow* and *TempEntry* arrays are copied into the appropriate half of the *BoardRow* and *BoardEntry* arrays. Now for an explanation of the code.

First is the label *XRayCreateBoardRetry*, which is where we end up again if the arrangement fails the integrity check – back to the very beginning. Next we have a quick loop that raises the 8 high-order bits of each index of *#TempRow* ($ff00), so now I'll explain what these extra 8 bits are for.

Each of the 8 low-order bits, as in each bit of each *BoardRow* index, is raised to indicate a diffuser is present in that cell. As with the Binary representation, Bit 0 is for the cell farthest to the right, and Bit 7 is for the cell farthest to the left. But the high-order bits, only necessary during the integrity check, are initially raised to set what I call "bread crumbs" in all the cells.

What is this "integrity check" I keep mentioning? It begins in the code after the above snippet, and it simply fires all the lasers at each of the numbered Entry Points in sequence, and records the outcome in the *TempEntry* array. In the case a laser exits the grid at another Entry Point than the one from which it entered, that other Entry Point is appropriately marked, and is then skipped when the Iterator reaches it (because we already know that outcome). While travelling through the grid, each laser "sweeps up the bread crumbs" of all the cells it examines to look for a diffuser. Then, when it's all done, we use a series of Bitmasks in a loop to see if any cells on the board are occupied by both a diffuser and a bread crumb. If so, the board configuration is rejected, because there's at least one diffuser that can't be found.

Once we have a valid configuration, we no longer care about the bread crumbs. By copying a 16-bit variable (an array index) to an 8-bit one, we lose the 8 high-order bits where the data about the bread crumbs was stored.

After all that explanation, we now come to another loop which initializes the *TempEntry* array to values of 0. That value becomes nonzero when a laser either enters the grid or exits at the appropriate Entry Point.

Now we can randomly place the diffusers. *FOR Iteration = 1 TO Arg* should be obvious. Inside of the *DO* loop are three lines, the first of which uses the *RANDOM* function to select one of the 64 cells on the board, and the next two lines to parse the column and row for that cell into *Temp* and *Temp2*. For the column, you see *USR POWEROF2* which I explained earlier, so now I can show you a practical example of its use.

RANDOM(64) gives us the 6 lower bits either raised or not raised at random (the other 2 bits are not raised). *AND 7* is a bitmask which retains only the 3 lower bits, giving us the range 0-7. By feeding *Temp AND 7* as the argument for *POWEROF2*, we get only that bit number raised (Bit 0-7), and save that bit configuration to *Temp2*.

After that, we divide *Temp* by 8, which is the same as shifting its Binary bits three positions to the right. This is the number of the row, or the index of the #*TempRow* array. It's the following line that illustrates my original point about optimization.

LOOP WHILE should be self-explanatory, as would be *LOOP UNTIL* if we were using that. In the case of *WHILE*, if the following expression evaluates to TRUE, then we go back to *DO* and execute the three lines again. (*UNTIL* would go back to *DO* if the expression were to evaluate to FALSE.)

But what is the expression? #*TempRow(Temp) AND Temp2* doesn't look at first glance like something that would be either TRUE or FALSE. That is where the Binary conversion to TRUE or FALSE comes into play. First, *Temp* gives us the index in the #*TempRow* array, which we are examining to place one of the diffusers. *#TempRow(Temp)* is then the Binary representation of the row on the board we are setting up, each of the low 8 bits of which indicate whether or not there is a diffuser there already. *Temp2* has only one bit raised, which is the Bit number (0-7) that corresponds to the column. Therefore, the value of *Temp2* behaves as a Bitmask by use of the word *AND*. If there is a diffuser there, then this "expression" will be nonzero, which evaluates to TRUE, and so we have to try again to find a random cell that is unoccupied.

In the line below, we know we have an empty cell, so now we perform a little more Binary gymnastics to occupy that cell with a diffuser. The reason we use *XOR* as opposed to *OR* is because ...

E.3.2 The Intellivision CPU does not have native Logical-OR instructions

Whenever we use *OR*, IntyBASIC performs an extra step to simulate *OR*, through a combination of AND to zero out the bit, followed by XOR to raise it again. There are a few times when *OR* is absolutely necessary, but the trick is to keep it to a minimum.

There's no need for me to dredge up an actual code example here, but I've used *IF* in this manner before:

```
IF (Temp = 1) XOR (Temp = 3) THEN
     ' Do stuff.
ELSE
     ' Do other stuff.
END IF
```

In this case, we know these two expressions in the IF line can't both be true. Temp can't be equal to 1 and equal to 3 at the same time. That's why we can get away with using *XOR* as a substitute for *OR*. It wouldn't work if we had multiple conditions that could be true though, because an even number of TRUE expressions would cancel each other out.

While proofreading this book, I noticed Oscar had a better idea — use "+" instead. That brings us back to conversion to Binary. Notice we have parentheses around each of the two conditions in the example above, which gives us two separate expressions. *(Temp = 1)* evaluates to TRUE, which you now know has a value -1, if *Temp = 1*. *(Temp = 3)* evaluates to TRUE (again, value -1) if *Temp = 3*. If neither condition is true, we get 0, which means FALSE. If either condition is true, we get -1, which is nonzero, meaning TRUE.

But what happens in cases where multiple conditions that we check for could be true? Here's a modified example:

```
IF (Temp = 1) + (Temp2 = 3) THEN
    ' Do stuff.
ELSE
      ' Do other stuff.
END IF
```

If Temp = 1 and Temp2 = 3, then we have two TRUE conditions, which would add up to -2. It's still nonzero, and still evaluates to TRUE. This works, whereas *XOR* would reverse all the raised bits, giving us 0, evaluating to FALSE.

E.3.3 Operator Precedence

When you were in Math class, you might have heard the mnemonic "Please Excuse My Dear Aunt Sally." In case you were asleep at the time, that translates to "Parentheses, Exponents, Multiplication, Division, Addition, Subtraction." That's the sequence in which complex math expressions are evaluated.

Why does that matter? Consider this expression: "3 + 3 × 3". What is its value? If you had guessed 18, you would be wrong. The reason you might have guessed 18 is probably because you used what is called "Left-to-Right Evaluation" which means you went in sequence from left to right, and if you "showed your work" it would look like this:

$$\underline{3 + 3} \times 3$$

$$\underline{6 \times 3}$$

$$18$$

The correct answer is 12. That's because "Operator Precedence" is the correct way to evaluate the expression, which looks like this:

$$3 + \underline{3 \times 3}$$

$$\underline{3 + 9}$$

$$12$$

For the correct answer to be 18, we could add parentheses, which are evaluated first:

$$\underline{(3 + 3)} \times 3$$

$$\underline{6 \times 3}$$

$$18$$

What does that have to do with writing code? If you're familiar enough with Operator Precedence, you will know when parentheses are necessary, and more importantly, when they are not. Not using parentheses when not necessary is a good optimization technique to shave a few CPU cycles off your game engine's performance. If you've ever played Atari 2600 Dragster competitively, you know that every hundredth of a second matters.

Let us see an example from DILLIGAS: Background Scanning.

There are a few things I should explain about DILLIGAS, which is a bonus game bundled with X-Ray, before we dive into code examples. First, an explanation of the 2-Player mode. DILLIGAS uses Colored Squares Mode to draw part of the background using black and white quadrants. At the start of the game, one of four monochrome background images is selected at random and drawn on both halves of the screen.

The object is to collide a shared "Zapper" with one of the 7 colored bouncing bubbles to capture it. Who collects that bubble depends on the color of the background tile that the center of the Zapper is pointing to at the moment it hits the bubble. It goes into the reservoir whose color is the same – one player's reservoir is black, and the other is white. The winner is the first player whose reservoir is full of bubbles.

Another thing that bears mentioning is that I use 8.8 floating-point arithmetic to maintain all the objects' position in space. It's the same way early Intellivision games maintained sprite positions through the Executive ROM. The 8 high-order bits determine the actual sprite pixel position on screen, and the 8 low-order bits are only retained for "sub-pixel precision." That is how the 5 enemy squadrons in Space Battle move slowly on the map toward the center of the screen – they are given speeds and a target position, and the Executive ROM calculates their new position every 3 video frames. In addition, all 16 positions on both controllers' Directional Discs are used to offset the current trajectory of the Zapper (again, same as with early Mattel games), which is why sub-pixel precision was necessary.

Now the trick during collision handling is to determine which quadrant in the background to scan to determine its color. I would have included text that explained Colored Squares Mode in more detail, because that was missing from the original book. But it is already explained in this book, and so I left it out. Here is the part of the code that executes in the 2-Player mode of DILLIGAS to handle collision between the Zapper and any of the bubbles.

```
IF (State AND $70) = STATE_MODE_DILLIGAS2 THEN
    Snap = (#ZapperPosX / 256 + 3) AND $f8
    Snap2 = ((#ZapperPosY + $80) / 256 + 3) AND $f8
    Snap = (Snap2 / 8) * 20 + (Snap / 8) - 21 ' Cardtab position
    IF (#ZapperPosX + $280) AND $400 THEN ' p1 or p3 quadrant
        IF (#ZapperPosY + $280) AND $400 THEN ' p3 quadrant
            #Temp2 = $2600
        ELSE ' p1 quadrant
            #Temp2 = $38
        END IF
    ELSEIF (#ZapperPosY + $280) AND $400 THEN ' p2 quadrant
        #Temp2 = $1c0
    ELSE ' p0 quadrant
        #Temp2 = $7
    END IF
    IF #backtab(Snap) AND #Temp2 THEN
        … ' White reservoir
    ELSE
        … ' Black reservoir
    END IF
END IF
```

I'll start by explaining the variables here. *State* contains 8 bits which direct the flow of the program; bits 4-6 (hence the bitmask *State AND $70*) are used to determine which of the games we're currently playing (or whether we're at the menu) and whether the game is over. *Snap*, *Snap2*, and *#Temp2* are incidental. *#ZapperPosX* and *#ZapperPosY* contain the X and Y positions of the Zapper. They are 16-bit variables for the reasons I mentioned above; it's the 8 high-order bits that give us the actual pixel position on screen.

I included these lines of code for a reason. Starting with the *IF* statement, notice the parentheses around *State AND $70*. These are necessary because *State AND $70 = STATE_MODE_DILLIGAS2* (without the parentheses) causes a mis-evaluation. *$70 = STATE_MODE_DILLIGAS2* would be evaluated first as TRUE or FALSE, and then the code would check the value of State to see if it is zero (FALSE) or not, and then *AND* combines the two expressions.

Don't get too bogged down in the next three lines. I just want to point out here that the two instances of */ 256* shift the actual pixel coordinates of the Zapper into range, and the two instances of *+ 3* and *AND $f8* are to isolate the center pixel of the Zapper.

As for *#ZapperPosY + $80*, that's because the Zapper is a minimum-Y-sized double-resolution sprite whose image uses less than all 16 pixel rows, and so I have a second image which is redrawn to be "half a pixel" lower vertically. I choose one of the two images each video frame depending on its "half-pixel vertical position" to simulate double-resolution sprite placement, which is a neat trick but extremely hard for the player to notice. I use the same technique with the "MIDNIGHT BLUE INTERNATIONAL" text as it pans down from the top of the title screen in its flattened state, making it move half as fast as in earlier games, but twice as smoothly. I still had a little room left over for more graphics in the ROM.

But the important thing here are the parentheses. The bitwise operator *AND* would be evaluated first before the mathematical division and addition operators. Because I want that to be evaluated last, I have to wrap parentheses around *#ZapperPosX / 256 + 3*. Since division takes precedence before addition, I do not need additional parentheses around *#ZapperPosX / 256*. However, in the line just below, I have two sets of parentheses to ensure + *$80* is evaluated before */ 256* and that I save *AND $f8* for last.

There's only one thing I want to point out in the next line, regarding *- 21*. Recall that sprites fully visible in the top left corner of the screen have X and Y pixel positions of 8 (assuming there are no border extensions), not 0. Pixel positions between 1-7 place the sprite partially off-screen. With my calculations so far, I'm looking one card below and to the right of where I want to be. Subtracting by 20 offsets it one card higher, and by 1 more offsets it one card to the left. I use a similar trick in FUBAR when calculating the position of each paintbrush every time it paints onto the canvas.

Now Snap is pointing to the appropriate card. We still have to get the quadrant. *#Temp2* will store the bitmask for the three bits that set the color in that quadrant. I don't need to go into any further detail here, because it only covers topics I discussed already.

Getting to the last *IF* statement in this example, we have another instance of something that doesn't look like an expression, but will evaluate to FALSE if its value is 0. In this case, 0 represents the color black, so the code execution falls to *ELSE* in the case we see a black square. Any other color found in the three bits from *#Temp2*'s bitmask would be white, because that's all we're using for the background.

E.4 Defs (definitions)

You might not find much of a use for these, but I have a handful that I created, which makes code a little easier to write. Where they are most useful is with use of Flash for saving and loading data. The important thing to note is that they are supposed to be a single line in length, which is why I use the colon and backslash characters from IntyBASIC's syntax. I prefer camelCase to distinguish them as defs.

```
' Input
DEF FN getInput = \
    DO: WAIT: \
        Input = CONT.KEY: \
```

```
      LOOP WHILE Input = 12: \
      DO: WAIT: \
      LOOP UNTIL CONT.KEY = 12 ' Keypad value saved to Input

' Sound
DEF FN callHush = \
      SOUND 0, 0, 0: \
      SOUND 1, 0, 0: \
      SOUND 2, 0, 0: \
      SOUND 5, 0, 0: \
      SOUND 6, 0, 0: \
      SOUND 7, 0, 0 ' Delete these last three lines if not using ECS.

DEF FN callTick = \
      WAIT: SOUND 2, $2b, 15: \
      WAIT: SOUND 2, 0, 0 ' Note E9 for NTSC, F#9 for PAL.

' Graphics
DEF FN hideSprites = \
      SPRITE 0, 0, 0, 0: \
      SPRITE 1, 0, 0, 0: \
      SPRITE 2, 0, 0, 0: \
      SPRITE 3, 0, 0, 0: \
      SPRITE 4, 0, 0, 0: \
      SPRITE 5, 0, 0, 0: \
      SPRITE 6, 0, 0, 0: \
      SPRITE 7, 0, 0, 0
```

Nothing too exciting so far. Now that we've gotten warmed up, let's add parameters.

```
' Flash
DEF FN readRow(FSector, FRow) = \
      FLASH READ FLASH.FIRST + FSector * 8 + FRow, VARPTR #FlashRow(0)
DEF FN writeRow(FSector, FRow) = \
      FLASH WRITE FLASH.FIRST + FSector * 8 + FRow, VARPTR #FlashRow(0)
DEF FN eraseSector(FSector) = \
      FLASH ERASE FLASH.FIRST + FSector * 8
```

Everything else I have so far is specific to my games, and wouldn't do you any good.

E.5 Multithreaded programming

In case you're not a Computer Science graduate, I'll explain in brief that "threads" are essentially modules of code execution, more than one of which can run concurrently and can share resources. Fortunately, Oscar discusses that a little in this book, using the procedure that is executed each video frame. I'll demonstrate what my "main.bas" file in each project typically looks like:

```
' FUBAR
' By Michael Hayes
' http://www.midnightblueinternational.com
' "Once we accept our limits, we go beyond them." - Albert Einstein
' Last modified on September 6, 2019
OPTION WARNINGS ON
OPTION EXPLICIT ON
INCLUDE "projects/fubar/const.bas"
INCLUDE "projects/fubar/vars.bas"
INCLUDE "projects/fubar/defs.bas"
' One-time initialization goes here, before actual code.
FLASH INIT SIZE NumSectors
ON FRAME GOSUB GameLoop
'STACK_CHECK ' Replaced with "ASM DIS" and "ASM EIS"
INCLUDE … ' Titles, graphics, and music
ASM ORG $a000
INCLUDE … ' Menu System and AI routines
ASM ORG $c100
INCLUDE … ' Game Engine
ASM ORG $f000
INCLUDE … ' Lookup data, text, and metadata
```

All I've left out here are the actual filenames beyond the Constants, Variables, and Definitions listings. But otherwise, this is main.bas in its entirety for FUBAR. The first three Include files do not contain any code, which is why I can get away with putting them first, before the *FLASH INIT* and *ON FRAME* lines. Notice I commented out *STACK_CHECK*, which I always had done anyhow before a game goes into production, but I also added a comment that it was replaced with something else, which I'll explain in a moment. The only other thing to point out is that you cannot execute code in the $f000 address range, so this is a good place for data, graphics, large blocks of text, and so on.

Getting back to *ON FRAME*. You should already know about that from the previous book. In this case, I'm calling the procedure *GameLoop* which executes every video frame. When that code is finished, the main code execution resumes for the remainder of the video frame. This is an example of "multithreaded programming" because there are two threads of code execution happening in tandem, to say nothing of other threads like IntyBASIC's music engine. The Executive ROM for early commercial games allowed for up to six time-based routines to be defined.

This book's examples merely use their time-based procedure as a sound engine. In X-Ray, I used the timed procedure to handle game events like moving objects, while the main thread handled events like generating a new board, which couldn't be done from start to finish in a single video frame. In my implementation of RobotFindsKitten, I put these two main threads to clever use as well, handling input from up to 4 players with one thread while handling collisions with the other thread.

E.5.1 Alternative to STACK_CHECK

What's wrong with *STACK_CHECK* and why did I replace it with something else while developing FUBAR? I'll quote my entire comment from AtariAge[17] which you can read here:

Fun facts while re-developing FUBAR:

1. I was getting the "Stack overflow" message and didn't know it. I had written the code so everything happened inside of the "*ON FRAME*" procedure, using a variable to know what to do that frame (between rounds, etc.), and leaving the main code execution in an infinite loop. When starting a new round, it took longer than a single frame to do everything, so I chopped it all up into multiple frames, knowing I had 2 seconds to get everything done before the action started.

   Why I didn't know the message was there was because initializing the canvas caused the text to appear white-on-white, perfectly blending in with the canvas. But then the AIs would start to "paint over the text" which caused all kinds of interesting screen artifacts, for example

---

[17] https://atariage.com/forums/topic/314714-intybasic-stack-overflowcheck/?do=findComment&comment=4702589

having the *NEXT_COLOR* bit become raised, which is not used in Colored Squares Mode for that purpose.

2. As a workaround, I commented out *STACK_CHECK* as I normally do before a game goes into production, and I replaced it with *ASM DIS* at the beginning of the *ON FRAME* Procedure and *ASM EIS* at the end. That way, using too many CPU cycles during the procedure causes the screen to be blank on intermittent frames instead. I discovered that simply using IntyBASIC's *PRINT* command to display seven 3-digit numbers took more than a single frame, so I wrote a little code of my own to replace that.

3. Just to be sure I wasn't living in a fool's paradise just before the game went into production, I uncommented *STACK_CHECK* and suddenly was running into trouble again. Turns out the few extra cycles used by the Stack Check subroutine were enough to go overboard, due to my meticulous cycle count while rewriting the AI code (slowdown was one of the reasons I didn't come back to FUBAR until after JLP came onto the scene). I left *ASM DIS* and *ASM EIS* intact, despite a comment to remove those lines before production. Letting the game run all day for the two days of RetroGameCon 7 with no issues was more than enough evidence to me that it works fine.

So there you have it. The first line of code in the GameLoop procedure is *ASM DIS* and the last line is *ASM EIS*. *DIS* stands for Disable Interrupt Service and *EIS* stands for Enable Interrupt Service.

E.6 About *PRINT*

E.6.1 Don't use it in your game engine

PRINT is a very useful command in IntyBASIC. It has a lot of functionality that compares to other high-level languages, like printf in C. But as with other languages' standard text output commands, all that functionality comes at a price – speed.

I discovered that when I was building the core game engine for FUBAR. The prototype was designed to use the Executive ROM, and I fixed the speed of the game loop to run 5-6 times per second. In the released game, using IntyBASIC, the game loop is 10 video frames in length, making it run just as fast as in the prototype. Of those 10 frames, 8 of them are dedicated to handle each of the players, in case there's an 8-AI demo taking place. All the time available is needed to handle the AI core, pretty much down to the last CPU cycles, as I mentioned in that AtariAge post.

That leaves 2 frames for everything else: the music engine (I used my own legacy music tracker because of the meticulous CPU cycle count I mentioned for the AI core) and updating the paint count display and internal team ranks. At first, I dedicated one frame to updating the paint count display, leaving the music engine and ranks update for the other frame. I used *PRINT <.3>* to draw the paint counts in each team color. In the worst-case scenario where all 7 teams were active, I tripped the Stack Overflow watchdog (which I still had enabled at the time).

That meant I had to write some code to manually display the paint counts, which thankfully didn't require more Assembly code. (Fun fact: The Assembly module from the prototype to (un)paint the squares on the canvas is mostly intact, the only change being to pass back a 4-nybble (half-byte) 16-bit binary sequence in R0 and then update the internal paint counts outside the procedure, whereas I originally updated each appropriate paint count immediately as I went along.)

Example From FUBAR: Bypassing *PRINT.*

```
' Update paint counters.
'PRINT AT 20 * 10 + Iter * 5 + 6 COLOR Iter, <.3>#TeamCounter(Iter)
Temp = Iter * 5
#backtab(20*10+6 + Temp) = 0 ' Blank out the first two digit spaces.
#backtab(20*10+7 + Temp) = 0
#backtab(20*10+8 + Temp) = 0
#Temp = #TeamCounter(Iter)
IF #Temp THEN
    #backtab(20*10+8 + Temp) = (#Temp%10+16)*8 + Iter
    IF #Temp >= 10 THEN
        #backtab(20*10+7 + Temp) = (#Temp/10%10+16)*8 + Iter
        IF #Temp >= 100 THEN
            #backtab(20*10+6 + Temp) = (#Temp/100+16)*8 + Iter
        END IF
    END IF
END IF
```

The only changes I made here were to abbreviate *Iteration* to *Iter* and eliminate some spacing in the calculations, just to fit each line of code in the width of the page. This block of code is running inside of a *FOR* loop (*FOR Iter = 0 TO 6*) which handles all 7 teams. The *FOR* loop also has code to update the internal team ranks, leaving the 10th video frame alone for the music engine.

You'll notice the *PRINT* line is commented out and replaced with all the lines that follow. You might think that's more code to execute and would therefore take longer, but it doesn't. Add to that the fact I'm also recalculating the team ranks in this loop, and you get an idea how much slower *PRINT* can be! By all means though, use *PRINT* outside your main game loop, like in menus, so your code is easier to read.

Let's break this down though, in case you have a need to borrow this code for your own game engine.

First, the variables. *Temp*, *#Temp*, and *Iter*(ation) are incidental. All that's left is the *#TeamCounter* array, with 7 indexes, one for each possible team. It's a 16-bit array because the paint counters could go higher than 255. (The released version of FUBAR uses JLP, which gives us all the extra 16-bit memory I need for the AI core and the 8 AI configurations. Those configurations are user-defined; otherwise I could just fetch values from ROM.)

Temp is set to point to the location on screen, offset from the start of the paint counts display, where that team's paint count is drawn. In case that team's paint count diminished since the previous game cycle to where it's now one digit shorter in length, I blank out each digit first. Then we have *#Temp*, which fetches the value to be displayed, from the appropriate *#TeamCounter* index.

The outer *IF* statement just has *#Temp* as its expression to evaluate, which as you know by now means we'll skip drawing any number at all if the value is 0 (which is the case if there are no active players on that team). In the next line, we know there's at least one digit to draw, and it's offset so the numbers to display are right-justified – notice we have *20*10+8 + Temp* in this line, followed by *20*10+7 + Temp* for the second digit and then

20*10+6 + Temp if there's a third digit. (The canvas is comprised of 800 squares or 40*20, so there's no need for a fourth digit.)

You might be wondering if we're adding time by having to calculate *20*10+8* to get 208. In fact, IntyBASIC at compile-time is smart enough to know that's a fixed value, and calculates it for us – so the game engine is only adding the value of *Temp* to 208. What comes after the equal sign is the screen representation of the digit to display. The percent symbol is a Modulo operator, which is "remainder after division". Since JLP also has the ability to perform multiplication and division in real-time (which requires a large number of CPU cycles if done using the Executive ROM, as I had to do in the prototype, being the chief reason for slowdown issues), we get the last digit's value right away, add 16 which is the position of '0' in the Graphics ROM (GROM), multiply 8 since the last three bits are for the color, and finally add the value of the team's color.

Now we repeat the process with a nested *IF* statement to check if the counter is 10 or higher, meaning there's another digit to display. The calculation to get this digit is only slightly different, but I'll point out now the use of parentheses in the math expression. This is the minimum necessary due to Operator Precedence as I discussed earlier. Because the Modulo operator is essentially division, first we evaluate *#Temp / 10* to eliminate the first digit we already drew, and then use *% 10* to isolate the "ten's place" digit that we want. The one set of parentheses is necessary because we want to evaluate addition *+ 16* before multiplication ** 8*.

Finally, we check to see if the value is 100 or higher, which would necessitate the third digit. Since that's the last possible digit, the calculation only involves division without the Modulo operator.

E.6.2 "\0601"

What the heck does that mean, "*\0601*"? It's how I remember suggesting an update to IntyBASIC that Oscar implemented in a recent version. If you've written in C, C++, Java, Python, or a similar language, you may recognize the backslash character as what is called an "escape character". That means instead of drawing a literal backslash, the respective *PRINT* command for that language knows that you want to do something else, like start a new line in the case of "\n".

But what if you do want the actual backslash character? You just use two backslashes instead, "\ \". An example of that is in the folder specifications in the "config.py" file within my Windows port of PIDEjL, a front-end I wrote for my Portable Intellivision Development Environment to have a jzIntv Launcher, and subsequently ported to Windows (with a little help from "jenergy" on AtariAge).

As a shameless sidebar plug, since I'm almost done here, that front-end is available on my website[18]. Here is a screenshot from Windows 8:

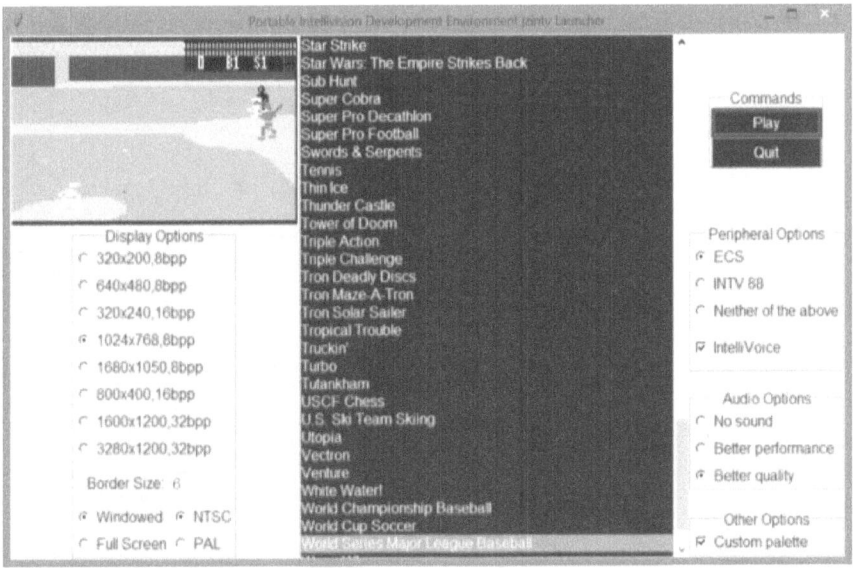

The feature to use "\ \" to get a backslash character wasn't available in earlier versions of IntyBASIC; you could only supply a number, and IntyBASIC would fetch the indicated character from GROM. As I was reimplementing RobotFindsKitten in IntyBASIC, I wanted that character for a few of the NonKitten Items (NKI). As a workaround, Oscar said to use "\60" since 60 is the number of the backslash character's position in GROM.

---

[18] http://www.midnightblueinternational.com/pide.php#pidejlw

I thought about that for about one and a half seconds before I realized somebody might want to display an actual numeric character immediately after the backslash, as in "*1*". Right away I asked Oscar how that would work. He made another change so IntyBASIC limits the number of digits to 3. That means by using "*0601*", IntyBASIC only interprets *060* to draw the backslash, leaving the *1* to be displayed as the character following the backslash.

Appendix F

About the author

Óscar Toledo Gutiérrez (Mexico, 1978) is an experienced computer programmer.

He has written hundreds of programs in several programming languages, collaborates in the design of the Fenix Operating System and the Biyubi Internet Browser, gives talks at universities and does game design and programming consulting.

He is also the creator of the world's smallest chess programs written in C, Java, Javascript, x86 and 6502 machine code, and also the first Mexican to win the IOCCC (International Obfuscated C Code Contest): Best Game (2005), Best of Show (2007), Best Small Program (2007), Most Portable Chess Set (2007) and Best Non-chess Game (2012), and 2nd place winner at the first JS1K contest (2010).

One of his hobbies is working on classic consoles. He has developed games for MSX, Colecovision, Intellivision, Atari 2600, Sega Master System, Memotech, Spectravideo and Tatung Einstein. His games Princess Quest and Mecha-8 are included in the ColecoVision Flashback console by AtGames and he created the IntyBASIC language for programming Intellivision consoles.

He is also the author of the books "Toledo Nanochess: The Commented Source Code", "Programming Games for Intellivision", "Programming Boot Sector Games", "More Boot Sector Games", and tweetstar with short stories in Spanish published in @historiasmini and now collected in 3 books.

www.ingramcontent.com/pod-product-compliance
Lightning Source LLC
Chambersburg PA
CBHW021350210526
45463CB00001B/57